OUTCOMES ASSESSMENT
IN HIGHER EDUCATION

OUTCOMES ASSESSMENT IN HIGHER EDUCATION

Views and Perspectives

Edited by
Peter Hernon and Robert E. Dugan

LIBRARIES
UNLIMITED
A Member of the Greenwood Publishing Group

Westport, Connecticut • London

Library of Congress Cataloging-in-Publication Data

Outcomes assessment in higher education : views and perspectives / edited by Peter
  Hernon and Robert E. Dugan.
    p. cm.
  Includes bibliographical references and index.
  ISBN 1–59158–098–6 (alk. paper)
  1. Education, Higher—United States—Evaluation. 2. Educational tests and
measurements—United States. I. Hernon, Peter. II. Dugan, Robert E., 1952–
LB2331.63.O88 2004
378.1'67'1—dc22   2004041799

British Library Cataloguing in Publication Data is available.

Library of Congress Catalog Card Number: 2004041799
ISBN: 1–59158–098–6

First published in 2004

Libraries Unlimited, 88 Post Road West, Westport, CT 06881
A Member of the Greenwood Publishing Group, Inc.
www.lu.com

Printed in the United States of America

∞™

The paper used in this book complies with the
Permanent Paper Standard issued by the National
Information Standards Organization (Z39.48–1984).

10 9 8 7 6 5 4 3 2 1

Contents

Figures

Preface

With the price of earning a college education sharply increasing and with an undergraduate degree no longer being sufficient for entry into a number of professional careers, the federal government (the White House, Congress, and the department of education), state legislatures, state departments of education, regional accrediting organizations, professional associations, parents, and students, among others, now demand that higher-education institutions—like primary and secondary schools in the public sector—demonstrate that they are meeting their stated educational missions and goals and that the supporting evidence they provide is objectively and continuously gathered and reported. Furthermore, that evidence should offer direct and indirect indicators that educational programs make a difference: students, at both the undergraduate and graduate level, learned as a direct result of those programs. As U.S. Congressman Howard P. McKeon, a Republican from California, wrote, "The last thing that I want to do is to tell colleges how to run their businesses, but I will not stand idly by as they continue to raise their prices each year. Nor will I be an accomplice to this growing problem by providing more and more federal aid without some form of accountability." Equally as blunt, he demanded that institutions of higher education "ensure that low-income families are not priced out of the market."[1]

During the debate over the renewal of the Higher Education Act in 2003, a consistent theme has been the need to hold all institutions of higher education receiving federal support more accountable for the quality of the undergraduate and graduate education provided. Roderick R. Paige, the secretary of education during the Bush administration, has stated:

> The same principles that guided legislation to improve elementary and secondary education by demanding greater accountability and performance from public schools—a law known as the No Child Left Behind

Act—would guide the administration's "future legislative proposals, in areas including special education, vocational education, and *higher education*." (italics added)[2]

The focus on accountability increasingly centers on the appropriate and proper use of taxpayer funds, evidence that students receive a *quality* education at an affordable price, " 'the effectiveness of postsecondary institutions' in retaining students and graduating them 'in a timely fashion,' " and the need to lower the student dropout rate.[3] Naturally, this focus has not been well received in some quarters. Nils Hasselmo, president of the Association of American Universities, for instance, wrote that "if the administration [and Congress] delved too deeply into issues of institutional quality, . . . [they] would assure an adversarial relationship with the higher-education community from the outset of the reauthorization process [for the Higher Education Act]."[4]

The purpose of this book is not to enter the debate and take sides. In fact, institutional quality and effectiveness, and a demand for greater accountability, are issues that have existed before the debate over the renewal of the Higher Education Act. Accountability and institutional effectiveness are concerned, in part, with measuring institutional efficiency, such as fiscal accountability, and educational quality and improvement, including student learning. As a result, there is an interest in answering questions such as "What should students learn?" "How well are they learning it?" and "How do institutions gather evidence of quality and use that evidence to improve their programs, courses, approaches to learning, and institutional effectiveness?" Results-oriented questions such as these have served as catalysts in higher education's systematic application of processes for outcomes assessment in the effort to measure, report, and improve institutional effectiveness.

Institutions of higher education have reported outcomes for years. However, those outcomes actually comprise outputs (e.g., graduation rates, retention rates, transfer rates, and employment rates for a graduating class). Now, accrediting organizations are saying that such measures are insufficient; institutions of higher education must set student learning outcomes, provide evidence that those outcomes have been achieved, and use the evidence gathered to improve, in an ongoing manner, educational quality.

The uniqueness of this book is its broad, cross-disciplinary perspective on the discussion of educational quality as reflected through outcomes assessment, or the application of student outcomes and student learning outcomes to ensuring institutional effectiveness. Contributors include individuals from accrediting organizations and associations that expect academe to embrace outcomes assessment, university administration, and institutional research, as well as faculty members and academic librarians. Regardless of their position or source of employment, the message of the various authors is the same: outcomes assessment is here to stay (it is not a fad for institutions to either ignore or discard). Outcomes assessment links institutions to their stakeholders by providing evidence of accountability, and it enables courses and programs to link to the institutional mission and to demonstrate that learning actually occurred. Outcomes assessment applies at the institutional, program, and course levels; and libraries are not exempt from involvement in such assessment. Outcomes assessment, in summary, represents an opportunity for libraries, academic departments, and others to form partnerships and work toward the same ends—enriching the educational experience and turning college and university graduates into lifelong learners.

Peter Hernon and Robert E. Dugan
November 2003

NOTES

1. Howard P. McKeon, "Point of View: Controlling the Price of College," *The Chronicle of Higher Education* (July 11, 2003): B20.
2. Stephen Burd, "Bush's Next Target?" *The Chronicle of Higher Education* (July 11, 2003): A19.
3. Burd, "Bush's Next Target?"
4. Burd, "Bush's Next Target?"

CHAPTER 1

Keystones of Regional Accreditation: Intentions, Outcomes, and Sustainability

Ronald L. Baker

Once viewed as a social utility to develop human capital, American higher education is increasingly regarded as an economic utility to strengthen competitive commercial advantage. The social utility model of higher education emphasizes access to educational opportunities to foster personal growth and development in the belief that society as a whole benefits from the aggregation of realized individual human potential. In contrast, the economic utility model of higher education is viewed as a strategic investment of resources to produce benefits for business and industry by leveraging fiscal and human capital to produce a direct, immediate, and positive financial return on those investments.[1] As competition increases for funding to support basic and critical societal needs, decision makers are allocating scarce resources based more upon evidence of organizational accomplishments in effectively fulfilling intentions and achieving intended outcomes than adherence to historical funding patterns. When considering funding requests for higher education, financial backers seek evidence of educational quality, student achievements, and institutional accomplishments to foster confidence in higher education's ability and capacity to produce meaningful educational results in an effective and efficient manner.

The call for evidence from external stakeholders is not limited to financial providers. Institutional constituencies, including employers, increasingly express doubts regarding the efficacy of traditional academic measures such as grades, certificates, and degrees to evaluate and document students' knowledge, skills, and abilities.[2] Higher education has been slow to respond to the heightened stakeholder interest in matters previously considered to be the sole domain of higher education. As a result, some constituencies have concluded rightfully or wrongfully that the academy is unable or unwilling to provide evidence of accomplishments to enable meaningful external judgments of educational quality and institutional effectiveness.[3] The perceived lack of a meaningful response from the higher educational community to this unmet need has produced considerable external pressure for institutional accountability in the form of explicit data-driven evidence of student learning achievements and institutional accomplishments.[4]

TRADITIONAL VALUES

Quality and effectiveness in achieving intended outcomes are two of higher education's most deeply held values. Yet, the characteristics of educational quality and the criteria to evaluate effectiveness in achieving identified educational and institutional outcomes are not easily identified, clearly understood, or universally accepted. This should not be surprising, given the diversity and contextual nature of educational outcomes in American higher education. Nonetheless, colleges and universities nearly always include a reference to quality or excellence in their mission statements.

Educational accomplishments in general and student learning outcomes in particular might appear to be common platforms to measure educational quality and effectiveness. However, the considerable variance in constituent perspectives and institutional philosophies, characteristics, cultures, and missions makes it difficult to articulate common operational definitions of quality and effectiveness appropriate for all stakeholders. Without a set of common definitions, identification and implementation of a single set of prescriptive criteria for use by all colleges and universities and their constituencies to measure educational quality and effectiveness are difficult to achieve.[5] In recognition of the complexity of the matter, higher education's external constituencies usually deferred judgments of educational quality and institutional effectiveness to the academic community. Consequently, higher education's role as the primary adjudicator of educational quality and institutional effectiveness remained fundamentally unchallenged.[6] However, recent shifts in societal attitudes toward higher education are causing America's colleges and universities to share, rather than own, that authority and responsibility.

In past generations, judgments from within the academy regarding quality and effectiveness were more often based on informal perceptions of institutional reputations, resources, and implications than explicit evidence based on analysis of data-driven assessments of student and institutional achievements. Heightened expectations of external constituencies, however, are pressuring colleges and universities to move away from judgments determined by institutional descriptions, anecdotal perceptions, and inferences of accomplishments. Higher education's stakeholders now expect claims of educational quality and institutional effectiveness to be supported by evidence in the form of analytic data-driven assessments of achievements of intended outcomes. The pressure to move from anecdotal to analytic evidence of quality and effectiveness is not limited to colleges and universities. Quality assurance organizations, such as those providing accreditation, are experiencing similar pressures from their stakeholders.

ROLE OF ACCREDITATION

Accreditation is the oldest and best-known seal of collegiate quality. It is the cornerstone of self-regulation in America's colleges and universities.[7] Receipt of accreditation is public recognition that an institution or program meets the accrediting agency's established requirements. An accrediting organization may grant preaccreditation (candidacy) status to an institution or program that is not yet accredited but is progressing toward accreditation if there is reasonable expectation that the institution or program will satisfy the agency's expectations regarding compliance with its accreditation criteria within a prescribed period of time.

As practiced in the United States, accreditation has dual purposes of fostering quality improvement and providing assurance regarding the quality and effectiveness of educational programs and institutional services.[8] Accrediting organizations fulfill their dual purposes through a collegial process of analytic institutional self-assessment and critical peer review based upon criteria established by voluntary nongovernmental associations. Although an accreditation evaluation is not an institutional audit, it does ensure that the institution meets peer and publicly accepted minimum standards of quality and effectiveness.[9]

There are three primary types of accreditation: regional, national, and specialized.[10] Regional accrediting organizations primarily accredit comprehensive colleges and universities. They make a decision on the accreditation status of the institution following a review of all major institutional functions. Accreditation criteria are requirements in the form of qualitative statements that emphasize quality and effectiveness in achieving institutional mission and goals at acceptable standards as determined by the academic community and representatives of the public. Although educational programs and institutional units are reviewed as part of the evaluation process, regional accreditation organizations accredit institutions as a whole and do not specifically monitor or accredit individual educational programs, subject content areas, or operational units within the institution. National accrediting agencies evaluate institutions that are frequently single-purpose in nature, such as business or information technology institutes, or that have a clear thematic mission, such as faith-based institutions or liberal arts colleges. Like regional accreditation, national accrediting agencies accredit entire institutions rather than individual educational programs. Specialized accrediting agencies evaluate individual educational programs with regard to program-specific standards. Educational programs accredited by specialized accrediting agencies may reside within comprehensive institutions or within single-purpose institutions. An institution may not be accredited by more than one regional accrediting organization. It may, however, be accredited by both a regional accrediting organization and a national accrediting agency and/or have one or more of its academic programs accredited by specialized accrediting agencies.

Regional accreditation is grounded in traditional academic values of self-regulation, academic integrity, and collective responsibility.[11] It operates under the principle that analyzing quality and effectiveness of individual educational programs and institutional units is insufficient to make a determination of the quality and effectiveness of the institution as a whole. Judgments of institutional quality and effectiveness are made by analyzing individual educational programs and institutional units, reviewing relationships among the programs and units, and synthesizing findings into a judgment of the institution as a whole. Therefore, analytic evaluations of all major institutional units are a necessary, but not sufficient, condition in rendering a judgment regarding the overall quality, effectiveness, viability, integrity, and sustainability of an institution.

ACCREDITATION CRITERIA

Historically, decisions regarding educational quality and institutional effectiveness were based on inferences drawn from perspectives of institutional infrastructures, resources, and processes. It was generally presumed that quality, educational outcomes, and institutional effectiveness mirrored institutional characteristics, intentions, and assets.[12] In the context of current expectations, however, indirect inferences of quality and effectiveness are not by themselves sufficient to meet the expectations of institutional stakeholders or regional accrediting organizations. Institutions must now purposefully assess and explicitly document *achievement* of intended outcomes to substantiate claims of quality and effectiveness.

Regional accreditation criteria are agreed upon by member institutions as characteristics of educational quality and institutional effectiveness. They are catalytic rather than prescriptive and serve as a framework that applies equally to all accredited and preaccredited institutions. The criteria provide sufficient flexibility to enable institutions with divergent values, characteristics, and educational philosophies to demonstrate that the principles of quality and effectiveness embedded within the criteria are preserved. Further, they provide a basis for examination, feedback, and assistance to institutions as they seek to fulfill their own missions and goals. While remaining appropriately broad and deliberately general to accommodate the diversity of institutions in American higher education, regional accreditation criteria require institutions to evaluate and document achievement of educational outcomes and institutional effectiveness in addition to assessing the adequacy, appropriateness, and availability of institutional resources and processes. The accreditation criteria do not, however, explicitly define *adequacy*, *appropriateness*, and *availability*, because those characteristics must be determined within the context of the institution's characteristics, mission, and goals.

The form of accreditation criteria varies from region to region but typically consists of eligibility requirements, standards, and related policies. Collectively they foster analytical, evidence-driven peer judgments regarding quality and effectiveness in achieving identified institutional and educational outcomes. Eligibility requirements are institutional characteristics and conditions required for initial and continuing accreditation. They reflect critically important principles embedded within the accreditation standards and policies, and form the nucleus for institutional self-assessment, peer review, and decisions on the accreditation status of an institution. Standards and related policies are the primary accreditation criteria by which quality and effectiveness are evaluated. They are structured to enable an evaluation of all major units of the institution. The standards and related policies form an integrated framework to underscore the interconnected nature of the institution. They require an analysis of each major institutional unit as well as a synthesis across those units to yield a judgment of the institution as a whole. Taken in total, eligibility requirements, standards, and related policies for accreditation assist institutions, peer evaluators, and accrediting agencies in making judgments on educational quality and institutional effectiveness.

An evaluation by a regional accrediting agency is a mission-centric process that begins with the conduct of a thorough institutional self-analysis and the publication of a self-study report of findings. The self-study report assesses institutional strengths and challenges, and articulates the institution's plan for improvement. Peer evaluators validate the content of the report by reviewing the institution's supporting documentation and interviewing institutional stakeholders. They analyze and synthesize their findings to produce an evaluation report that draws conclusions regarding institutional strengths and areas in need of improvement with regard to the accrediting agency's evaluation criteria. Judgments of the institution are determined by accreditation decision-makers in relationship to the accreditation criteria and the institution's characteristics, mission, and goals; adequacy and efficacy of its infrastructure and resources; and degree to which it fulfills institutional mission and educational program objectives at levels generally accepted by the academic community and the public.[13]

In addition to addressing issues of institutional compliance with accreditation criteria, regional accreditation encourages purposeful change and improvement of educational quality and effectiveness in fulfilling institutional missions and goals. As a result, recognition as a regionally accredited institution warrants confidence of the educational community and the public with regard to the institution's performance, quality, and integrity by ensuring that an accredited institution: (1) has clearly defined and appropriate educational objectives (intentions), (2) has conditions under which institutional objectives can reasonably be achieved (infrastructure), (3) appears to be substantially accomplishing its objectives (outcomes), and (4) is reasonably organized, staffed, and supported to continue to do so (infrastructure).[14]

INTENTIONS—INSTITUTIONAL MISSION AND GOALS

An institution's mission is its statement of purpose and intentions. It serves as a covenant with its constituencies and a contract with its students. Regional accrediting organizations do not determine institutional missions or goals, nor do they specify institutional, program, or student learning outcomes, because those decisions are properly the domain of the institution and its stakeholders. However, they do require each accredited or preaccredited institution to define its mission clearly, set goals that lead to fulfillment of the mission, and identify indicators of mission and goal achievement. Thus, institutional mission is the kernel of regional accreditation and one of the major considerations when making an accreditation decision regarding institutional quality, effectiveness, and compliance with accreditation criteria.

By placing the institutional mission at the center of the accreditation process, regional accreditation honors the diversity of institutions that is the hallmark of American higher education. However, in allowing for variations of institutional values, missions, and philosophies, quality cannot always be defined in precisely the same terms for all institutions. An evaluation of educational quality and institutional effectiveness in the context of regional accreditation must necessarily include a consideration of an institution's characteristics and the purposes it seeks to accomplish as reflected in its mission and goals. Therefore, in addition to addressing external expectations for accountability, regional accreditation provides a means to judge an institution in terms of its own expectations of itself.

OUTCOMES—ASSESSING ACHIEVEMENTS

Assessments of educational quality have always been and remain key components of the accreditation process. However, quality should not be determined solely on the basis of economy, productivity, and efficiency.[15] Quality, for purposes of regional accreditation, must be evaluated primarily in terms of institutional integrity with regard to the degree to which institutional intentions match institutional accomplishments. Consequently, institutions are evaluated with regard to the manner and degree to which they fulfill their missions and goals. Inherent in that evaluation is a determination of the institution's success and quality in achieving its intended educational and institutional outcomes.

In that context, assessment—the process of gathering and assembling data in an understandable form—is an important tool in determining achievements of outcomes.[16] It is also useful in providing documentation to support institutional claims of quality and effectiveness. Regional accreditation requires institutions to collect and analyze assessment data in forming judgments that are used to inform and improve planning, decision making, and actions. More than episodic exercises, assessment is expected to be conducted regularly and systematically to produce meaningful information regarding institutional and educational accomplishments. Further, the institution's assessment processes should be planned and implemented as a major contributing factor in the creation of a culture of evidence to demonstrate that an institution is willing and capable of examining itself on an ongoing basis.[17]

Past institutional evaluation procedures focused almost entirely on institutional processes, structures, and resources such as the academic degrees held by faculty members, the number of books in the library, and the size of institutional budgets. Judgments of institutional quality and effectiveness of outcomes were based on the assumption that more than contributing to achievements of acceptable levels of educational quality and institutional effectiveness, institutional infrastructure and resources (inputs) were directly responsible for institutional outcomes. As external constituencies become increasingly skeptical of the validity of judgments of quality based primarily upon a review of institutional intentions and resources, they demand evidence of achievement of intended educational outcomes and fulfillment of institutional mission and goals.[18]

Current regional accreditation evaluation criteria require each accredited and preaccredited institution, as well as units within the institution, to continuously examine goals, operations, and achievements by engaging in ongoing, systematic, and substantive planning and assessment to provide evidence of how well, and in what ways, it is achieving its mission and goals. Institutions are expected to develop and implement strategies and methods to assess their effectiveness by gathering and evaluating assessment data that are used in an ongoing cycle of planning and evaluation. Regional accrediting agencies do not prescribe specific methods, nor do they dictate the characteristics, form, or tools used in assessment and evaluation. They do, however, stress outcomes assessment as an essential part of institutional planning, decision making, and actions that translate plans into effective results. Therefore, in accord with its mission, organization, and characteristics, each accredited or preaccredited institution is expected to formulate and implement plans that provide for a comprehensive assessment of institutional and educational outcomes and, further, to incorporate the results of assessments to improve planning that leads to fulfillment of mission and goals.

Assessment and evaluation can be conducted in a variety of ways and based upon a variety of data sources. Because culture, characteristics, and mission are unique to each institution, a wide range of assessment systems is used to effectively demonstrate educational quality and institutional effectiveness. Some assessment systems are more formalized than others; some are more quantitative while others are more qualitative; some are well developed and others are evolving; some are adopted from outside the institution while others are developed internally. Regardless of the specific strategy selected by the institution, assessment strategies and methods should be adapted to the unique context of the institution to produce multiple indices of quality and effectiveness to document the institution's effectiveness in fulfilling its mission and goals.

As an example of the importance placed on assessment by regional accrediting agencies, the Northwest Commission on Colleges and Universities, the regional accrediting organization for the seven-state Northwest region, includes an explicit reference to assessment, evaluation, measurement, or judgment of quality and effectiveness in its eligibility requirements and each of its standards for accreditation. In demonstrating the achievement of mission and goals, institutions accredited and preaccredited by regional accrediting organizations are expected to build a convincing case that accomplishments are consistent with intentions. More than an emphasis on meeting minimum indicators of quality and effectiveness, regional accreditation focuses on an institution's capacity and its will, culture, and ability to assess itself continuously and to act on the results from those assessments to enhance quality and effectiveness.[19]

SUSTAINABILITY—INFRASTRUCTURE, RESOURCES, AND PROCESSES

Regionally accredited institutions offer certificate and degree programs that range from one to four years or more in length. Given the span of time required to complete an academic program, college and university stakeholders in general, and students in particular, are keenly interested not only in determinations of program quality and institutional effectiveness at the time of initial enrollment, but also in the institution's ability and capacity to assure persistence of program quality and institutional effectiveness throughout the duration of their course of study. Therefore, in addition to past accomplishments and current evidence of educational quality and effectiveness in achieving intended program outcomes, perceptions of institutional constituencies and enrollment decisions by students are influenced by indicators that warrant confidence in the ability and capacity of the institution to sustain achievement of program outcomes at acceptable levels of quality and effectiveness into the foreseeable future.

Predictions of future levels of quality and effectiveness based solely on evaluations of institutional intentions and current achievements are insufficient to provide reasonable assurance that intentions will be realized and outcomes will be maintained, or improved, over time. Therefore, in addition to reviewing an institution's mission, goals, and current educational and institutional outcomes, regional accreditation requires an evaluation of an institution's infrastructure and resources as a primary means to predict its ability and capacity to sustain achievement of institutional and educational outcomes at acceptable levels of quality and effectiveness over time.

PRESERVATION OF PRINCIPLES

Traditional American higher education principles of quality, effectiveness, autonomy, and self-regulation through voluntary peer review are manifested in accreditation criteria that reflect public expectations and expectations of the academic community itself. In response to shifting societal expectations, regional accrediting agencies have recently revised their accreditation criteria to more clearly emphasize assessment of achievements of institutional and student learning outcomes, as well as judgments of institutional intentions and capacity, in making accreditation decisions. In doing so, they preserve traditional higher education principles while responding to current societal expectations for accountability and quality assurance.

An example of regional accreditation's emphasis on function rather than form and its interest in balancing institutional intentions with evidence of institutional achievements can be found in the eligibility requirements of the Northwest Commission on Colleges and Universities. Before 2001, the commission's eligibility criteria reflected the generally accepted notion that a physical library was the primary way for institutions to demonstrate availability and access to requisite library and information resources to support an institution's academic programs. Consequently, the eligibility criteria included a requirement for institutions to have a least a "core library" as the means to support the institution's mission and the educational, research, and scholarly activities of students, faculty, and staff.[20]

Recent advances in technology and delivery systems, however, enable alternative means for institutions to demonstrate integrity with a basic accreditation tenet that library and information resources are essential contributors to the educational quality of college and university programs. In response to the expansion of delivery options, the commission revised its eligibility criteria in 2001 to require that accredited and preaccredited institutions "*provide* library resources, technology and services for students and faculty appropriate for its mission and for all of its educational programs wherever located and however delivered" (emphasis added).[21] The revision to the eligibility requirement preserves the principle regarding the importance of library and information resources to the educational quality of institutional programs while recognizing that institutions have multiple options to satisfy that principle in a manner that best meets the intentions and needs of the institution. This change reinforces the commission's values and principles of quality and effectiveness while putting them into a modern context that reflects a proactive response to a changing environment and societal expectations for relevant and meaningful evaluations of institutional quality and effectiveness.

In addition to considerations of function and form, the Northwest Commission on Colleges and Universities' accreditation criteria emphasize assessment as a means of determining effectiveness in achieving identified outcomes. In the area of library and information services, institutions are required to regularly assess the quality, accessibility, and use of library and information resources and services to determine their level of effectiveness in support of the educational program.[22] To reinforce the integrated nature of institutional units in fulfilling institutional missions, the accreditation criteria require each accredited or preaccredited institution to document that students effectively *use* library and information resources as an integral part of the learning process in the institution's academic programs.[23]

As evidenced by the examples cited above, regional accrediting organizations continuously review and revise their accreditation criteria to maintain principles of quality and effectiveness. In doing so, they adapt the forms of the criteria to reflect current internal institutional and external constituency expectations. More than focusing on ways and means that institutions provide educational programs and related services, regional accreditation criteria require evidence that principles of quality and effectiveness are realized at levels accepted by the academic community and the public. In requiring institutions to address questions such as "What do you claim to do?" "How well are you doing it?" and "What evidence do you have to support your judgments?" regional accrediting organizations are fulfilling their dual missions of providing quality assurance to interested stakeholders while encouraging continuous quality improvement within accredited and preaccredited institutions.

CONCLUSION

Assessment and evaluation are intended as means to document educational quality and institutional effectiveness, foster institutional improvement, and demonstrate accountability. Unfortunately, without a clear sense of the purpose for assessment, knowledge of what is to be assessed, and understanding of how the results will be used, assessment efforts all too often become an end in themselves.[24] If the results of assessment are not used to inform planning and decisions, colleges and universities often find themselves in positions of being data rich and information poor.

One way regional accreditation encourages the confidence of the public and the educational community is by requiring member institutions to conduct continuous, effective, and relevant self-assessment and self-evaluation of their intentions, infrastructure, processes, and outcomes to document clear and compelling evidence of achievement of results that correlate closely with institutional mission, goals, and characteristics. While not abandoning ongoing attention to inputs, regional accrediting agencies have responded to calls for evidence of accomplishments by adopting criteria that enable an evaluation of institutional outcomes as well as institutional inputs as part of the overall decision-making process regarding the accreditation of an institution.[25] The effect of this movement is that accredited and preaccredited institutions are required to provide substantive data-driven evidence of quality and effectiveness in fulfilling institutional and educational missions and goals. Given the diversity of America's colleges and universities, however, regional accreditation agencies do not dictate a particular form of assessment as the best or most appropriate means of determining quality and effectiveness. Decisions on specific methods and tools are most appropriately made by the institutions in light of their individual characteristics. Therefore, in evaluating educational quality and institutional effectiveness, institutions are evaluated in the context of institutional intentions supported by evidence of accomplishments based upon assessments of outcomes and achievements.

The recent emphasis by regional accrediting organizations on assessment and documentation of student and institutional achievements reflects a historic interest in improving educational quality and institutional effectiveness. It also constitutes a response to pressure from external constituencies to be more directly accountable for results rather than intentions and resources.[26] In turn, regional accrediting agencies are expanding their efforts to review and implement accreditation criteria and procedures that assure the public and the academic community that accredited and preaccredited institutions not only have appropriate resources and processes and are currently achieving their intended outcomes, but also that they assess, evaluate, and document their ability and capacity to sustain achievement of those outcomes over time. Consequently, institutions are more directly and systematically assessing themselves and their accomplishments to provide data-based evidence of achievement of student, programmatic, and institutional outcomes. Assessment data and the analysis of that data enable more informed analytic internal and external judgments of educational quality and institutional effectiveness, thereby enhancing public confidence that institutions are effective in achieving intended results. Further, assessment data and evaluation findings assist the public in making independent judgments regarding institutional accountability and stewardship of resources. The process of assessment and documentation also benefits institutions by providing important feedback regarding their progress in fulfilling their institutional and educational missions and goals.

By requiring evidence of achievements based upon assessments and evaluations of institutional and student performance, regional accrediting organizations foster development of meaningful documentation of quality and effectiveness in relationship to institutional values, characteristics, and missions at acceptable levels of quality and effectiveness to the academic community and public. In doing so, they provide meaningful assurance that distinctive institutional missions and the quality and effectiveness of educational programs and institutional services are both affirmed and advanced.[27] In addition to demonstrating accountability to external stakeholders, assessment and evaluation, in context with institutional intentions, ability, and capacity, help accredited and preaccredited institutions develop evidence to document fulfillment of institutional intentions as well as provide an outcomes-based, assessment-guided, evidence-driven foundation for future actions that lead to improvements in educational quality and institutional effectiveness.

NOTES

1. Peter T. Ewell, "A Matter of Integrity: Accountability and the Future of Self-Regulation," *Change* 26, no. 6 (1994): 24–29.

2. Roger Peters, "Some Snarks Are Boojums: Accountability and the End(s) of Higher Education," *Change* 26, no. 6 (1994): 16–23.

3. Ewell, "A Matter of Integrity," 27.

4. Ralph A. Wolff and Olita D. Harris, "Using Assessment to Develop a Culture of Evidence," in *Changing College Classrooms: New Teaching and Learning Strategies for an Increasingly Complex World*, ed. D. F. Halpern (San Francisco: Jossey-Bass, 1994), 271–288 (ERIC, ED 368307).

5. Kay McCullough Moore, "Assessment of Institutional Effectiveness," *New Directions for Community Colleges* 14, no. 4 (1986): 49–60.

6. James L. Hudgins, "Institutional Effectiveness: A Strategy for Renewal," *Community College Journal* 63, no. 5 (1993): 41–44.

7. E. Grady Bogue, "Quality Assurance in Higher Education: The Evolution of Systems and Design Ideals," *New Directions for Institutional Research* 25, no. 3 (1998): 7–18.

8. Ralph A. Wolff, "Restoring the Credibility of Accreditation," *Trusteeship* 1, no. 6 (1993): 20–21, 23–24.

9. Bogue, "Quality Assurance in Higher Education," 10.

10. Judith S. Eaton, *An Overview of U.S. Accreditation* (Washington, D.C.: Council for Higher Education Accreditation, 2002).

11. Ewell, "A Matter of Integrity," 28.

12. Thomas P. Hogan, "Methods for Outcomes Assessment Related to Institutional Accreditation," in *Accreditation, Assessment, and Institutional Effectiveness: Resource Papers for the COPA Task Force on Institutional Effectiveness* (Washington, D.C.: Council on Postsecondary Accreditation, 1992), 37–55 (ERIC, ED 343513).

13. Hudgins, "Institutional Effectiveness," 43.

14. Northwest Commission on Colleges and Universities, *Accreditation Handbook* (Redmond, Wash.: Northwest Commission on Colleges and Universities, 2003).

15. South Carolina Higher Education Assessment Network, *Recommendations for Defining and Assessing Institutional Effectiveness* (Charleston, S.C.: South Carolina Higher Education Assessment Network, 1994) (ERIC, ED 393384).

16. Gene Packwood, "Issues in Assessing Institutional Effectiveness," in *Assessing Institutional Effectiveness in Community Colleges*, ed. Don Doucette and Billie Hughes (Laguna Hills, Calif.: League for Innovation in the Community College, 1990), 45–51 (ERIC, ED 324072).

17. Peter T. Ewell, "Outcomes, Assessment, Institutional Effectiveness, and Accreditation: A Conceptual Exploration," in *Accreditation, Assessment, and Institutional Effectiveness: Resource Papers for the COPA Task Force on Institutional Effectiveness* (Washington, D.C.: Council on Postsecondary Accreditation, 1992), 1–17 (ERIC, ED 343513).

18. Hogan, "Methods for Outcomes Assessment," 38.

19. Ewell, "Outcomes, Assessment," 12.

20. Commission on Colleges and Universities, Northwest Association of Schools and of Colleges, *Accreditation Handbook* (Bellevue, Wash.: Commission on Colleges and Universities, 1999).

21. Northwest Commission on Colleges and Universities, *Accreditation Handbook*, 7.

22. Northwest Commission on Colleges and Universities, *Accreditation Handbook*, 70–71.

23. Northwest Commission on Colleges and Universities, *Accreditation Handbook*, 28.

24. Wolff and Harris, "Using Assessment," 275.

25. Hogan, "Methods for Outcomes Assessment," 38.

26. Ewell, "Outcomes, Assessment," 1.

27. Bogue, "Quality Assurance in Higher Education," 15.

CHAPTER 2

An Institutional Commitment to Assessment and Accountability

James Anderson

During the last decade, conversations about accountability in higher education have resonated across political, economic, legislative, and educational boundaries. Various stakeholders and audiences believe that their questions and expectations are of the highest priority and deserve attention from administrative and academic leaders. As expectations for public expenditures rise, so do public expectations for accountability of those expenditures.[1] Employers complain that recent college graduates are not prepared for the world of work. They suggest that graduates write and speak poorly, cannot work in cooperative teams, do not think critically, and cannot apply abstract knowledge in practical settings.

At no other time has there been a greater need for colleges and universities to agree upon and prioritize their indicators of accountability. In *Measuring Up 2000: The State-by-State Report Card for Higher Education*, the unit of analysis was the states and not individual higher education systems.[2] Yet, it would be foolhardy to believe that such a report card is not a precursor of institutional accountability reporting. States provide most of the direct support to and oversight of public institutions, and provide prominent support to private institutions. States also provide the organizational structure for public institutions and influence how and when these structures change.

The perceptions about higher education accountability often differ dramatically both within the academy and among those outside of it. The result of external conversations is that policy solutions, like national testing, are advanced before coherent conceptual frameworks occur. Undoubtedly, the lead-up to the reauthorization of the Higher Education Act in 2003 has engendered bipartisan commentary, some of which has spilled over into the accountability arena. Another strong external voice, the U.S. Department of Education, has pressed accreditation organizations to explain their timidness in terms of holding colleges and universities accountable for demonstrating that students learn, achieve, graduate, and become productive citizens.

Higher education leaders seek to sustain quality while stretching their budgets, but business and political leaders feel that colleges and universities have received adequate appropriations; these leaders are demanding better results, especially results that are meaningful to them.[3] Adding to this pressure are the growing public concerns over spiraling tuition costs and the pressure placed upon higher education to integrate information technology into the curriculum and instructional practices. Many higher education professionals have not been trained or educated to be accountable to the public.[4] This does not imply a lack of integrity or credibility on their part. Instead, their attention has been internally focused and they have often relied on traditional and/or easy-to-access performance indicators to demonstrate quality and effectiveness.[5]

STATEWIDE TESTING AND ACCOUNTABILITY

While only a small number of states actually engage in mandated, statewide testing of undergraduates, an increasing number are taking a close look at linking such testing to accountability. As Peter Ewell and Dennis P. Jones—vice president and president, respectively, at the National Center for Higher Education Management Systems—suggest, statewide testing will reflect two important characteristics: (1) it will be tailored to the culture and history of a particular state, and (2) it will be designed to meet a different set of objectives in each state.[6] Moreover, the large-scale implementation of a testing program presents enormous logistical and organizational challenges. One would expect that state policymakers would not rush to judgment in favor of implementing testing and chance that a new and costly layer of bureaucracy would emerge. Yet, testing offers an attractive incentive because of the perception that it allows for uniformity across institutions, that it provides equitable standards for achievement, that it is cost-effective, and that it eliminates the subjective nature of institutionally generated assessment and accountability efforts.

The development of statewide testing has strategic significance for faculty and academic departments not only as it applies to accreditation but also in terms of how it will impact critical feedback, like course-based assessment, which informs faculty work and program improvement.

Higher education leaders must become more focused on the importance of providing results to internal and external stakeholders. Faculty will tend to prefer locally designed and administered assessment methods because they incorporate their own values and preferred outcomes. Legislators and policymakers may prefer external assessments like standardized tests that allow for interinstitutional or national comparisons. In either case, a range of valuable resources exists that can assist campus leaders in making informed decisions about their choice of assessment approaches and tools.

Peggy Maki, then a senior scholar at the American Association of Higher Education, provides examples of course material that facilitates the assessment of general education outcomes.[7] Such assessments are valuable because they provide faculty with feedback on how students learn and develop throughout their undergraduate careers, and they allow for cross-curricula comparisons. Some sources focus on the types of assessments and their relationships to certain skills and competencies, while others emphasize methodological soundness and usefulness. All authors of source material agree on one important point: good practice in assessment involves the utilization of multiple methods to assess student learning.

PROMOTING FACULTY RESPONSIVENESS

The responsibility of campus leaders, academic and administrative, is to harness the available wealth of information (e.g., inputs, relational databases, student performance indicators, and outcomes-based information) for faculty use.[8] This will facilitate the development of conceptual frameworks and paradigms that are both discipline specific and that cut across academic areas. Too often, faculty are hesitant about moving beyond their own frames of reference to assess higher-order learning outcomes that seem complex, seem unrelated to their work and instructional strategies, and have not been presented in a meaningful language to them.[9] Such factors must be taken into account when faculty are asked to engage in more assessment activities and to discuss them publicly outside of their discipline.

In the context of enhancing faculty confidence, how assessment results are reported out becomes as important as the assessment tools that are utilized. Academic departments differ in terms of the degree to which they want their assessment results made public at different stages of the process. At North Carolina State University, a team of reviewers provides feedback to departments and programs when they initially submit their program review portfolio. The portfolio is a collection of material that reflects continuous and ongoing planning, information gathering, self-review, and use of assessment results. The portfolio captures a program's ongoing outcomes-assessment efforts and seeks to answer the following questions:

- What are we trying to do?
- How do we know?
- How do we use the information to improve?
- Do the improvements work?

The feedback is translated into changes as the portfolio is formally submitted. Some departments are adamant about confidentiality during this review/feedback process. Other departments are more willing to have their work made public. While uniformity is important for certain aspects of the assessment process, administrators have learned to respect department sentiments concerning portfolio reviews.

How can an institution promote department-based accountability among faculty? Faculty confidence is enhanced when they perceive an assessment process to be well planned, systematic, and meaningful to their values and work. Literally, what is initially put in their hands or provided during training can make or break a commitment to program review. For example, a sequence of activities implemented at North Carolina State University facilitates faculty involvement. That sequence includes the following:

- The presentation of a flexible outline for assessment plans along with an explanation of the characteristics of a good assessment plan

- Training and practice at writing measurable and meaningful outcomes that involve faculty who are novices and those who are more expert
- Consistent feedback to faculty and departments about their progress (both individual and comparative) via a variety of communication modes (e.g., electronic, paper, committees, and small groups)
- Submission of a practice assessment plan that meets the requirements of a criteria checklist
- Utilization of a rubric to evaluate the assessment process

Finally, faculty are provided with evidence that administrative and resource support are and will be available.[10]

Peter Gray, associate director of the Center for Instructional Development, Syracuse University, has the notion that academe should not downplay the potential of the assessment movement because it has not transformed higher education or because faculty buy-in is limited.[11] Rather, academe should embrace a more realistic and positive set of assumptions:

- All organizations and individuals need to change and grow in order to adapt to current conditions.
- Faculty are professionals who are curious and intrinsically motivated to question; hence, they have a propensity to embrace the purpose of assessment, which is to bring about continual improvement.
- Faculty members will understand that engaging in assessment can be in their own self-interest, because it can provide them with valuable information.

The imperative that is associated with assessment and accountability should motivate institutions to make proactive and assertive statements about their commitment and level of involvement. The set of affirmations in the following section could underscore the leadership vision of an institution that seeks to grow, change, and continually improve.

INSTITUTIONAL AFFIRMATIONS

Accountability means that institutions have a duty to:

- Educate students
- Continually improve the process for educating them
- Assess what they learn and how well they learn it
- Make the results public
- Demonstrate that assessment results are used to inform decisions about change and improvements

Accountability should address the diversity among educational environments that reflects varying missions, goals, priorities, and student characteristics. Academe can accomplish this by generating conceptual frameworks that account for these variations.[12]

Accountability should also address how an institution expands its public presentation of what it values and what it does to include evidence that key decision-makers and appropriate constituents can understand how higher education contributes to student learning.[13] Furthermore, accountability should address how an institution ensures that the process of providing evidence of learning is systematic and continuous.[14] For example, at what point should the search for technological solutions in gathering and reporting data be curtailed because it is no longer cost-effective?

Accountability means that those closest to the learning paradigm (i.e., faculty) must also have a sense of public accountability, for it is they who determine the knowledge to be learned, establish and communicate the process for learning, determine the responses that indicate learning has occurred, and decide the programmatic changes necessary to promote better learning. Accountability also means that faculty must set and agree upon their own benchmarks and communicate to others, internally and externally, what these benchmarks mean.[15]

Accountability means that assessment and evaluation should adhere, to the degree that circumstances allow, to standards of social science research and good practice. Furthermore, accountability means that institutional leaders take responsibility for assessment-based results and the consequences that follow.

NEGOTIABLE ISSUES

While the perception might be created that proactive assertions about assessment and accountability are nonnegotiable, within programs and departments both faculty and staff can negotiate the more fundamental aspects of an assessment plan. Each department can tailor:

- The purpose of the assessment effort
- Who will be involved
- The criteria for assessment
- Who will do the study
- The design of the study
- The consultation needed
- Interpretations of the findings
- Recommendations for policy/practice[16]

Perhaps the most significant subjective starting point is "What are the most important questions to ask or address?" A particular program, department, or college may focus on general questions such as "What do you expect your students to know and be able to do by the end of their education?" or "How can you help students make connections between classroom learning and experiences outside of the classroom?" Questions can also be posed that use the learners as the focal point for examining learning outcomes:

- Can the interpersonal transactions that occur in the everyday lives of the students and that reflect their cultural orientations serve as a basis for potential new models of critical thinking?
- What curricular experiences will promote this skill development?

Faculty must be convinced that they control the assessment process and, ultimately, that they are held accountable for student learning and development.

THE IMPORTANCE OF REGIONAL ACCREDITATION REFORM

One of the most significant reforms that is occurring in higher education over the last few years involves the decision by the eight regional accrediting commissions to change their practices. These organizations assign an accredited status to institutions that meet compliance standards and that provide evidence of educational effectiveness. While reaffirming that an institution is in compliance with basic operational standards is important, it is more important to demonstrate its capacity to improve and sustain educational excellence and effectiveness.

The current reform is more than a simple revision of accreditation standards. Instead, it is a public call to institutions to raise the bar of accountability and to reestablish their commitment to the mission, goals, and institutional objectives that they publicize and rest their image and reputation upon. This reform represents the long-needed blood transfusion that can and, in many cases, will serve as the catalyst to energize campuses to become risk-takers and to embrace an institutional paradigm shift.

Accreditation reform has six features that are intended to enhance the role of accreditation while expanding its capacity to meet current institutional needs:

1. Revising accreditation standards to focus on quality improvement
2. Using regional accreditation to address national quality-review needs
3. Attending to quality review of distance learning
4. Expanding international quality-review activity
5. Expanding attention to teaching and learning
6. Achieving greater efficiency through coordination across accrediting organizations[17]

Needless to say, many institutions will perceive that regional accreditors are placing new demands upon them—demands that will undoubtedly require new resources, new ways of operating, and even a new vision for the future. Such valid realities must be addressed, but they cannot be used as barriers to the implementation of a process that not only will enhance quality and effectiveness, but also will make accountability the norm and not the exception.

PROMOTING THE PROCESS OF ASSESSMENT AND ACCOUNTABILITY

In a perfect world, the optimal scenario would be to create a culture of assessment and accountability at colleges and universities. Two of the most critical aspects of such a culture are reflected in the faculty's conversations about and commitment to the "process" upon which that culture is built. Therefore, mechanisms should be in place that promote the process among all constituents who are actively involved in such a culture. The following eight examples represent suggested ways that the process associated with assessment can be promoted:

1. Continually remind each other of the benefits of assessment and its role in accountability reporting;
2. Share examples across departments and programs irrespective of whether one is a novice or expert;
3. Advertise your assessment goals, decisions, and what you are learning and be accepting of constructive critiques;
4. Articulate your college-wide assessment expectations;
5. Incorporate students in all facets of assessment planning and implementation;
6. Acknowledge and address barriers to assessment;
7. Understand your role as an administrator, faculty representative, or researcher in this process and try not to step too far beyond that role; and
8. Have answers for the question, "What happens if I don't engage in assessment?"[18]

At the college level, it is important to anticipate the most relevant questions and to promote broad-based discussions about the potential answers. Those questions include:

1. Will the college have its own timeline for the implementation of the process or does the institution or external bodies drive the schedule?

2. Whose internal and external expertise can you leverage?

3. Will there be someone doing the "regular" data collection (e.g., enrollment figures, retention and graduation rates)?

4. Will there be someone coordinating the assessment planning process?

5. Will there be someone in charge of the documentation?

6. How can you use assessment to inform other aspects of planning and/or performance indicators in the college?

7. Can key assessment coordinators get release time to get the process established?

8. How will you manage college expectations for data with faculty and program expectations of assessment?

9. How will you use the assessment results?[19]

TRANSFORMATION AND ACCOUNTABILITY

Among the many indicators that a culture of assessment and accountability is emerging, the presence or absence of "transformational characteristics" is clear evidence of institutional commitment. Based on work authored or inspired by various authors,[20] these characteristics are:

- Shared purpose
- Collaboration across the institution
- Leadership/commitment from administration and faculty
- Rituals, practices, and symbols
- Education, support, reward, and recognition
- Evidence of depth and pervasiveness
- Sustainability[21]

A variety of measures can be utilized to gauge the degree of transformation. For example, one could use surveys and self-evaluations, Web site utilization, documentation usage evaluation, testimonials, observation, document analysis, and evaluation of assessment plans.

The institutional commitment to assessment and accountability begins with the conceptual agreement throughout the college/university community about what is valued. This agreement forms the shared purpose, which consists of:

- Common language;
- Shared conceptual understanding;
- Improving student learning;
- Assessment plans;
- History of evidence-based decision making;
- Results driven decision making;
- Expectation of assessment; and
- Shared outcomes.[22]

CONCLUSION

Once a shared purpose of assessment is established at an institution, participants can move forward with conversations regarding the innate interests of the faculty and their desire to improve what they do. The commitment toward continuous improvement can be seen in decisions that have an impact on the assessment process, and those commitments and decisions lead to a far different atmosphere from the compliance-oriented atmosphere, which is established by setting deadlines, insisting on rigid rules, and punishing those who err in an accreditation-driven process. The alternative is an atmosphere where faculty develop and grow with the assessment process, realizing the value and benefit of its continuous, iterative nature.

NOTES

1. Dean L. Bresciani, *Explaining Administrative Costs: A Case Study* (Ph.D. diss., University of Arizona, 1996), UMI Dissertation Services, 9713408.

2. See National Center for Public Policy and Higher Education, *Commentary on Measuring Up 2000* (Washington, D.C.: National Center, n.d.), available at http://www.highereducation.org/commentary (accessed March 1, 2004).

3. Bresciani, *Explaining Administrative Costs.*

4. Marilee J. Bresciani, *Expert Driven Assessment: Making It Meaningful to Decisionmakers*, ECAR Research Bulletin 21 (Boulder, Colo.: Educause, 2003).

5. Bresciani, *Expert Driven Assessment.*

6. Peter Ewell and Dennis P. Jones, *Indicators of Good Practice in Undergraduate Education: A Handbook for Development and Implementation* (Boulder, Colo.: National Center for Higher Education Management Systems, 1996).

7. Peggy Maki, "From Standardized Tests to Alternative Methods," *Change* 33, no. 2 (March–April 2001): 28–31.

8. Marilee J. Bresciani, "Creating a Universitywide Assessment Plan," submitted for publication to *Assessment Update* (2002).

9. Bresciani, *Expert Driven Assessment.*

10. See North Carolina State University, Division of Undergraduate Affairs, *Assessment for the Division of Undergraduate Affairs* (Raleigh, N.C.: North Carolina State University, 2001), available at http://www.ncsu.edu/undergrad_affairs/assessment/assess.htm (accessed March 1, 2004).

11. Peter J. Gray, "Viewing Assessment as an Innovation: Leadership and the Change Process," *New Directions for Higher Education* 100 (1997): 5–15.

12. Bresciani, *Expert Driven Assessment.*

13. Bresciani, *Expert Driven Assessment.*

14. Bresciani, *Expert Driven Assessment.*

15. Bresciani, *Expert Driven Assessment.*

16. See North Carolina State University, Division of Undergraduate Affairs, *Assessment for the Division of Undergraduate Affairs*, available at http://www.ncsu.edu/undergrad_affairs/assessment/assess.htm (accessed March 1, 2004).

17. Judith S. Eaton, "Regional Accreditation Reform," *Change* 33, no. 2 (March-April 2001): 38–45.

18. Bresciani, "Creating a Universitywide Assessment Plan," 2.

19. Bresciani, "Creating a Universitywide Assessment Plan," 4.

20. Trudy W. Banta, "Characteristics of Effective Outcomes Assessment: Foundations and Examples," in *Building a Scholarship of Assessment*, ed. Trudy W. Banta and Associates (San Francisco: Jossey-Bass, 2002), 260–283; Marilee J. Bresciani, "The Assessment of Assessment" (submitted for publication to *Assessment Update*, 2002); Marilee J. Bresciani and Keri Bowman, "Assessing the Impact of Our Assessment Process," paper presented at North Carolina State University Assessment Symposium, Raleigh (2003); Ewell and Jones, *Indicators of Good Practice*; Cecilia López, "Assessment of Student Learning: Challenges and Strategies," *The Journal of Academic Librarianship* 28 (2002): 356–367; Peggy Maki and Marilee J. Bresciani, "Integrating Student Outcomes Assessment into a University Culture," paper presented at the American Association of Higher Education Faculty Forum on Roles and Rewards Conference, Phoenix, Arizona (January 2002); and Catherine A. Palomba and Trudy W. Banta, *Assessment Essentials: Planning, Implementing, and Improving Assessment in Higher Education* (San Francisco: Jossey-Bass, 1999).

21. Bresciani, "The Assessment of Assessment," 1.

22. Bresciani, "The Assessment of Assessment," 1.

CHAPTER 3

A Decade of Assessing Student Learning: What We Have Learned, and What Is Next

Cecilia L. López

The Commission on Institutions of Higher Education (now called the Higher Learning Commission) of the North Central Association of Colleges and Schools (NCA) introduced its Assessment Initiative by issuing its first "Statement on Assessment and Student Academic Achievement" in 1989. That statement was the first public expression of the commission's growing belief that, if its member institutions were to serve learners of the twentieth century successfully, they would need to become student centered. Today, the commission's vision is that all of its affiliated colleges and universities will recognize the value of becoming student-centered learning organizations committed to continuous improvement in the quality of the education achieved by their students. It strengthened the criteria for accreditation so that each affiliated institution would plan and implement a program to assess student learning and discover for itself the power of assessment to transform institutional culture.

The commission's first step was to ask that every affiliated institution

This chapter is adapted from Dr. Cecilia L. López, "A Decade of Assessing Student Learning: What We Have Learned; What's Next," a paper on assessing student learning presented at the 1999 annual meeting of the Commission on Institutions of Higher Education. Available at http://www.ncahigherlearning commission.org/AnnualMeeting/archives/ASSESS10.PDF.

develop a plan for a program to assess student academic achievement within five years. Next, it asked that each institution implement the program it had planned and begin to use the results of assessment to improve its students' learning. At the ten-year milestone, the commission took stock of where the NCA Board of Trustees and its member institutions were in relationship to that vision. The commission has come far enough to see clearly the impediments that it still needs to overcome in order to arrive at its destination and to recognize that it already possesses the tools to overcome all obstacles if it will use them.

THE COMMISSION'S ASSESSMENT INITIATIVE: A BRIEF OVERVIEW

The commission issued its first "Statement on Assessment and Student Academic Achievement" in October 1989. That statement made explicit two fundamental points in the commission's position on the assessment of student learning: first, that assessing student achievement is a critical component of evaluating overall institutional effectiveness, and second, that "assessment is not an end in itself, but a means of gathering information that assists institutions in making useful decisions about improvement."

In 1996, the commission strengthened its statement by adding that an effective assessment program should be structured, systematic, ongoing, and implemented. It also clearly stated that an acceptable assessment program should be based on explicit statements published by the institution regarding its faculty's expectations for student achievement and should provide evidence that it uses the information gained from the systematic collection and examination of assessment data gathered at the academic program level both to document and to improve student learning.[1]

WHAT THE COMMISSION HAS LEARNED AND ACHIEVED FROM THE FIRST TEN YEARS OF THE ASSESSMENT INITIATIVE

After ten years of steady effort, the major lesson the commission has learned from its Assessment Initiative is that it is not easy to gain universal acceptance of the efficacy of assessing student learning. This explains why it has been so difficult to have all NCA colleges and universities plan, introduce, and fully implement structured and ongoing assessment programs—even over a ten-year period. Indeed, the number of institutions that have actually taken each of those steps and are now using the results of assessment to develop and test ideas for how to improve the level of student learning in each academic program is still relatively small. The number of institutions that have yet to engage each of their academic departments in every aspect of assessment is disappointingly large.

On the other hand, the commission can point to several significant achievements. First, it has been successful in communicating the importance it places on the assessment of student learning. The message has been heard! No NCA institution is unaware that the commission's commitment to assessment is strong and will last. Assessment is not a fad, and it will not go away. Instead, the emphasis upon assessment of student learning will continue to increase because assessment is the foundation upon which a student-centered learning institution must build if it is to improve continually the education its students achieve.

The commission's second achievement has been to expand greatly the number of institutions familiar with assessment, with what good practice in assessment is, and with the ways in which a sound assessment program can be valuable to institutions and their students. Ten years ago, less than a dozen institutions had any significant experience with ongoing, structured, and systematic processes to assess student learning across all academic programs or understood how the results of assessment could be used to improve continually their educational programs. Today, because of the Assessment Initiative, virtually all affiliated colleges and universities have at the very least gone through the discipline of planning and then starting assessment programs. As a result, there is now a broad base of institutions within NCA that has firsthand experience in the assessment of student learning. These colleges and universities will testify to the value that assessment activities on their campuses have added to their students, faculty, and institutions.[2]

Finally, although the Assessment Initiative has not moved ahead as rapidly as originally envisioned, the commission can claim as a significant achievement that its emphasis on the importance of assessing student learning has begun to have a major impact on the culture of many colleges and universities. Specifically, the Assessment Initiative has provided the impetus for a growing number of affiliated institutions to fulfill their potential by becoming student-centered learning institutions that use assessment to improve continuously the education their students obtain. This is evidence that the NCA—the commission and member institutions together—is actually accomplishing a shift in the accreditation paradigm from one that emphasized evaluating institutional inputs to one focused on assessing student outcomes. This basic change in paradigm frees institutions to keep pace with the profound social and technological transformations higher education is undergoing, while improving educational quality.

WHAT INSTITUTIONS HAVE LEARNED FROM PLANNING AND IMPLEMENTING PROGRAMS TO ASSESS STUDENT LEARNING

What NCA colleges and universities have learned from planning and implementing programs to assess student learning is as important as the lessons the commission has learned. Their most difficult lesson has been to discover that simply being made aware of the characteristics of an effective assessment program has not been sufficient for some institutions to plan and implement an effective assessment program successfully. From an examination of numerous evaluation team reports and self-study reports, it is clear that institutions that do not have a fully operational assessment program after ten years of work are almost surely being held back by some combination of three factors: (1) basic misunderstandings about the purpose and nature of assessment, (2) emotionally based resistance to assessment from those responsible for it, and (3) inadequate information and skills needed to conduct assessment.

How Far Have NCA Member Institutions Come?

The 1998 team reports indicate how far the 989 institutions that comprise the NCA commission have come in ten years toward realizing the commission's vision. Virtually all institutions accredited by NCA are now actively working to complete implementation of their assessment programs. Some are still trying to introduce missing components in their programs, some are trying to engage academic departments that have lagged behind, and a small but modest number have complete and well-established assessment programs. Their assessment programs fall along a continuum of implementation and reflect varying degrees of commitment to continuously improving student learning.

By comparing the number of assessment program elements an institution has in place and the proportion of its academic departments that conduct assessment across each program it offers, it is possible to describe institutions as having reached one of three levels of implementing their assessment programs.[3] Each level has a distinguishing cluster of characteristics that (1) depict the level of program implementation a college or university has reached and (2) reveal its institutional priorities. The levels accurately reflect where improvement of student learning and assessment, as the critical means to that end, falls within those priorities. Institutions that are at Level One, "Beginning Implementation," have still not agreed on effective means to assess student learning in general education competencies and skills or to document learning across each of their majors or any other academic programs. Institutions at Level Two, "Some Implementation," have a substantial number of the essential components of an assessment program in place, demonstrating that assessment and improvement of student learning are becoming an institutional priority.

Institutions that have reached Level Three have fully implemented assessment programs; they are engaged in "Ongoing Implementation." Level Three colleges and universities have typically progressed to a point where their mission and purpose statements include explicit language about the importance that the institution places on the assessment of student learning and student outcomes. Faculty in academic programs regularly recommend and introduce changes to increase students' academic achievement and track the results of those changes. In short, an effective assessment program has transformed each college and university at Level Three into a student-centered organization focused on students' learning that uses the results of assessment to continually improve the learning its students achieve.

What lessons can we learn from the institutions that encountered problems early on and are now "stuck" at Level One, or from those now at Level Two but making slow progress toward implementing their assessment programs? What can we learn from the other institutions that have encountered very similar problems but have overcome them and, with implemented programs in place, are now able to concentrate fully on *using* assessment results to improve learning? Fortunately, there is a rich store of information about common difficulties that colleges and universities have met, the reasons why some institutions have been blocked by these problems, and the positive and creative ways that faculty and administrators have found to overcome them.

The problems most frequently described as preventing or slowing an institution's progress toward reaching full implementation of its assessment plan fall into eight broad areas:

1. Difficulties in involving faculty and students in assessment
2. Difficulties in developing program goals and measurable objectives
3. Difficulties in selecting or developing direct and indirect measures aligned with program goals and measurable objectives
4. Difficulties in collecting and interpreting data
5. Difficulties in disseminating assessment data and information because of insufficient or incomplete feedback loops
6. Difficulties in obtaining or reallocating the funds needed for assessment activities
7. Difficulties in linking the assessment processes with operational planning and annual budgeting processes
8. Difficulties in understanding and providing for the collaborative roles of academic administrators and faculty

What Institutions Have Learned and Taught Us about Involving Faculty and Students in the Assessment Program

For assessment to become an integral permanent component of campus culture, faculty need to recognize its potential value, be committed to its inclusion in the regular ongoing processes of their institution, accept ownership and responsibility for the assessment program, and participate fully in all of its components. However, as soon as institutions began to respond to NCA's request for their assessment plans, not all faculty were immediately enthusiastic about the Assessment Initiative. Although many faculty were quick to embrace assessment of student learning and could see its possibilities, others were antagonistic, fearful, or passive when faced with the request to introduce it. In those colleges and universities in which key faculty have not claimed ownership or participated wholeheartedly and in large numbers, institutions have had great difficulty in launching and developing their assessment programs. Institutions repeatedly remark on three factors that make it difficult to draw faculty into the assessment effort on their campus:

1. Misunderstandings about the nature and purpose of assessing student academic achievement and about what constitutes an assessment program, academic program review, and evaluation of institutional effectiveness

2. Strongly negative reactions to the idea of "measuring" learning and the thought that assessment results could be used to actually improve students' learning

3. Lack of the information and technical skills needed to understand and implement assessment

Problems Caused by Misunderstandings

Three frequently encountered misunderstandings account for much of the difficulty some institutions have had in recruiting faculty to participate in planning and implementing their assessment programs. One has been misunderstanding on the part of faculty and administrative officers about the purpose of assessing student learning. Some college and university personnel have assumed the purpose of NCA's increased emphasis on assessment of student learning was to force colleges and universities to comply with additional regulations, or thought it was only a new fad among accrediting bodies that would pass. Institutions at which faculty or administration have reacted to the Assessment Initiative as an intrusive imposition by outsiders or a bureaucratic chore, rather than as a useful tool for the purpose of effectively accomplishing educational goals and intended student outcomes, were slow to plan an assessment program and have been even slower to carry out the plan. They have resisted taking advantage of what is known about learning and how to measure it. Even now, a few still seem far from recognizing the benefits of the Assessment Initiative that so many of their peer institutions are beginning to reap.

In contrast, institutions that understood early on that the motivation for NCA's Assessment Initiative was to help colleges and universities carry out their respective educational missions and reach their own goals for the improvement of student learning seized the opportunity to build a useful assessment program. They have moved rapidly to formulate or reaffirm an educational philosophy and agree upon a statement of purpose for the assessment program that would guide faculty and academic administrators as they began to plan and then implement the program. In these colleges and universities, faculty wrote clearly expressed educational goals and precise descriptions of what students were to demonstrate they knew, believed, and could do at the completion of every educational program. They understood that their statements would be the markers for determining how much students learn of what their faculty value most. Today, these institutions are well along in implementing their assessment programs. Many report that soon, for the first time, faculty will discover how close or far their students are from meeting the educational goals and measurable objectives they set for graduates of their programs.

A second very different misunderstanding initially prevented other institutions from being able to attract faculty to join colleagues in developing assessment plans and implementing acceptable assessment programs. Faculty and academic administrators in this second group of colleges and universities were confused about the difference between assessment of student learning and evaluation of overall institutional effectiveness. For instance, they often erroneously described evaluation of instruction and faculty performance as measures they would use to document student learning.

They did not understand that neither the quality of teaching nor any other aspect of faculty performance measures what students know and can apply, although they are important to conducting academic program review. These institutions typically needed to resubmit plans demonstrating that they could differentiate between how well faculty teach and how much students learn. In contrast, successful plans dealt exclusively with the assessment of student learning, or showed that the college or university understood assessment of student learning to be one of several separate but related components of the institution's total program for evaluating its overall effectiveness.

A third misunderstanding that caused some faculty, and particularly chairs of academic departments, to draw back from participating in developing assessment programs was the mistaken impression that assessment of student learning would be duplicative of academic program review. They did not see either the difference or the connection between academic program review and the assessment program. They did not recognize, for instance, that academic program review is typically resource oriented and episodic, whereas a program to assess student learning is outcomes centered and ongoing. In institutions where this misunderstanding existed, evaluation teams noted that even assessment committees were perplexed about how to report the outcomes of assessment of student academic achievement in a form that would be useful to faculty in recognizing areas where student learning could improve and, in turn, in suggesting ameliorative changes. Faculty in those institutions were often slow to recognize that an academic department could submit assessment results and documentation of initiatives intended to improve learning as one among the many kinds of evidence that peer evaluators would consider during program review.

Problems Caused by Negative Beliefs

Misunderstandings about the nature and purpose of assessment and those about its relation to institutional evaluation and program review are relatively straightforward to resolve. While they can directly inhibit faculty participation in assessment if not addressed, institutions typically do find the necessary external help to clear up these confusions. There is, however, a greater obstacle to faculty participation that institutions are reluctant to bring up in conversation or written documents, and that can only be overcome within a campus community itself. This obstacle is the active or passive opposition of influential faculty who have intensely personal reasons for resisting institution-wide assessment and who refuse to take any constructive role in it. Strongly negative, emotionally charged positions held by even a few powerful campus figures can be a potent hindrance to gaining the cooperation of other faculty in developing, or participating in, the assessment program. If left unaddressed, it can be the most persistent and deleterious. The influence of faculty leaders who ignore or refuse to introduce assessment at the department level or speak negatively about the institution-wide program can slow progress on both fronts for a very long time. When a college or university has such a problem, its institutional leaders need to acknowledge the nature of the difficulty and deal directly and sympathetically with its human sources.

Some faculty fear that the results of assessment, especially those that may reveal how many students have not learned what faculty had assumed, will somehow, someday, be used against them professionally. They believe the results of any assessment of student learning at the program level will be taken into account during faculty evaluation and could affect tenure, promotion, or salary decisions. A few refuse to participate because they view assessment of student learning as an additional time-consuming responsibility not included in the duties specified in their union contract and therefore an infringement on academic freedom. Some faculty and academic administrators are reluctant to commit their own or their department's human and financial resources to assessment because they believe that nothing any faculty can do individually or collectively within a department will ever make a *real* difference in improving students' learning. They assume that, because students are endowed with differing degrees of academic aptitude, motivation, and preparation, some will never "be good students" or learn much.

Some faculty have come to believe that it is impossible to assess, let alone quantify, what students are learning about the "really important things." They may be unaware of the differences between qualitative and quantitative research and know little about psychometrics. Others hold tenaciously to an unexamined belief that grades within individual classrooms attest to academic achievement across an entire academic program and that no other kind of assessment can add anything useful to faculty perceptions about what their students are learning. And, some faculty, particularly those in large decentralized universities, are unwilling to help introduce any new institutional program because they are convinced that nothing can or should change the culture of the department, college, or school in which they work.

However intransigent these men and women may appear, most are fiercely loyal to the institutions where they teach, and they are devoted to their students. They can usually be persuaded to give assessment a fair trial if the colleagues they most highly regard make a personal request for their cooperation and assistance. Concerned and informed peers need to engage each individual who clings to these kinds of negative beliefs in ongoing dialogue. Every erroneous belief needs be countered with facts each time it is expressed until at last it loses its energy and can no longer contribute to the delay or prevention of full implementation of assessment.

Three examples suggest the kinds of information that faculty and administrators might use to help colleges and universities correct misinformation or erroneous beliefs that have held them back from participating in their institution's assessment effort. In the first instance, an institution might need to address a campus rumor that documentation of student academic achievement is going to be used to discredit or penalize faculty whose students have scored less high than others. Such rumors would certainly be unsettling to many faculty, who then would very likely express their discomfort by ignoring or rejecting efforts to get them to become active in departmental and institution-wide assessment activities. In such a case, the assessment committee and all other faculty and administrators in the institution who understand assessment would have a responsibility to strenuously rebut the rumors that the results of assessing student learning were to be used against individual faculty. They would need to reiterate that NCA does not have, nor will it ever have, a policy that could link assessment with decisions about faculty promotion, tenure, or compensation. They would also need to assure worried colleagues that the results of assessment are always to be used solely as the basis for improving student learning across entire academic programs and would never be used for the evaluation of individual faculty. Of course, even in institutions where no such rumor exists, everyone, from the president and board members through the administrative ranks and department chairs, needs to remind constantly faculty, students, and all other constituents about the purpose of assessment and the uses that will be made of its results. The mantra on every campus must be "assessment is about student learning; it is *not* about faculty evaluation."

A second example of a situation where an institution might use peer interaction and authoritative information to correct erroneous beliefs would be if there were a need to respond to the allegations of some faculty that to require or strongly encourage them to participate in assessment of student learning would be an infringement on academic freedom. Colleagues with expertise in contractual matters might be asked to meet with concerned faculty to revisit the 1940 Statement of Principles on Academic Freedom and Tenure with 1970 Interpretive Comments,[4] the language of the letter of initial appointment, the institution's faculty handbook, or any contract between the institution and a faculty union that describes the responsibilities and rights of individual faculty members. They could point out that virtually none of these documents describes participation in institutional or departmental academic affairs as "overload" or even as part of compensated workload.

The statement of the American Association of University Professors (AAUP) refers specifically to faculty entitlement to conduct research on any subject, to publish the results of that research, and to discuss controversial topics related to their subject in the classroom. It does not refer to faculty participation in departmental, programmatic, or institutional processes, including assessment activities and the use of assessment results to improve student learning. Faculty working with concerned colleagues could also remind them of the faculty's traditional responsibilities as set forth by the AAUP.[5] Seen in this light, to refuse to accept a primary role or participate in the development and implementation of programs and processes related to the educational process (including their institution and department's assessment programs) is to abdicate a fundamental faculty responsibility.

A third example of a situation where collegial discussion and exposure by a colleague to new information that could be used to correct erroneous beliefs about assessment of student learning would be if some faculty on a campus were to hold that any college student who received poor grades in a course taught through lecture and readings is either lazy or of limited ability. Faculty might be able to induce colleagues to consider the potential of assessment to improve student learning by making them aware of studies showing that students have the capacity to achieve higher levels of competence and personal growth than may have been realized. Assessment committees, department chairs, and academic administrators might also help change the perspective of colleagues by holding faculty seminars on multiple intelligences[6] and on differing learning styles.[7] Participation could open them to the possibility that faculty have been successful in teaching students who possess less recognized kinds of intellectual giftedness. They might profit from discussion of why many students who are considered slow learners may in fact be bright people who learn better by doing than by listening.

They could also be invited to brown-bag faculty lunches and campus lectures by visiting scholars on constructivism. Hearing from other scholars that learning can be defined as "an active process of constructing rather than acquiring knowledge"[8] might help many faculty to understand better the potential of students not easily reached by a single, oral mode of instruction such as the lecture. Becoming familiar with research and theory in those three areas could reduce some faculty's pessimism about the possibility of enabling students to learn more. It could also move some faculty to adopt pedagogies of active learning such as problem-based learning,[9] collaborative learning, student-faculty partnerships,[10] service learning, and engaging undergraduate students in faculty research.[11]

Faculty know that the image of the student as an "empty vessel that passively gets filled" is not an accurate portrayal and never has been. Most faculty have discovered that "teaching as telling" and "learning as memorizing" do not work very well for most learners. Yet, some may not be aware of the evidence that when students are actively engaged in learning, they are more likely to apply and demonstrate the knowledge and skills they have acquired. The educational process that achieves these results invigorates both faculty and students. Faculty need to convey to their colleagues who are pessimistic about the likelihood that student learning across entire programs could be demonstrably improved that, as an academy, we know a lot more than we used to about how adults learn. They need to persuade them that what is known should make faculty realistically hopeful that their students can learn more but only if their faculty are willing to assess their academic achievement, determine where improvement is needed, and try new ways to involve and assist them in their learning.

Problems Caused by Lack of Information or Skills

Misunderstandings about assessment and negative attitudes toward it have not been the only deterrents to faculty participation in the construction and operation of successful assessment programs. A widespread lack of information and skills basic to carrying on assessment has been an equally formidable obstacle that many colleges and universities have had to face.

In many institutions, faculty and administrators were unfamiliar with good practice in institutional processes and structures. In some, individual faculty members knew a considerable amount about assessment but declined to assist in setting up their college or university's program because they recognized that to assess learning across academic programs would require a level of professional and technical advice and assistance beyond that which they or any individual in their department was qualified to give.

Faculty and other campus leaders who had never had an opportunity to participate in well-organized, participatory institutional processes in their college or university often did not know to include provisions in the assessment plan for essentials such as administrative leadership, clear lines of authority, faculty ownership and student participation, a carefully structured process with a realistic timetable, and adequate funding. In contrast, faculty and academic administrators who had taken part in effective planning and budgeting processes or similar complex institutional governance processes were not daunted by the challenge of helping establish an institution-wide assessment program. They were both willing and able to transfer their prior knowledge directly to the design of their institutional assessment program.

When most colleges and universities began to develop a plan for an assessment program, few, if any, of their faculty had technical information and skills in testing, research design, and statistics, all areas they would need if they were to take a significant part in developing and executing an assessment program beyond the early phase of working out educational goals and measurable objectives. This made it particularly difficult for their institutions to encourage faculty to participate in the implementation of the next phases of the assessment program. Faculty members who had neither training nor experience in areas such as psychometrics were typically unable to distinguish accurately between direct and indirect measures of student learning, found it difficult to move beyond the assessment of easy-to-quantify skills, did not understand the meaning of or purpose for using multiple measures and methods, and did not grasp the necessity for valid and reliable instruments. They were at a loss about how to select or create tests or other measures that aligned with the educational goals and measurable objectives. In institutions where there have been few, if any, faculty with the knowledge to provide leadership and teach their colleagues, it has often been slow and difficult to educate faculty about good practice in measuring student academic achievement and about the potential benefits of assessment to their institution and its students. In contrast, institutions that had faculty and administrators on staff already familiar with the literature of adult learning and the construction of tests and measures were able to involve them in planning the proposed assessment program and later as assessment committee members. These institutions have moved forward in implementing their programs and are conducting sound and useful assessments of learning across all or nearly all of their academic programs.

Faculty Development as the Primary Solution to Problems in Faculty Participation in Assessment

Self-studies and team reports indicate that the vast majority of NCA colleges and universities had to grapple with some or all of the types of problems just described as they attempted to get their faculties to assume ownership of institutional and departmental assessment programs. A number of institutions have found it possible to interest faculty and students in assessment and gradually build a knowledgeable, enthusiastic cadre of faculty who are actively engaged in all aspects of the assessment program.

Roles of Assessment Committees in Increasing Faculty Involvement in Assessment at the Departmental Level

Not surprisingly, the most effective way a majority of colleges and universities have found to build broad faculty participation in their assessment programs has been to arrange for all faculty and academic administrators to learn about assessment from persons knowledgeable in the field. They have found that training cannot be accomplished in just one session, but requires any number of different kinds of opportunities to learn about various aspects of assessment over several years. Institutions that have been successful in educating their faculty about assessment have high rates of faculty involvement in the assessment program at both the institutional and departmental levels.

The administrators of most institutions provide and fund opportunities for faculty development in assessment of student learning through the standing assessment committee. Some of these committees have found it possible to integrate assessment into the culture of the academic departments by bringing to campus trained, experienced departmental chairs and faculty from comparable colleges and universities. Because they are peers, these guest consultants will be accepted as authorities when they speak at workshops for departmental chairs and faculty on how to measure student learning across academic programs, and they are credible when they describe the ways in which assessment has proven beneficial at their institutions. They help the host departments design their departmental assessment programs, or single components of it, on an "as-needed" basis and are available to give practical advice on any perplexing assessment activities.

Assessment committees at a number of institutions have reported that, in addition to the usefulness of bringing outside peer consultants to work on campus with individual departments or groups of departments, it has proven valuable to have their own members work one-on-one as consultants on assessment. They report that they often do this first with individual department chairs. Once individual chairs have become receptive to learning more about assessment, the assessment committee or one or more of its members hold workshops for all chairs and seminars for the faculty and chairs of single departments or divisions.

Some assessment committees have found that their members are able to serve individually as respected peer advisors to any faculty members who are known to be misinformed, suspicious, or critical of assessment. They report that although this process is time-consuming, it markedly contributes to developing a climate of trust in the assessment process. They have learned that when their members work privately with individual faculty members and department chairs, they find it is often possible to persuade faculty that they will personally benefit if they obtain program assessment results, and will be able to use the results in ways that will not only increase their students' learning but also serve the best interests of the department and the institution as a whole.

Assessment committees report in self-studies that arranging for external consultants and having their members serve as mentors to individual faculty are only two of the ways in which they help educate faculty about assessment. The third way is simply by carrying out the ongoing responsibilities set forth in their original charge. They point out that as they coordinate, monitor, and review institutional and academic departmental assessment activities, they are constantly educating, reassuring, and encouraging faculty. Many assessment committees form review teams drawn from their membership to systematically review and comment on all aspects of departments' assessment programs and activities and on their annual assessment reports. Typically, the review teams of the assessment committee make a written response to every document sent to them by the departmental faculty. When responding to the annual reports, the committee tells the department what level of implementation of its assessment program has been reached and what it could do next to gain more benefit from its work.

Assessment committee review teams also provide suggestions for specific activities and/or recommend how to use the assessment results included in the department's reports as the basis for discussion of changes that could improve student learning. The review teams have found that when they include this information in the assessment reports they routinely distribute throughout the institution, faculty gradually become more comfortable with assessment. As faculty read the committee's assessment reports, they become more interested in assessment and begin to borrow ideas from other departments to try on their own. Assessment committees have also observed that as faculty respond to their committee's suggestions for improvement, departmental assessment programs begin to yield more useful formative and summative information about their students and their graduates. As faculty discover for themselves the usefulness of assessment results, they become more enthusiastic about assessment. Evaluation teams have noted that, when assessment committees provide this kind of peer review of individual departmental assessment programs, participation in the assessment programs at both the institutional and departmental levels increases.

For assessment committees to perform numerous functions optimally, its members need to be trained in all aspects of assessment. They also need to be well respected and, in some types of institutions, senior faculty. Having highly regarded peers on the assessment committee greatly improves the likelihood that its members will be able to reduce the reluctance or hostility of some individuals and draw them into their program. Admired and respected faculty members on the assessment committee have also proven to be effective assessment tutors and resources to chairs and department faculty. Having them in this position also increases the probability that faculty and department chairs will respect the process by which the assessment program has evolved and will believe the committee's statements that the call for assessment of student learning is from peers, not a requirement imposed on faculty by administration. It also encourages faculty to trust the assessment committee's reports on assessment activities and accept its suggestions and recommendations for improvement, and to turn to that group for whatever kind of assistance they need in their assessment program activities.

Uses of Financial Incentives and Rewards to Engage Faculty in the Assessment Program

A large number of institutions report that they have found financial incentives and rewards to be particularly effective as a means to increase faculty knowledge about assessment and to engage them, as individuals and as entire academic departments, in all aspects of the institution's assessment program. Institutions have been able to build faculty interest in the assessment program by funding assessment committee members and other individual faculty members to participate in statewide, regional, and national assessment conferences. They have established summer grants for faculty to design assessment activities and provided stipends for those who carry out a particularly heavy load of assessment activities in addition to their regular duties. They have also subsidized travel for faculty to present results of their assessment activities at conferences and workshops.

Many institutions have found that to get faculty's continued support and participation in assessment activities it has been necessary to provide each academic department with increased resources by setting up a line designated for assessment expenses in their annual operating budgets. They reward departments by increasing their budgets for assessment if they have made documented progress in assessment activities during the previous year and have developed operational plans that include initiatives to introduce changes to increase student academic achievement in areas where assessment results indicate improvement is possible. One institution, for example, found that "challenge grants" provided a significant impetus for departmental faculty to (1) develop assessment plans, (2) revise assessment plans prior to starting data collection, (3) "collect data on identified measures related to specific indicators in their assessment plans," and (4) "implement carefully considered new practices and to achieve performance goals."[12]

Students

Involving them in assessment has proven no less challenging for institutions than engaging faculty, and it is equally important if an assessment program is to work well. How to get students to take assessment seriously has been a topic discussed widely both in papers and in informal conversations at assessment conferences and workshops. Students can be strong advocates and goodwill ambassadors for the assessment program, but for this to happen, they need to understand the purpose and content of the assessment program and they need to receive results (data and interpretations) from the assessment activities in which they participate.

When students in an institution appear cynical or negative about assessment, it is usually because they have been disenfranchised; their representatives had not been involved in the discussions and decisions that led to the development and implementation of the assessment program. Students in colleges and universities where they have not been purposively educated about their institution's assessment program are poorly informed and likely to feel alienated. They have no way to make the connection between a nationally normed test and the published goals for the curriculum. They have no idea what the results of the assessment show or how results will be used. As a group, these students seem totally unaware that the mode of instruction they are receiving could be changed, or its quality improved in any way. Not surprisingly, without any real information, students form ambivalent or negative impressions of assessment and are likely to "blow off" tests that are part of the assessment program.

Institutions that have been successful in gaining positive student response to the introduction of assessment have actively solicited student input into decisions about the assessment program from its planning stage forward. These colleges and universities have involved their students by arranging for them to work closely with faculty in the design and implementation of processes and procedures for carrying out assessment activities such as formulating the rationale for assessment and designing locally developed tests. On campuses where students are kept fully informed and given opportunities to share responsibility with faculty for the planning and implementation of the assessment program, they appear to take the assessment process and its intended outcomes seriously and consider the measures rigorous and worth their time.

Institutions have described a variety of approaches that they find valuable in successfully raising students' enthusiasm about assessment and attracting their participation in assessment activities. Many have found that to gain student support, it is necessary to include the rationale and philosophy for assessing students' learning in the catalog to signal its importance. A growing number of institutions are finding it effective to publish information about assessment at the program level on their Web pages and in their catalogs. When students read this information on the Web and in catalogs, institutions find that they are more likely to understand that the assessment program is integral to every academic department and to the institution as a whole. When they recognize its importance, they are more interested in participating in assessment activities.

Some institutions with large numbers of part-time or transfer students have decided that it is not feasible to involve students in planning or implementing the assessment program. These colleges and universities often have mandated annual assessment of students' academic achievement at the beginning and completion of their first year, and then with each successive year, rather than measuring the value added between entry into and completion of an entire program. Typically, these institutions require new students to enroll in introductory seminars that include the rationale and explanation for assessment as well as guidance in understanding the faculty's expectations for the assessment program.

A growing number of institutions have mentioned in self-studies that their students are more willing to participate in assessment activities in part because faculty regularly provide them with individualized reports of their scores on the standardized tests they have taken so that they can compare them to nationally normed groups. Voluntary participation by students appears to rise in institutions where faculty advisors or counseling staff share assessment results with them in individual advising sessions or in senior seminars. Colleges and universities with relatively high rates of student participation in assessment also report that students' motivation both to do well on tests and to participate in other assessment program activities is heightened by well-publicized assessment days devoted to assessment activities and to honoring student achievement. Not surprisingly, faculty attitudes toward assessment have a direct impact on the level of student involvement. Institutions have observed that high levels of student interest and participation in assessment activities are closely associated with faculty advocacy of and contributions to the assessment program. It appears that one unexpected reward for an institution's investment in faculty professional development in assessment is greater student participation in the assessment program.

In summary, from the beginning of the Assessment Initiative, NCA has consistently stressed that, for an institution's assessment program to be successful, it must be faculty owned and faculty driven. It should also have the support and participation of students. Recently, a faculty member from a small private liberal arts college wrote an e-mail message to an NCA staff liaison stating:

> The best thing we can do for our students and our faculty is bring them to a place where they can see for themselves not only what they are learning and teaching, not only why they are learning and teaching certain things, but how this process is taking place, for what end, and to what level of success. As a teacher, I've often found that students who struggle do so more often than not because they have never been given the confidence that they can actually learn, and have never been shown in any practical way that they actually are learning.

Developing Program Goals and Measurable Objectives, and Selecting Measures of Student Learning

A second area in which institutions have learned important lessons from developing an assessment program is that of coming to agreement on program goals, measurable objectives, and instruments to measure student learning. Consultant-evaluators say that after engaging the faculty and academic administrators in planning and mounting the assessment program, the next major challenge most institutions encounter is the need for academic departments to develop common educational goals for their academic programs and to agree upon measurable objectives for each of those goals. In virtually all NCA colleges and universities, the single most important lesson faculty and administrators have learned from that exercise is that goals and objectives need to focus on *students*, on what students will be able to demonstrate that they know, believe, and can do, not on what the institution or its faculty provide, offer, or do for students.

This usually calls for faculty to make a major adjustment in their thinking about the nature of the institution and its work. Some faculty have experienced the shift in emphasis to be painful. They have found it difficult to write new educational goals and measurable objectives from the perspective of student learning rather than faculty offerings, primarily because it was unfamiliar and caused them to rethink their own long-held assumptions about what education is and about the role of the institution and faculty in education. But many other faculty have described the process of developing educational goals and measurable objectives as exciting and satisfying. They have enjoyed working with other members of their departments to sharpen their expectations of what students who complete each of their undergraduate programs and graduate programs will have learned. They report finding it stimulating to join colleagues from other disciplines to work on the general education program and examine, discuss, define, and finally operationalize such "fuzzy" domains as "critical thinking" or "global perspectives."

In this area, as in that of attracting faculty to participate in creating and operating the assessment program, a number of colleges and universities have discovered that their academic officers as well as their faculty and participating students needed seminars designed for faculty to master the vocabulary and techniques of quantitative and qualitative research. They have also learned that after providing this basic preparation, they needed to arrange for faculty to attend professional development workshops in assessment in order for them to progress further and build the skills needed to develop and implement departmental programs in assessment. In these workshops, faculty have learned how to formulate educational goals for a course and then "translate" each goal into a sequence of measurable objectives that they can include in the course syllabus. Institutions have found that once academic department members have become individually adept at formulating goals and measurable objectives for their own courses, the entire department has a common basis on which they can work together at the program level. They are prepared to arrive at educational goals and measurable objectives for general education, a major, a graduate program, or a professional degree program because they now have the tools to work out and articulate their common hopes and expectations for student learning across an entire program.

Colleges and universities have discovered that even after faculty have agreed upon educational goals and measurable objectives for a program, they find it a formidable task to select sound measures that align well enough with one or more of their objectives for each goal to yield meaningful information about value added, that is, about the student learning that will have occurred across an entire academic program. They have seen that faculty find it difficult and time-consuming to arrive at decisions about whether to use a nationally normed standardized exam, a locally developed test, a combination of the two, or performance-based measures such as portfolios, internships, and capstone projects. In institutions where a core of faculty possess the expertise needed for assessment, some or all are appointed to the assessment committee. These committees have become an invaluable resource for everyone involved in this aspect of assessment. Some have developed assessment manuals, workbooks, guides, or handbooks that provide guidance on how to select measures and that describe the conceptual and structural framework needed for departmental and institutional assessment activities.

As described earlier, in their role as in-house consultants, assessment committees meet with departments on an ongoing basis and are able to provide faculty and students working to develop a departmental assessment program with a comfortable environment in which to ask questions about any aspects of assessment they are having difficulty with. One of the areas in which their assistance has been welcome and successful has been in assisting departments to align program goals and measurable objectives with reliable measures that will yield useful assessment data and information.

Collecting and Interpreting Data

Institutions have discovered that when departmental faculty have been able to agree upon educational goals and measurable objectives and have selected the best measures for each, they will have taken the first steps toward collecting evidence of how close students' actual learning comes to meeting faculty's expected outcomes for any given academic program. Institutions have learned that even after faculty have taken advantage of opportunities for professional development in the area of assessment, they usually need both senior administrative oversight and the technical support of trained professional staff to carry out the actual assessment process. This is particularly true for institutions where few, if any, faculty have previous experience in assessment and where there is little disciplinary knowledge and skill to transfer to assessment activities. Then, unless the institution provides direct assistance or supervision, some academic departments are likely either to ignore the call for assessment or to submit easily obtained data that may not be responsive to the critical questions of what has and has not been learned and by what cohort of the student population that has completed a particular program.

Institutions have found that even when assessment committee members and colleagues in the fields of higher education and the social sciences have served as consultants and introduced faculty to the basic concepts and vocabulary of assessment and have helped them develop program goals and measurable objectives and select valid and reliable measures, some may not have gained adequate expertise or have the necessary time to design and carry out assessment projects for their departments. They find they are unable as an assessment committee or as an academic department to administer the tests and then collect, score, and analyze the data as provided for in their assessment program. Many institutions have found that when this is the case, they need to employ specialized professionals with training, experience, and expertise in assessment to be support staff to the assessment program as a whole and to individual academic departments.

In spite of these difficulties, some institutions that had not previously made extensive or systematic use of assessment are now making steady progress in their implementation of a well-planned assessment program. Teams have discovered that in these colleges and universities, faculty and administration have developed a number of ways to ensure sound practice in their assessment efforts. Small institutions have in some cases appointed one of their own faculty members with a strong background in statistics, tests and measurements, or psychology to be the institution's resource person on anything having to do with assessing student learning. She or he is available to academic units and individual faculty and administrators when they need help with aspects of their assessment program. The faculty member is typically given release time or a reduction in workload for a specified number of academic years to act as the institutional in-house consultant on assessment.

Larger or more affluent small institutions have appointed one or more individuals with training and experience in assessment to provide consultative advice and technical support to the assessment committee and academic departments. These professionals assist faculty in designing and carrying out assessment at the departmental level and in coordinating institutional and departmental assessment projects with one another and with the planning and budgeting processes and timetables. They also are expected to decide on such matters as methodology, research design, appropriate sampling design techniques, validity and reliability of instruments, item analysis, and scoring protocols and rubrics. They frequently administer and score the results of the measures selected by departments and also write analyses of the data in a form that can be understood and used by faculty at the departmental and institutional levels.

Colleges and universities with operating budgets adequate to staff and fund an office of institutional research typically have that office offer all of the technical support and services needed for monitoring and operating the institution's assessment program at every level. A number of institutions that already had an office of institutional research when they started their assessment program report they have formally expanded the office's responsibilities to include the provision of ongoing assistance with the assessment activities of all departments and programs and support for institutional aspects of the program. Some institutions with a well-established office of institutional research have reported that they have needed to add research staff to support the assessment effort.

Large decentralized universities are those that most often have needed to expand their office of institutional research so that it is able to provide all the kinds of support, instruction, and technical assistance needed to carry on assessment at every level of the institution.

The office of institutional research can be of great value to the institution when it is ready to conceptualize how to evaluate the entire institutional assessment program, including the efficacy and effectiveness of all components of the institutional assessment efforts. It can be equally helpful to departments when they need to develop and carry out parallel evaluations of their departmental assessment programs.

Feedback Loops: Communicating Information about the Outcomes of Assessment

The absence of a system of "feedback loops" is often associated with lack of progress in implementing an assessment program. Conversely, successfully implemented assessment programs characteristically include a carefully designed feedback system that ensures an accurate and timely flow of information. Assessment committees have emerged as the hubs of these systems, communicating meaningful information about assessment activities and results throughout the college or university. How well these committees carry out their communications function has much to do with how rapidly institutions progress toward implementing their assessment programs. As described earlier, the assessment committee's responsibilities for communication include reporting regularly on new developments in the institution's assessment program, on all assessment activities throughout the institution, on upcoming deadlines in the assessment timetable, and on the results of departmental assessment efforts.

Assessment committees use both written and oral, formal and informal, presentations to the entire institutional community, to academic departments individually, and to all committees directly involved in assessment. The annual report is typically the most widely distributed of all its reports. It usually includes the actual assessment programs of all departments, gives assessment results for each degree program, identifies areas where the levels of documented student academic achievement suggest improvements are needed, and describes how the results have led faculty to propose changes in curriculum, instruction, academic support services, or other areas that could increase student learning. Some assessment committees use an annual report to document changes that have been proposed, funded, and instituted by each department and to describe any apparent effect a change has been documented to have had on student learning over several years.

Many assessment committees send out executive summaries or progress reports between issues of the extensive annual report. The summary or progress reports provide an overview of all assessment projects and activities in progress throughout the institution and an update of assessment findings from a number of projects. In this way, an assessment committee is able to keep the entire institutional community apprised of developments in the assessment program as they occur. Assessment committees also prepare special reports on individual major assessment activities and distribute them to senior administrators, deans, and academic chairs who, in turn, circulate the reports to their offices and academic departments. These reports focus exclusively on a single assessment project, explain its purpose, and give the findings.

A number of assessment committees issue assessment newsletters distributed directly to individual faculty members and administrators during the course of the academic year. The newsletters include matters of general interest about the assessment program, findings from important assessment projects, and information about specific assessment topics. The assessment committee may also submit abstracts of assessment studies for inclusion in university publications. Finally, the assessment committee encourages departments to share the results of assessment projects through presentations and discussion throughout the institution.

It is critical to the success of the assessment program that institutions have well-functioning feedback loops (i.e., to provide information generated by assessment activities in a form that can be readily understood and used by academic departments and administrative personnel to make reasonable proposals for improvements in curriculum, in instructional delivery, or in other areas that faculty feel could increase student academic achievement). Furthermore, to keep students positive and involved in assessment, the assessment committee and office of institutional research need to provide feedback to individual students. Whether feedback is intended for faculty, administrators, students, or all three, it needs to be specific and provided in a form that can be readily comprehended and delivered as promptly as possible so that the recipient can use the information transmitted to improve current performance.

Another important lesson is that some institutions have adequate provisions for feedback in their assessment program processes, but they show little or no progress in improving student learning because departments are failing to "close the feedback loop." For example, some departments report assessment data to the assessment committee but then do not use the information they have obtained about their students' academic achievement to consider what modifications could be tried to improve learning across the program. Failure to provide for and use a well-designed communication system in the assessment program is one of the most common reasons why many of the institutions that have not yet fully implemented their assessment programs are having difficulty in carrying out an otherwise acceptable plan.

Costs, Revenues, and Reallocation of Resources for Assessment Activities

Some administrators and faculty are concerned that operating a fully implemented assessment program can be an added expense to institutions already coping with limited resources. However, the commission has said that an assessment program should be "cost-effective," not "costly."[13] "Cost-effective" means the program must be designed so that maximum information is gathered for the time and money given to all assessment staffing and activities. That there are real costs associated with operating an effective assessment program is an indisputable reality. Evaluation teams have observed that institutions that have demonstrated improvements in their assessment programs have administrators who recognize that assessment activities require an investment of institutional dollars. These administrators have typically approved budget lines for assessment in departmental and institutional annual operating budgets affected by assessment activities so that the financial requirements for carrying out assessment will be considered in the context of the institution's total needs and resources. When there is a number of competing requests for new or additional money, they give highest priority to those that show the greatest potential of improving student learning.

Successful assessment programs can only be mounted and sustained when there is strong institutional commitment to the primary importance of student learning, hence to any programs or activities that support it. For this reason, evaluation teams have observed that inclusion of funds for assessment activities in successive annual budgets is always an indicator of strong institutional commitment to the improvement of student learning. In institutions where the assessment program is a high priority of the administration and is strongly supported by the faculty, they find that the approved annual budget for the assessment committee will be adequate to meet the costs of institutional assessment activities such as faculty development, speakers and consultants, incentives to faculty who have made outstanding contributions to institutional-wide assessment activities, and monetary recognition of departments that have made improvements in their students' learning across one or more programs they offer. They note, in addition, that there will be lines for assessment-related expenses in the annual operating budget request forms completed by academic departments and that the approved departmental budgets will be adequate to meet the costs of departmental assessment activities.

In the social and economic climate within which colleges and universities operate, few will be able to raise new funds for assessment. However, some institutions have been able to increase their revenues by adding an "assessment fee" to cover direct costs of assessment. This has occurred in institutions in which there are stringent operating budgets and very little flexibility to reapportion limited fiscal and human resources but a strong faculty, administrative, and student belief that, because assessment can be an effective means to improve students' learning, funds need somehow to be raised to meet the costs. Some colleges and universities have added two fees: one to fund the assessment activities of academic units, and another to meet the costs of institution-wide assessment projects. In some instances, the fee may be per capita (e.g., $5 per student per term, regardless of hours enrolled). In other instances, the fee may be a small amount (e.g., $1 or less attached to each credit hour for which a student registers).

In some colleges and universities where adding a fee is not an option, or where the revenues generated by a specific fee are not sufficient to cover the costs of assessment, institutions have had to reallocate their existing resources in order to carry on their assessment programs and accomplish their goals for improving student learning. It has long been recognized that how an institution uses its resources is a direct reflection of its values. As Darrell Krueger, president of Winona State University (Minnesota), is quoted as having said: "What is measured is what is valued; what is valued is what is funded."[14]

As institutions experience the positive effects of their assessment program on students' learning, they are likely to reconsider their former budget priorities and give preference to expenditures for assessment. In some institutions, when departmental faculty propose changes they believe could increase student learning based on assessment results, high priority is assigned to those proposed expenditures in their annual budget requests in order to ensure that they can be tested and evaluated for their effect on academic achievement. As colleges and universities actually experience the value of assessment to their students and faculty, many find themselves becoming student-centered learning organizations committed to constantly finding ways to improve student academic achievement. As this occurs, many will view reconfiguration of their former funding patterns as an appropriate reflection of the change in their institutional culture.

Linking Assessment with Operational Planning and Budgeting

Linking the assessment process of an institution with its operational planning and budgeting processes is essential to the ongoing success and cost-effectiveness of every assessment program. Yet, a number of institutions remain perplexed about what is meant by "linking" the three processes or, in some cases, how to connect them.

The reasons for linking assessment, planning, and budgeting are to ensure that assessment, like the planning and budgeting processes, will be an ongoing process, and that its results will be used to improve student learning. For that to occur, each project within the assessment program and every proposed change based on the results of assessment need to be sequenced and timed so that they can be included in the operating plan, and if there are costs associated with the proposed change, into the requested budget of the assessment committee or of the appropriate department for the following academic/fiscal year. Unless that happens, requests cannot be funneled into the institutional planning and budgeting cycles in a timely fashion. The risk of long delays between requests and authorizations can badly damage morale and progress.

Stated in practical terms, refocusing the culture of a college or university on how students' learning can be improved requires that both departmental and institutional processes of the assessment program, the operational planning process, and the annual operating budgeting process be integrated into a single, seamless system with a common calendar of events and flowchart to guide the institution through each cycle. When there is an integrated system that encompasses assessment, action planning, and annual budgeting, requests for expenditures to support ongoing assessment activities and agreed-upon changes intended to improve student learning can be considered in the normal institutional processes. In a student-centered learning institution, they are likely to be given priority in the allocation of resources and appear in the approved departmental and institutional action plans and budgets for the next academic year.

In colleges and universities where the expression "linking assessment to planning and budgeting" is not understood, there is always the danger that no special funds will be set aside for the assessment program and that activities it generates will have to be delayed for two or even three years. If that occurs, the assessment program is likely to lose its momentum, and disaffection will replace the satisfaction that faculty experience when they are able to propose, document, test, and evaluate the effects of a change that could increase students' learning within one academic year. Figure 3.1 depicts the relationship of assessment of student academic learning and the evaluation of other operational units to operational planning and budgeting.

Figure 3.1
Institutional Effectiveness: Conceptualizing the Relationship of Assessment and Evaluation Processes to Operational Planning and Budgeting

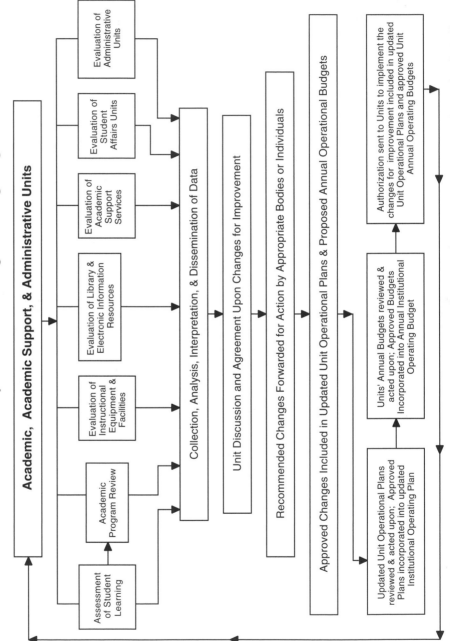

Like the processes of assessment of student learning and academic program review, evaluation of academic and nonacademic administrative units and programs is conducted through a prescribed annual cycle of actions. The cycle typically includes:

1. Review of the unit's purpose, goals, and objectives
2. The collection, analysis, interpretation, and dissemination of data
3. Discussion among unit personnel of the data collected followed by agreement upon changes to improve the performance of the unit
4. The recommendation for changes that personnel believe will improve performance are forwarded for action
5. Inclusion of approved changes in updated unit operational plans and proposed annual operational budgets
6. Preparation of proposed annual operating budgets

Once the updated unit operational plans have been reviewed and acted upon, they are modified or approved and incorporated into the updated institutional operating plan. If changes in the unit's plan would require reallocation of funds or additional resources, requests are prepared for inclusion in the departmental budget for the following fiscal year. Proposed annual budgets based upon unit plans are then reviewed and acted upon through the institutional budget process. Unit budgets are incorporated as approved in the institution's annual operating budget. When units receive authorization to implement some or all of the changes they have recommended in their plans, and any associated costs have been included in their approved operating budgets for the coming year, the cycle begins again. When the process of evaluating institutional effectiveness works well, the result is continuous improvement of the college or university's total educational enterprise.

Collaborative Roles of Administrative Officers and Faculty in Successful Assessment Programs

Although financial resources adequate to cover the direct and hidden costs of assessment have been found important for implementation of assessment programs, generous funding could never alone ensure their long-term success. For an assessment program to be successful, both faculty and administrators need to understand the purpose of assessment and agree upon the necessity of documenting what students know and can do by the end of an academic program. Both must take active and positive parts in advancing assessment goals and activities, and both must contribute energy, time, and leadership so that assessment becomes part and parcel of an institution's way of life, its culture. To bring this about, faculty and administrators need to work collaboratively to fulfill the purpose of assessment, which is to increase the quality of education their students achieve.

In the operations of assessment programs, as in institutional governance, institutional planning and budgeting, and institutional self-study and evaluation, the chief academic officer (CAO), the deans, the academic department heads, and the faculty each have specific roles. Some of their roles are shared; some are separate but complementary. All are essential in establishing and maintaining an effective assessment program.

What academic officers and faculty are doing, separately and together, is to build, operate, and continuously strengthen assessment programs in those institutions that have shown the greatest progress in shifting their attention from institutional inputs to student outcomes. Institutions that do not have all of the elements of a complete assessment program or have not been able to involve all of their academic departments in assessing student learning may find it useful to review the lessons we have learned concerning the respective contributions that academic officers and faculty have made to planning and building strong assessment programs and that they will need to continue.

Institutions that have a strong assessment program in place have chief academic officers who work collaboratively with faculty to:

- Lead the governing board and CAO to an understanding of the meaning and importance of assessing student learning
- Provide opportunities and support for faculty and academic administrators to be trained in every aspect of assessment
- Appoint a standing assessment committee and a chair who reports directly to the CAO, and provide each with a written charge and adequate budget
- Establish a line and allocate sufficient resources in the annual education and general operations budget to sustain ongoing as-

sessment efforts for the institution as a whole and for each academic program

- Add "responsibility for assessment" to the position description of each academic department and program chair and assign the chair sufficient authority and resources to be effective

- Expand the written responsibilities of the office of institutional research (or broaden the position description of an administrator or faculty member assigned responsibility for those functions) to include technical and staff support to the administrators, the assessment committee, and the departmental and program faculty engaged in assessment of student learning

- Support the ongoing operation of a campus-wide, systematic data-collection process

- Ensure that the findings from the assessment of student learning at the program level are incorporated into the review of each academic department or school

- Require departments to describe provisions being made for assessing student learning on their applications for approval of new courses and approval of new or revised programs

- Integrate the timelines of the assessment process, the planning process, and the budgeting process into a single calendar to be followed by academic units and the institution as a whole

Institutions with a strong assessment program have faculty who work collaboratively with the CAO and other academic administrators to:

- Give thoughtful consideration to the reasons for and uses of measuring student academic achievement across entire academic programs, and continue to discuss these in departmental and full faculty meetings and informally with peers

- Take advantage of opportunities and support offered by the administration to be trained in various aspects of assessment of student learning

- Become fully conversant with the institution's total student academic achievement program, including its structure, components, and annual cycle (timetable)

- Participate in their academic units' assessment programs by:

    a. Formulating a rationale to guide assessment activities

    b. Helping to develop goals and measurable objectives for each academic program within the department

    c. Ensuring that the objectives include what the faculty agree students will have learned in knowledge, skills, and attitudes (values) by the program's completion

    d. Stipulating the percentage of students who shall have attained and can demonstrate a particular level of competency in each domain as indicators for the faculty to gauge how well their objectives are being met

- Accept responsibility for ensuring that:

    a. Measures are linked to measurable objectives

    b. Multiple measures are used because no one instrument can successfully measure the range of student achievement

    c. Both quantitative and qualitative measures (including capstone experiences, student senior projects and research, and/or supervised internships) are used

    d. Direct measures of student learning are employed

    e. Instruments are reliable and valid

    f. Measures yield useful results

    g. Results of assessment are used to make changes intended to improve student learning

- Investigate instruments or measures other than those currently in use, and suggest any that seem to be a "better fit" in meeting the department's objectives for student learning or could yield more useful information be pilot-tested

- Become engaged in departmental discussions of the data gathered from the administration of measures of student learning and the interpretation of these data

- Contribute ideas for making changes in mode of instruction, curriculum, library holdings, academic support equipment, and personnel and/or introduce innovations that could increase student learning whenever comparison of the results of measuring student learning with the faculty's educational goals and objectives for the program have suggested improvement is needed

- Ensure that procedures are in place for:

    a. Prioritizing proposed changes for inclusion in departmental or program plans and budgets

    b. Determining whether or not the changes introduced correlate with actual improvements in student learning

    c. Documenting the changes that have been recommended, funded (if required), and implemented

- Make provision for external evaluation of all assessment efforts to ensure the best possible process (methodology) and use of results, and to establish a high level of credibility among the institution's internal and external constituents

"CONNECTING THE DISCONNECTS": WHAT REMAINS TO BE DONE

Nearly ten years after the Assessment Initiative began, too many member institutions either have just begun to implement their assessment programs or have only been able to implement their programs partially. Many have yet to realize a level of ongoing assessment that could position them to become a student-centered learning organization committed to continuous improvement of the education their students obtain. Institutions that have not achieved as much as they had hoped to typically want to understand why their progress has been slow and what actions they might take to move from the early stages of implementation to full implementation of their assessment programs. Institutions that have fully implemented assessment programs are eager to know what remains to be accomplished. NCA has provided a wealth of information and advice intended to be helpful to institutions at every stage in the development and operation of their assessment programs.

What Remains to Be Done by Institutions Beginning to Implement Their Assessment Programs

The reports of NCA teams that have evaluated assessment programs provide institutions with an extraordinarily rich array of accepted good practice in assessment, of commonly encountered obstacles to assessment, and of practical suggestions for how to overcome them. Earlier sections of this chapter summarize a considerable amount of their information and wisdom. Administrators and faculty leaders from institutions that are still struggling to implement various components of their assessment programs or to engage nonparticipating departments may want to return at a later time to those sections for insights and practical information. They may also find assistance by referring to the many publications dealing with assessment programs that NCA has released over the past ten years.[15]

Wherever institutions may be along the continuum from partial to full implementation of their assessment programs, they may find it helpful to review the characteristics associated with levels of implementation proposed by NCA staff.[16] When they have done that, they may want to ask themselves questions such as:

- Have we used every means known to be effective in involving faculty and student in the assessment program?

- Have we appointed or elected respected senior faculty to serve on the assessment committee? They become the assessment program's goodwill ambassadors and the tutors and mentors for other faculty.

- Have we done all we can to help every department agree upon program goals and measurable objectives and the measures that align with them? Have we provided opportunities for faculty development so that faculty understand the vocabulary and concepts of measuring student learning with reliable and multiple measures of learning?

- Have we provided faculty with the technical support they need to select multiple, valid, and reliable measures of learning, and to collect and interpret data?

- Have we established and published a system of feedback loops for reporting the results of assessment activities to all types of internal and external constituencies, and for capturing the decisions on how student learning could be improved that result from departmental discussion of the results?

- Have we instructed the governing board about the purposes of assessment? Have we kept the governing board informed about the institution's assessment results and its efforts to use them to improve student learning? Have we gained active board and senior administration support for the assessment program? Their support is vital to the success of an assessment program.

- Have we integrated the assessment process, the planning process, and the budgeting process into a single timetable and made certain that all faculty and administrators understand the sequence of steps and dates?

- Have we made certain that faculty and academic administrators know their roles in assessment? Are we promoting collaborative efforts between them? Collaboration is essential, even if not sufficient, for successful implementation to occur.

What Remains to Be Done by Institutions That Are Implementing Their Assessment Programs

When an institution has fully implemented a structured, systematic, and ongoing assessment program, it will typically have become a student-centered learning organization that is committed to continuously improving the education its students obtain. Because its culture is focused on student learning, assessment is woven into the fabric of everything its faculty, staff, and students regularly do. For these institutions, there are other exciting challenges to be faced.

Developing Strategies to Increase Student Learning

Some institutions with fully implemented assessment plans have collected a considerable amount of data but may not be sure what steps to take next. Good practice suggests that they systematically watch for any indications of an appreciable gap between the faculty's measurable objectives of educational goals for a program and evidence provided by assessment of what students completing the academic program have learned and can do. Whenever a gap is found, their faculty can then consider the possibilities of what could be changed or instituted that might help students learn more in that particular area. There has been a tendency for some departments to concentrate on interventions such as modifying the program's curricular design or the contents of an individual course.

Over time, however, institutions that are student-centered learning organizations are likely to consider the possibility that students' learning in some areas could be increased by improvements in other areas. They may propose changes in the library, in physical space and equipment, in electronic information systems, and in academic support services such as tutoring and academic advising, areas that have traditionally been recognized to support teaching and learning. Departments could also consider and propose changes to improve or enrich student life, extracurricular activities, student residences, and campus events as means to increasing some kinds of learning.

As an institution becomes increasingly adept in obtaining useful information about what its students have learned from books, lectures, and seminars, its faculty and administrators are likely to become interested in scholarship that explains the multiple intelligences of their students and the variety of their learning styles. They may also want to test strategies for engaging students in active learning and to explore the possibilities of interactive, computer-mediated instruction. When this occurs, faculty are likely to need to develop new means to assess how much students have learned from these less familiar strategies and sources of instruction. Similarly, they will need to find new ways to improve learning in areas where results from these new assessment techniques suggest students are not meeting the objectives set. Take the case of a faculty that has introduced active learning into its curriculum, or a department that is offering one or more courses and degrees online. In each case, the faculty will want to discover ways to evaluate what and how much students have obtained from the active learning experience or from the asynchronous mediated instruction.

In a number of institutions, after faculty have introduced a strategy to provide students with an opportunity for active learning, they have begun to explore innovative ways by which they could assess the outcome. The faculty of one university, for example, is pilot-testing an assessment tool for measuring the effectiveness of its learning communities. They have defined the term *learning community* as a curriculum device for linking two courses from different disciplines. It is characterized as student centered and focused on collaboration and the construction of knowledge.[17] It is particularly interesting that in the faculty's definition, they have operationalized *learning communities* by using such active learning dimensions as student-student collaboration, student-faculty collaboration, academic involvement, interdisciplinary learning, and knowledge constructivism, thereby establishing identifiable areas and measurable objectives by which to assess their students' learning.

At another university, faculty have chosen to explore ways to evaluate the impact that "interactivity" in Web-based courses has on cognition, knowledge construction, skills acquisition, motivation, perspective, or adoption of group learning strategies. Interactivity is defined as the interaction between (1) the student to the content, (2) the student to the faculty mentor/content specialist, (3) the student to other students, and (4) the student to his or her environment, physical and/ or virtual.[18]

As Figure 3.1 indicates, regardless of the kind of changes faculty propose on the basis of assessment results, in most institutions, groups and individuals (e.g., departmental or college curriculum committees, advisory bodies, and academic administrators) need to review and act on a proposed change in any academic or nonacademic unit. Once approved, a proposed change needs to be included in the departmental operational (action) plan. If the change would require additional dollars or the reallocation of existing dollars in a department's budget, the department needs to include the request in its next annual budget request before the request is forwarded for action through the normal annual budgeting process of the institution as a whole. In many institutions, budget requests far exceed available revenues and new requests for expenditures on items that could improve learning must compete with each other as well as with other pressing needs of the institution. This requires careful consideration of which interventions are both cost-effective and most likely to produce a significant improvement in student academic achievement. Whether only a few or most of the approved recommendations for change based on assessment outcomes data are ultimately included in any given budget, the departments and assessment committee will need to closely monitor subsequent assessment results to see whether the funded changes can be shown to have a direct effect on or correlate positively with improved student learning.

Benchmarking and Its Uses

Faculty and academic administrators in an institution that has fully implemented its assessment program face a second challenge. They question what their specific goals for their students' learning in each domain should be in each department's programs. They ask what percentage of students completing a program should perform at what level and against what (or whose) standards for them to be satisfied with the evidence of students' learning generated by assessment across the academic program or major. They may also be concerned about how the results of assessing their students' level of learning in a given program compares with the results of student achievement in programs by the same name at institutions with whom they compete for students.

How will the student-centered institution respond to faculty who ask questions such as "What *is* the desired state?" and "On what basis do we decide that a sufficiently high percentage of our students have been shown to have learned a sufficient amount for us to say, 'This is good enough'?" One means to answer those questions is to use benchmarks or comparative data sets.

Benchmarks are useful for accurate assessment of current student achievement and for setting goals that assist faculty and students to "stretch" to achieve them. Comparing student performance and overall institutional performance relative to comparable student populations and to comparable, competing institutions provides valuable information for colleges and universities interested in maintaining or improving their competitive edge. Comparative information and data on the results of student assessment from other colleges and universities assist decision-makers in knowing where the institution stands relative to comparable institutions.[19] Comparative information and data also allow the institution to set "stretch targets" for where it would like to be. Such comparative data sets can provide the impetus to stimulate innovation in strategies for improving teaching and learning and can signal changes occurring in educational practice. In short, comparative information and data sets constitute an effective external driver of improvement that may be valuable to institutions committed to the continual improvement of their educational programs and/or those who want to become student-centered learning organizations.

Even among institutions that have now fully mounted their assessment programs, many have little useful data concerning the academic performance of various populations of students in comparable institutions; some do not know how to collect or use such information and data. For these colleges and universities, the next great challenge will be to form networks with comparable institutions, agree on the data to be shared, ensure that the data corresponds from one institution to another, and learn how to collect and use information from other institutions.

CONCLUSION

NCA's Assessment Initiative has consumed extraordinary amounts of the time and energy of faculty, staff, and administrators in its member institutions. It has:

- Confused some, invigorated others
- Breathed new meaning into the mission statements of many institutions

- Become the rationale for rethinking the general education curriculum of numerous colleges and universities
- Provided the opportunity for institutions to publicly state what their faculty, administration, and governing boards truly value by formulating and publishing educational goals and measurable objectives for all their undergraduate and graduate programs
- Stimulated lively debates on campuses across nineteen states about what faculty know they have always cared about but have kept private too long—student learning

The Assessment Initiative has also given institutions principles of good practice and tools to demonstrate that students are learning what is stated or implied in their catalogs, viewbooks, and program brochures. It has made it possible for academic departments to use the demonstrated learning of their students and graduates as the basis for curricular revisions, for modifications of academic plans, and for annual budgets that reflect that improvement of student learning is of primary importance to the faculty and the institution. In short, an emphasis upon the assessment of student learning helps to transform an academy from one focused on what institutions and faculty *offer to* or *do for* students to one focused on what students can demonstrate they *know* and can *do*.

NOTES

1. North Central Association of Colleges and Schools, *Handbook of Accreditation*, 2nd ed. (Chicago: Commission on Institutions of Higher Education, 1997).

2. North Central Association of Colleges and Schools, *A Collection of Papers on Self-Study and Institutional Improvement* (Chicago: Commission on Institutions of Higher Education, 1999).

3. Cecilia L. López, *Assessment of Student Learning: A Progress Report*, paper presented at the 103rd annual meeting of the North Central Association, Commission on Institutions of Higher Education, Chicago, 1998; and Cecilia L. López, *Assessment of Student Learning: An Update*, paper presented at the Working Conference of the Association of American Colleges and Universities, Tampa, Florida (Chicago: Commission on Institutions of Higher Education, February 1999).

4. American Association of University Professors, *Policy Documents and*

Reports (Washington, D.C.: American Association of University Professors, 1990).

5. American Association of University Professors, *Policy Documents and Reports*, 3–4.

6. H. Gardner, *Frames of Mind: The Theory of Multiple Intelligences* (New York: Basic Books, 1993).

7. See, for example, D. A. Kolb, *Individual Learning Styles and the Learning Process* (Cambridge, Mass.: MIT Press, 1971); and S. Messick, "The Matter of Style: Manifestations of Personality in Cognition, Learning and Teaching," *Educational Psychologist* 29 (1994): 121–136.

8. T. M. Duff and D. J. Cunningham, "Constructivism: Implications for the Design and Delivery of Instruction," in *Handbook of Research for Educational Communications and Technology*, ed. David H. Jonassen (New York: Macmillan, 1996), 170–198.

9. C. H. Major, "Connecting What We Know and What We Do through Problem-Based Learning," *AAHE Bulletin* 51, no. 7 (March 1999): 7–9.

10. R. R. Jenkins and K. T. Romer, *Who Teaches? Who Learns? Authentic Student/Faculty Partners* (Providence, R.I.: IVY Publishers, 1998).

11. R. Edgerton, *Education White Paper* (Philadelphia: Pew Charitable Trusts, 1997).

12. S. R. Hatfield, *Best Practices in Assessment: Building an Assessment Culture*, presentation at the Minnesota State Colleges and Universities (MNSCU) Assessment Day Workshop, St. Paul, April 1999.

13. North Central Association of Colleges and Schools, *Assessment Workbook* (Chicago: Commission on Institutions of Higher Education, 1991), 38.

14. North Central Association of Colleges and Schools, *A Collection of Papers on Self-Study and Institutional Improvement* (Chicago: Commission on Institutions of Higher Education, 1996), 88.

15. Cecilia L. López, "Classroom Research and Regional Accreditation: Common Ground. Special Insert," *Briefing* 14, no. 3 (1996): 1–4; Cecilia L. López, *Opportunities for Improvement: Advice from Consultant-Evaluators on Programs to Assess Student Learning* (Chicago: Commission on Institutions of Higher Education, 1997); López, *Assessment of Student Learning*; López, *Assessment of Student Learning: An Update*; North Central Association of Colleges and Schools, *Assessment Workbook*; and North Central Association of Colleges and Schools, *A Collection of Papers on Self-Study and Institutional Improvement* (1999).

16. López, "Classroom Research and Regional Accreditation."

17. J. Chesebro, K. Snider, and A. Venable, "Measuring Learning Community Effectiveness: Conceptions, an Instrument, and Results," paper presented at the Conference of the Consortium for Assessment and Planning Support (CAPS), Monroe, Louisiana, April 1999, available at http://courses.ncsu.edu/info/f97_assessment.html (accessed March 2, 2004).

18. J. Joseph Hoey, "Effectively Sharing Knowledge in Cyberspace: A Comparative Analysis of Faculty Experiences, Student Attitudes and Student Outcomes in Web-Based Courses within the Research University Setting," paper presented at the Conference of the Consortium for Assessment and Planning Support (CAPS), Monroe, Louisiana, April 1999, available at http://courses.ncsu.edu/info/f97_assessment.html (accessed March 2, 2004).

19. D. Oehler and D. Sergel, "Performance-Based Assessment of General Education in Missouri: Common Outcomes across Institutions," paper presented at the Conference of the Consortium for Assessment and Planning Support (CAPS), Monroe, Louisiana, April 1999.

CHAPTER 4

Institutional Assessment Planning

Robert E. Dugan

The systematic institutional assessment process has become a critical means for higher education to respond to the increasing public demand for accountability and effectiveness. Education quality is one component of institutional effectiveness. The institutional mission statement, one of the institution's planning documents, is a primary vehicle for identifying student learning objectives that are used by institutional members to create general and specific performance indicators and related measures. When these educational standards are implemented and measured in classrooms, the compiled and analyzed results are reported with the intent to improve student learning processes and address the public's questions concerning educational quality and institutional effectiveness.

INCREASING ACCOUNTABILITY

Planning is an essential function for every higher education institution. The institutional planning process and its documents guide its budgeting and other decision making. These documents also inform its stakeholders and communities served (e.g., prospective students and their parents, current members of the institution's community, funding agencies, and academic accrediting organizations) about what the institution expects to accomplish when stated as a mission, values, a vision, and strategic goals and objectives.

Accrediting organizations comprise a major reviewer and evaluator of the institution's planning efforts. One of their roles is to manage an institution or program accreditation review process intended to assure other stakeholders of the institution's academic quality and ongoing financial and operational stability, oftentimes depending upon both institutional self-analysis and follow-up, on-site peer reviews.[1] In the recent past, accrediting decisions were most often based on "institutional reputation and resources rather than from explicit evidence of achievement of intentions and implied outcomes."[2] As such, the quality of institutional outcomes depended on the quality of quantifiable institutional inputs such as the qualifications of faculty and size of institutional budgets.[3]

However, the general public and stakeholder groups began to question the relevance of the most obvious outcome—a degree from an accredited institution—as values shifted from the perspective of higher education as a social good to one as an important and immediate contributor to the economic system.[4] As a result, stakeholders increasingly demand that higher education institutions prove that students actually learn what they have been promised as graduates from these institutions.

It should come as no surprise that stakeholders want to hold institutions accountable and responsible for student performance. The perceived high cost of postsecondary education, in part, influences heightened scrutiny. In addition, stakeholders feel powerless to individually confront higher education's existing practice to regulate itself through the accreditation process. Reports from accrediting organizations concerning institutions, and the details in those reports, are for the most part not made public; only the accreditation status of the institution is available to the general public. As a result, parents, education consultants, and others seek to change the self-regulating accreditation process and mandate accountability through changes in federal and state statutes and regulations. Examples of this demand for increased accountability are abundant and include:

• Congressman John A. Boehner, the Ohio Republican who chairs the House Committee on Education and the Workforce, said that it was appropriate for the federal government, among others, to ask questions about the quality of higher-education institutions. According to him, "Many parties have a stake in higher education, as graduates appropriately fuel our nation's economy." Representative Boehner asked, "How, then, can institutions provide all of these stakeholders with an assurance that the investment made in postsecondary education will be returned to them in the form of a strong, viable, and educated work force?"[5]

• John Immerwahr, senior fellow with Public Agenda, found that "business leaders are already upset over the quality problem, and now Congress is too." Some in Congress favor institutional report cards, others would link minimum graduation rates to grant aid, and still others would test college students to ensure quality. Congressman Howard "Buck" McKeon (R-CA), chairman of the House Education and Workforce subcommittee, introduced the College Affordability Act in October 2003 to track tuition increases as part of the renewal of the Higher Education Act for 2004.[6]

• In July 2003, Florida's Board of Governors, which oversees the state's public universities, considered requiring its students to take a standardized test before they graduate to determine whether they learned anything.[7] "When citizens pay taxes, they expect a level of service," said Carolyn Roberts, the board's vice chairwoman; the Board of Governors seeks "proof of a return on investment."[8]

• Charles Miller, chairman of the Board of Regents of the University of Texas System, said that colleges should test students in their first two years of college "to measure student learning at the undergraduate level across academic institutions." While higher education may be filled with a diverse array of institutions and missions, he continued, "There is or can be a broad agreement on core curriculum content for the early college years—what undergraduates should learn in 'general education' courses."[9]

• The Career College Association, a major lobbying group representing for-profit colleges, is asking Congress to require colleges to publish annual "institutional report cards." Richard T. Jerue, vice president for government relations and corporate development for the Education Management Corporation (which operates for-profit art institutes and culinary colleges), states that "the federal government should make sure this happens if an institution desires to participate in federal student-assistance programs." Colleges could be asked to report their retention and transfer rates, and would be required to provide "outcome measures" to answer Jerue's question "What value added did the students receive from the education they just paid for?" Factors such as job-placement rates, average starting salaries, graduate- and professional-school admissions data, passage rates of students on competency tests or certification exams, student and alumni satisfaction surveys, and employer-satisfaction surveys could be considered.[10]

• The U.S. Department of Education states it would be negligent if it did not hold higher education institutions accountable because the federal government provides more than $70 billion in taxpayer funds for student aid and other support for postsecondary education.[11]

• A 2002 report published by the American Council of Trustees and Alumni found that although an institution's participation in the accreditation process was initially a voluntary initiative, the 1952 Higher Education Act linked eligibility for federal student aid funds to those institutions accredited by federally recognized accrediting organizations; as a result, the accrediting associations became "gatekeepers" of institutional eligibility for federal funds.[12] The report also found that accreditation was assumed to be a reliable indicator of education quality. However, the accreditation process ascertains that each institution has certain resources and procedures, but can give no assurances about the quality of individual courses or programs, and does not address rising college costs, such as tuition and fees.[13]

Several congressional legislative mandates already exist that focus on higher education accountability to meet stakeholder demands for educational quality and performance. Regional accreditors point to the Higher Education Act of 1992 and Title IV of the Higher Education Amendments of 1998 (P.L. 105–244), which require universities receiving federal monies to review the institution's success with respect to student achievement.[14] The Government Performance and Results Act of 1993 (P.L. 103–62) requires every government agency to establish specific objective, quantifiable, and measurable performance goals for each of its programs, including intergovernmental grants and other assistance.[15] Achievement reported by the institutions when complying with the receipt-of-assistance requirements becomes part of the federal agencies' annual report to Congress concerning success in reaching its legislated programmatic goals. However, the results produced by these mandates have not satisfied stakeholders, including members of Congress.

The pressure on higher education institutions to prove accountability has moved beyond the acceptance and reliance of self-reports and anecdotal evidence compiled during the self-regulatory accreditation process to an increasing demand from a variety of constituencies to demonstrate institutional effectiveness by focusing on quality measures, such as educational quality, and cost efficiencies. In the effort to address these concerns about effectiveness, and to slow if not eliminate additional federal and state intrusion into the self-regulatory accreditation process,[16] higher education governing and monitoring bodies such as the Council for Higher Education Accreditation (CHEA) and the American Association for Higher Education (AAHE), and the regional accreditation associations, have advocated the need to increase awareness for measuring and reporting educational quality by expecting each institution to prepare a plan to assess outcomes, to report their findings, and to incorporate the results of their evaluative processes into ongoing efforts to improve student learning.[17]

Accountability focuses on results as institutions quantify or provide evidence that they are meeting their stated mission, goals, and objectives. Institutional effectiveness is concerned, in part, with measuring:

- Efficiency, including institutional employee workloads and productivity indicators.
- Outputs: measures of the volume of a program's activity such as products created or delivered, people served, and activities and services performed. Outputs are most often numbers-based; for example, the number of prospective student applications reviewed, the number of students attending orientation, or the number of attendees to workshops or the number of workshops presented.
- Outcomes: focuses on people, such as their satisfaction with a program or service.
- Student outcomes: aggregate statistics on groups of students such as graduation rates, retention rates, transfer rates, and employment rates for a graduating class, and other measures such as how students spent their time, including extracurricular activities and studying. Such outcomes are institution-based and may be used to compare internal year-to-year institutional performance and as comparative measures with other institutions.
- Student learning outcomes: oftentimes referred to as educational quality and concerned with attributes and abilities, both cognitive and affective, which reflect how student experiences at the institution supported their development as individuals. Students are asked to demonstrate acquisition of specific knowledge and skills, generally:
  - What do students know that they did not know before?
  - What can they do that they could not do before?[18]

Objectives for institutional effectiveness must be identified, planned, and communicated widely, as must be the methods and process for their measurement. The measures are later compiled, reviewed, and evaluated against stated standards to determine if the objectives were effectively reached. Institutions then consider the measures, report the analysis to stakeholders, and apply the findings to the planning phase as a catalyst for revision and improvement.

INSTITUTIONAL PLANNING PROCESS FOR ACCOUNTABILITY EMPHASIZING STUDENT LEARNING OBJECTIVES AND OUTCOMES

Systematic assessment processes best guide accountability concerning institutional effectiveness and educational quality, with a specific focus on student performance indicators and measures. To meet the needs of the accrediting organizations and other institutional constituencies, student learning outcomes assessment should originate from an institutional planning process that is, in itself, systematic and ongoing. Outcomes assessment is a continuous process of institutional effectiveness focusing on planning, discovering, understanding, and improving student learning. It involves:

- Identifying educational objectives found in the institutional mission statement and restating them as learning expectations
- Converting these expectations into institutional educational objectives
- Creating clear and understandable performance standards supporting the educational objectives
- Identifying or otherwise creating appropriate measures concerning the performance standards
- Making those standards and measures known to students and faculty
- Systematically gathering and otherwise measuring, analyzing, and interpreting evidence to compare measured performance to the stated standards
- Reporting and considering the results of these measurements
- Using the information generated from the results to recommend changes that will improve student learning institution-wide, such as revising the stated standards, expectations, and objectives, and

improving learning performance by revising course content, methodologies, and pedagogy

As stated by Thomas A. Angelo, "When it is embedded effectively within larger institutional systems, assessment can help us focus our collective attention, examine our assumptions, and create a shared academic culture dedicated to assuring and improving the quality of higher education."[19]

Institutional effectiveness planners have abundant assistance to start the process. The American Association for Higher Education's Assessment Forum created nine Principles of Good Practice for Assessing Student Learning to facilitate the institution's effort (see Figure 8.3). Among them are the following:

- Assessment is most effective when it reflects an understanding of learning as multidimensional, integrated, and revealed in performance over time.
- Assessment works best when the programs it seeks to improve have clear, explicitly stated purposes.
- Assessment is most likely to lead to improvement when it is part of a larger set of conditions that promote change.[20]

Furthermore, a 2002 U.S. Department of Education report, *Defining and Assessing Learning: Exploring Competency-Based Initiatives*, identified practices shared by several higher education institutions that increase success when planning and assessing student learning outcomes to achieve institutional goals.[21]

To be successful, an institutional assessment process should:

- Display a commitment from institutional leadership
- Include members of the institutional-wide community
- State clearly and succinctly learning expectations from the institutional mission statement as performance standards within a general philosophy for education
- Conduct performance measurements using quantitative and qualitative measures, and analyze the results
- Apply the results institution-wide to refine expectations and improve learning

Initiating the Assessment Planning Process

Because of the focus of regional accrediting organizations, accountability for institutional effectiveness concerning educational quality must start at the institutional level. It is the institution as a whole that assures, with supportive data, accreditors and other constituents that students learn.[22] Institutional leaders must create an institutional environment in which teaching, learning, and student achievements of expected learning outcomes are high institutional priorities.[23] The program to assess student learning should emerge from and be sustained by a faculty and administrative commitment to excellent teaching and effective learning, working to achieve a consensus on the institution's philosophy of general education.[24]

A senior administrator may serve as the leader for creating an institutional culture for assessment, advocating the process of how student learning outcome objectives are identified, planned, implemented, measured, and reported to improve learning and to address stakeholder accountability needs. Institutional assessment planning should be collaborative and inclusive; the facilitator must involve the other stakeholders to define, develop, and reach consensus on clear, understandable competencies that can be measured and assessed.[25] Some of the campus stakeholders and communities served through institutional assessment and planning include:

- Senior administration including the president and board of trustees
- Institutional-level committees
- Individual faculty
- Faculty governing mechanisms (e.g., senate or assembly)
- Faculty standing committees
- Other institutional administrators such as institutional research departments
- Academic deans
- Program/departmental chairs
- Students

Generally, three models are more common than others when initiating the institutional assessment effort: an institutional-based model, a faculty-based model, and a hybrid of these two, usually accomplished by means of a committee with membership from both the institution and faculty levels.[26] A transformational effort to promote and improve learning requires those involved in the institutional effort to identify educational visions and goals collectively, share assessment language and concepts, and adopt or otherwise develop a list of guidelines for using assessment to promote learning.[27] The institution's culture strongly influences commencement and success of the assessment planning effort.

Student Learning Expectations, Objectives, and Measures

The assessment process links the institution's mission to the identified educational values and skills that students are expected to achieve.[28] Goals for student learning should be embedded within the context of the larger institutional planning process and its institutional mission, broadly stating what students are expected to learn, achieve, and master.[29] Therefore, the formal institutional mission statement is expected to identify learning objectives and become a critical means of publicly communicating these objectives as widely as possible to all constituencies, including students, faculty, funders (including parents and government), and accreditors.

Specific learning objectives are created from the general education learning expectations stated, or surmised, from the institutional mission statement. While the identification for student learning objectives may originate from the institutional level because institutions are being held responsible by the regional accreditors for educational quality, educational quality and its assessment are primarily a program-based effort implemented and even managed at the course level. Very few student learning objectives and outcomes are solely institutionally based; those that are institutionally generated are often general, aggregated student outcomes, or may actually be outputs such as retention levels or graduation rates. It is doubtful such institutional, aggregated outcomes would meet the tests for accountability as required by the regional accrediting organizations. To directly affect all students and faculty, these educational expectations should be reinforced by creating objectives and standards in the core (general education) curriculum; through school, program, and departmental plans; and finally through course-level syllabi.

Therefore, institutions depend upon student learning objectives and standards established and measured at the course level; compiled to the program, department, or discipline level; communicated to the school level; and finally summarized at the institutional level to demonstrate accountability supporting the values found in the mission statement. Institutions drive the need for outcomes; academic departments provide the evidence of learning required for accountability.

Student learning objectives are essentially performance indicators. What characteristics of a learning objective should an institution strive for when creating it? The objective must be relevant to the educational values found in the mission statement. It should be measurable and informative so that one knows if it is achieved and, if not, that there were early indicators that can be communicated to the student that the objective may not be met and corrective action is needed. Therefore, the objective must be valid and reliable in that it measures the skills or values that it is intended to measure. As a result, the measure should be flexible enough to be changed if found ineffective. It should be understandable to the student and fair in that what is expected is actually part of the instruction. Additionally, as few indicators as possible should be used to accurately compile results; however, one indicator should not be exclusively used to the detriment of others.[30] It should also be clear from the indicator which measurement instruments may be used, when they are to be used, and by whom.[31]

What general education skills and values does the institution want students to achieve, learn, and master? While the response will necessarily vary from institution to institution as do their missions and cultures, examples are abundant. Alverno College in Milwaukee, Wisconsin, identified the following ability areas from the institutional perspective based upon the mission statement:

- Analysis
- Problem solving
- Communications
- Valuing in decision-making context
- Effective citizenship
- Taking global perspectives
- Social interaction
- Aesthetic responsiveness[32]

Alverno College's academic departments integrate these institutional outcomes into the context of the discipline, program, and course, increasing the specificity of the subject's content, ideas, and processes as the student progresses through the curriculum.[33] As a result,

> Defining expectations [will impact] . . . an increasing level of specificity from the institutional level to the program level and . . . classroom results in curricular coherence. Alverno faculty members have found that this kind of coherence enhances students' abilities to transfer their learning from one course to another. Defining expectations at an institutional level also can raise the general quality of student performance across a curriculum.[34]

Other identified institution-based, noncontextual general learning outcomes include:

- Reading, writing, math, and reasoning skills
- Problem solving
- Critical thinking
- Decision making
- Acquiring knowledge
- Presentation
- Attitudes
- Behaviors
- Values
- Concepts
- Principles

Several institutions identify "key transferable skills" as institutional outcomes, such as the students' ability to:

- Communicate effectively
- Gather and organize information
- Use information technology
- Act independently
- Work in teams[35]

Understanding University Success, a joint project of the Association of American Universities and the Pew Charitable Trusts, describes foundational skills and content standards in English, mathematics, natural sciences, social sciences, second languages, and the arts. Each chapter addresses a discipline and comprises two sections: foundations and standards. The foundations section describes the skills, behaviors, and attitudes expected of incoming higher education students. The standards section lists the content knowledge that helps maximize the probability of success in entry-level university courses.[36]

Assessing and Reporting

The assessments of competencies are directly linked with the goals of the learning experience and the identified objectives. As the Middle States Commission on Higher Education observes, "Assessment should involve the systematic and thorough collection of direct and indirect evidence of student learning, at multiple points in time and in various situations, using a variety of qualitative and quantitative evaluation methods that are embedded in courses, programs, and overall institutional processes."[37]

Institutions are dependent upon faculty for assessing learning outcomes. Therefore, faculty and other constituent groups such as academic administrators must be involved in developing student learning indicators, determining educational standards, creating measures, and deciding which assessment instruments would be applied to measure specific competencies. The instruments could be commercially or locally developed approaches. According to Raymond Rodrigues, "Faculty members are much more likely to accept processes developed by their peers than those developed by some outside group without their input. Therefore it is essential to support faculty development of the assessment efforts in whatever ways possible."[38] Ongoing, multiple assessments using these instruments are necessary to provide useful and meaningful information. The institution should also experiment with new ways to assess identified and desired student competencies.[39]

After measuring course outcomes and compiling the findings, the results from these assessment efforts are gathered and reported in a meaningful way so that all constituent groups understand the findings. Faculty and institutional leaders must apply these assessment results to improving student learning. What has the institution learned about what, and how, its students have learned? Faculty and other institutional leaders use these findings to make strategic institutional decisions, including:

- Determining how well the actual learning experience matches up with the institution's stated mission and values statements
- Recommending changes in pedagogies, curriculum, course content, instructional resources, and academic support services in an effort to make a positive, measurable difference in their students' learning[40]
- Incorporating the recommended changes concerning learning and process into institutional and departmental planning and budgeting processes as priorities for funding and implementation[41]
- Evaluating the assessment process itself for its comprehensiveness and efficacy[42]

Continuous changes to improve student learning discovered during the evaluative feedback influences the planning process by providing the institution with an opportunity to refine its identity through revision of the educational values and objectives found in the institutional mission statement. Once the ongoing process concerning accountability of institutional effectiveness completes its cycle, it begins again.

CONCLUSION

The institutional planning process can be effectively applied to plan, implement, measure, and report student learning objectives, standards, and outcomes in the effort to address increasing concerns of education stakeholders of the effectiveness of higher education. Important to this process is the openness and involvement of the various institutional constituencies and stakeholders, the appropriateness of the identified standards and measures as related to the stated general educational values and objectives found in or culled from the institution's mission, and the reporting and application of compiled and considered results to improve student learning. To be effective, this process is continuous and not undertaken only when institutional self-studies are required for accreditation. The institution can apply the process to demonstrate its educational effectiveness, thereby providing direct evidence of accountability to its constituencies and stakeholders.

NOTES

1. Ronald L. Baker, "Evaluating Quality and Effectiveness: Regional Accreditation Principles and Practices," *The Journal of Academic Librarianship* 28 (January–March 2002): 3.

2. Baker, "Evaluating Quality and Effectiveness."

3. Baker, "Evaluating Quality and Effectiveness," 5.

4. Baker, "Evaluating Quality and Effectiveness," 3.

5. Stephen Burd, "Republican Leaders Stress Accountability and Cost Issues in Hearing on Higher Education Act," *The Chronicle of Higher Education* (May 14, 2003), available at http://chronicle.com/daily/2003/05/2003051401n.htm (accessed June 22, 2003).

6. Mark Clayton, "Backlash Brews over Rising Cost of College," *The Christian Science Monitor* (June 17, 2003), available at http://www.csmonitor.com/2003/0617/p15s01-lehl.html (accessed June 18, 2003).

7. Anita Kumar, "An FCAT for College Juniors?" *St. Petersburg Times* (July 24, 2003), available at http://pqasb.pqarchiver.com/sptimes/access/374842351.html?FMT=FT&FMTS=FT&desc=An+FCAT+for+college+juniors? (accessed August 12, 2003).

8. Anita Kumar, "A College FCAT? The Debate Begins," *St. Petersburg Times* (May 1, 2003), available at http://pqasb.pqarchiver.com/sptimes/access/331459891.html?FMT=FT&FMTS=FT&desc=A+college+FCAT%3f+The+debate+begins (accessed August 12, 2003).

9. Burd, "Republican Leaders Stress Accountability."

10. Stephen Burd, "Will Congress Require Colleges to Grade Themselves?" *The Chronicle of Higher Education* (April 4, 2003): A27.

11. Stephen Burd, "Accountability or Meddling?" *The Chronicle of Higher Education* (September 20, 2002): A23.

12. George C. Leef and Roxana D. Burris, *Can College Accreditation Live Up to Its Promise?* (Washington, D.C.: American Council of Trustees and Alumni, 2002), 1.

13. Leef and Burris, *Can College Accreditation Live Up to Its Promise?* 2.

14. Bonnie Gratch-Lindauer, "Comparing the Regional Accreditation Standards: Outcomes Assessment and Other Trends," *The Journal of Academic Librarianship* 28 (January 2002): 14.

15. Beverly Sheppard, "Outcome Based Evaluation" (Washington, D.C.: Institute of Museum and Library Services, n.d.), available at http://www.imls.gov/grants/current/crnt_obe.htm (accessed June 22, 2003).

16. Cecilia L. López, "Assessment of Student Learning: Challenges and Strategies," *The Journal of Academic Librarianship* 28 (November 2002): 367.

17. Baker, "Evaluating Quality and Effectiveness," 3.

18. Robert E. Dugan and Peter Hernon, "Outcomes Assessment: Not Syn-

onymous with Inputs and Outputs," *The Journal of Academic Librarianship* 28 (November 2002): 376–377.

19. Thomas A. Angelo, "Reassessing (and Defining) Assessment," *AAHE Bulletin* 48 (November 1995): 7.

20. AAHE Assessment Forum, "Principles of Good Practice for Assessing Student Learning," available at http://www.aahe.org/assessment/principl.htm (accessed June 8, 2003).

21. U.S. Department of Education, National Center for Education Statistics, *Defining and Assessing Learning: Exploring Competency-Based Initiatives*, NCES 2002–159, prepared by Elizabeth A. Jones and Richard A. Voorhees with Karen Paulson (Washington, D.C.: Council of the National Postsecondary Education Cooperative Working Group on Competency-Based Initiatives, 2002).

22. Oswald M. T. Ratteray, "Information Literacy in Self-Study and Accreditation," *The Journal of Academic Librarianship* 28 (November 2002): 374.

23. Charles D. Eisenman, "Faculty Participation in Assessment Programs," *North Central Association Quarterly* 66 (Fall 1991): 458–464.

24. Cecilia L. López, "Assessment of Student Learning," *Liberal Education* 84 (Summer 1998): 36–44, available at EBSCOhost, Academic Search Premier database (accessed June 6, 2003).

25. U.S. Department of Education, *Defining and Assessing Learning*, viii.

26. López, "Assessment of Student Learning," 359.

27. Thomas A. Angelo, "Doing Assessment as if Learning Matters Most," *AAHE Bulletin* (May 1999), available at http://aahebulletin.com/public/archive/angelomay99.asp (accessed August 12, 2003).

28. AAHE Assessment Forum, "Principles of Good Practice for Assessing Student Learning."

29. Middle States Commission on Higher Education, *Student Learning Assessment: Options and Resources* (Philadelphia: Middle States Commission on Higher Education, 2003), 3.

30. Sharon Markless and David Streatfield, "Developing Performance and Impact Indicators and Targets in Public and Education Libraries," *International Journal of Information Management* 21 (2001): 173–174.

31. Markless and Streatfield, "Developing Performance and Impact Indicators," 176.

32. Carole E. Barrowman, "Improving Teaching and Learning Effectiveness by Defining Expectations," *New Directions for Higher Education* 24 (Winter 1996): 104.

33. Barrowman, "Improving Teaching and Learning Effectiveness," 107.

34. Barrowman, "Improving Teaching and Learning Effectiveness," 110.

35. Joanna Allan, "Learning Outcomes in Higher Education," *Studies in Higher Education* 21 (March 1996): 93–109, available at EBSCOhost, Academic Search Premier database (accessed June 6, 2003).

36. David T. Conley, *Understanding University Success: A Report from Standards for Success, a Project of the Association of American Universities and the Pew Charitable Trusts* (Eugene: Center for Educational Policy Research, University of Oregon, 2003), 8.

37. Middle States Commission on Higher Education, *Student Learning Assessment*, 3.

38. Raymond Rodrigues, "Want Campus Buy-In for Your Assessment Efforts?" *AAHEBulletin.com* (September 2002), available at http://aahebulletin.com/member/articles/2002–10-feature02_pf.asp? (accessed June 8, 2003).

39. U.S. Department of Education, *Defining and Assessing Learning*, viii.

40. López, "Assessment of Student Learning," 358.

41. López, "Assessment of Student Learning," 358, 360.

42. Middle States Commission on Higher Education, *Student Learning Assessment*, 3.

CHAPTER 5

Developing an Assessment Plan to Learn about Student Learning

Peggy L. Maki

All too frequently higher education institutions view the commitment to assessing their students' learning and development as a periodic activity—most often driven by an impending accreditation visit. That is, about one to two years before an accreditation visit, institutions engage in a flurry of assessment activities—from creating assessment plans and committees to designing and implementing methods to assess student learning. Institutions hope these assessment efforts will satisfy accreditors' criteria for institutional effectiveness, an institution's capacity to verify that it is achieving its mission and purposes. Assessing student learning and development, that is, finding out how well students achieve educational objectives, is one of the primary means by which institutions demonstrate their institutional effectiveness.

Unfortunately, however, this periodic approach to assessment—a compliance approach—is based on an external motivator, namely accreditation, rather than on an internal motivator—institutional curiosity. Institutional curiosity seeks answers to questions about which students learn, what they learn, how well they learn, and when they learn; and it explores how pedagogies and educational experiences develop and foster student learning. When institutional curiosity drives

Reprinted from *The Journal of Academic Librarianship* 28 (1/2), Peggy L. Maki, "Developing an Assessment Plan to Learn about Student Learning," pp. 8–13, 2002, with permission from Elsevier.

assessment, faculty and professional staff across an institution raise these kinds of questions and jointly seek answers to them, based on the understanding that students' learning and development occur over time both inside and outside of the classroom. Assessment becomes a collective means whereby colleagues discover the fit between institution- or program-level expectations for student achievement and patterns of actual student achievement. These patterns may verify that certain cohorts of students achieve at an institution's level of expectation but other cohorts do not. When assessment results do not match institutional or programmatic expectations, that is, when they do not fit, then faculty and staff collectively have the opportunity to determine how to improve student performance. Assessment, then, becomes a lens through which an institution assesses itself through its students' work.

Innovations in pedagogy or integration of diverse methods of teaching and learning into a program of study, redesign of a program, reconceptualizing the role of advising, or establishing stronger connections between the curriculum and the co-curriculum represent some of the kinds of changes that faculty and staff may undertake to improve student learning and development based on their interpretations of assessment results.

How does this process of inquiry work if an institution is committed to learning about student learning to improve the quality of its education? The Assessment Guide, which is represented in three figures, is designed to assist institutions in conceptualizing a plan that integrates assessment into their cultures so that over time assessment becomes a systematic and organic practice. The guide consists of three major parts: (1) Determining Your Institution's Expectations; (2) Determining Timing, Identifying Cohort(s), and Assigning Responsibility; and (3) Interpreting and Sharing Results to Enhance Institutional Effectiveness. For purposes of discussion, each part is divided into subactivities that, in turn, include examples of how some institutions have responded to each of these activities. However, in reality, decisions across these subactivities are interrelated. Decisions about what to assess—*student outcomes*—are related to decisions about how to assess. These decisions, in turn, should be linked with what and how students have learned. Rather than prescribing a lock-step linear process, the figures identify major issues that an institution needs to address in its plan if it intends to integrate assessment into its culture as an ongoing, not an episodic, means of improving student learning.

DETERMINING YOUR INSTITUTION'S EXPECTATIONS

The columns in Figure 5.1 identify consensus-based decisions that faculty, staff, and administrators need to make about desired learning outcomes and the methods and criteria to assess those outcomes. Student learning outcomes state what students should know and be able to do as a result of their course work and educational experiences at an institution or in a program of study. These outcomes encompass areas of knowledge and understanding, abilities, habits of mind, modes of inquiry, dispositions, or values. They are drawn from an institution's mission and purpose statements, from the mission statement of an institution's general education curriculum, and/or from the mission statement of a major, program, or service. For example, in Column A of the figure, "State Expected Outcomes," a program or major might say that it expects its undergraduate students to "derive supportable inferences from statistical and graphical data." An institution that takes an interdisciplinary approach to general education might state that it expects students to "analyze a social problem from interdisciplinary perspectives." Key to describing expected outcomes are active verbs that capture the desired student learning or development, such as *design*, *create*, *analyze*, and *apply*. Outcomes describe an eventual expectation for student learning at the institutional or programmatic level, or they describe developmental expectations that enable faculty, staff, and administrators to track learning and development over time.

Along with stating expected outcomes, peers need to identify if, in fact, they provide sufficient educational opportunities inside and outside of the classroom to develop the desired outcomes they assert they teach or develop. If, for example, an institution asserts in its mission statement that it develops interdisciplinary problem-solvers, then identifying the range of educational opportunities that develops this kind of problem solving is essential. Courses may be one means, but not all students develop an ability at the same time or under the same pedagogies. Are there ample opportunities for students to practice the ways of knowing and modes of inquiry characteristic of interdisciplinary thinking, or are these opportunities addressed in only one or two courses? Do students practice or apply interdisciplinary modes of thinking, and deepen their learning, as they participate in services and programs that complement the curriculum?

Figure 5.1
Assessment Guide
(Part I: Determining Your Institution's Expectations)

A. State Expected Outcomes	B. Identify Where Expected Outcomes Are Addressed	C. Determine Methods and Criteria to Assess Outcomes	D. State Institution's or Program's Level of Expected Performance	E. Identify and Collect Baseline Information
For example:	For example, in:	Examples:	Examples:	By means of:
• Derive supportable inferences from statistical and graphical data.	• Courses	• Test	• Numerical score on a national examination	• Standardized tests
• Analyze a social problem from interdisciplinary perspectives.	• Programs	• In-class writing sample	• Numerical score on a licensure examination	• Locally designed tests or other instruments
• Evaluate proposed solutions to a community issue.	• Services	• In-class analysis of a problem	• Holistic score on ability to solve a mathematical problem	• In-class writing exercise
	• Internships	• In-class collaborative problem-solving project	• Mastery level score on a culminating project	• In-class case study
	• Community service projects	• Portfolio	• Mastery level score on writing samples	• Portfolio
	• Work experiences	• Performance		• Performance
	• Independent studies	• Simulation		
		• Focus group		

To assure that students have sufficient and various kinds of educational opportunities to learn or develop desired outcomes, faculty and staff often engage in curricular and co-curricular mapping. During this process representatives from across an institution identify the depth and breadth of opportunities inside and outside of the classroom that intentionally address the development of desired outcomes. Multiple opportunities enable students to reflect on and practice the outcomes an institution or program asserts it develops. Furthermore, variation in teaching and learning strategies and educational opportunities contributes to students' diverse ways of learning. Column B in Figure 5.1 provides a list of possible opportunities that might foster a desired outcome. That is, an institution has to assure itself that it has translated its mission and purposes into its programs and services to more greatly ensure that students have opportunities to learn and develop what an institution values. If the results of mapping reveal insufficient or limited opportunities for students to develop a desired outcome, then an institution needs to question its educational intentionality. Without ample opportunities to reflect on and practice desired outcomes, students will likely not transfer, build upon, or deepen the learning and development an institution or program values.

Consensus about methods of capturing student learning is another focal activity represented in Column C (Figure 5.1). What quantitative and qualitative methods, and combinations of these, will provide useful and accurate measures of student achievement (e.g., standardized tests, performances, computer simulations, licensure exams, locally designed case studies, portfolios, focus groups, interviews, or surveys)? Decisions about whether to use standardized tests or locally designed assessment methods, such as case studies, simulations, portfolios, or observations of collaborative problem solving, for example, should be based on how well a method aligns with what and how students have learned at an institution or within a program and how well a method measures what it purports to measure.

Standardized tests may measure how well students have learned information, but they may not demonstrate how well students can solve problems using that information. Using multiple methods of assessment contributes to a more comprehensive interpretation of student achievement. Some students may perform well on multiple-choice questions in a discipline but not well on writing assignments that require them to apply what they have learned in that discipline. No two programs or majors may choose the same method of assessment. Whereas members in one department believe that standardized test results enable them to understand how well students learn, members of another department might not select standardized tests, believing, instead, that results of a locally designed instrument or student portfolios provide more relevant evidence of student learning. Some institutions use standardized assessment methods that focus on students' general education outcomes; others use capstone projects to assess how well students integrate general education into their majors.

Developing agreement about scoring methods is related to making decisions about the methods of assessment to use. In the case of standardized or licensure examinations, faculty may rely on nationally normed scores against which to judge their students' achievement. When colleagues develop their own assessment methods, such as portfolios or case studies, they also need to develop a way to assess student performance. This consensus-based activity involves developing criteria that characterize achievement of an outcome and developing scoring ranges that identify students' level of achievement, known as rubrics. For example, mathematics faculty might identify four traits they desire to see students demonstrate in solving an advanced level mathematical problem: (1) conceptual understanding, (2) system of notation, (3) logical formulation, and (4) solution to the problem. In addition, they might identify four levels to score those characteristics: exemplary, proficient, acceptable, unacceptable. Or, these levels might be indicated through a numerical range, 1 to 4. Within a department or program, deciding on traits and scoring levels is best accomplished through the work of a team, often with representatives from relevant support areas, such as the library or student services, that contribute to students' learning. In the case of stating institution-wide outcomes, interdisciplinary teams often work together to achieve consensus about desired traits and levels of performance.

Column D (Figure 5.1) provides examples of some scoring methods that institutions or programs have used to assess their students' learning. In the first two examples, departments relied on criteria and scoring ranges established by national testing services or professional organizations. In the remaining examples in that column, however, institutions and departments created their own criteria and scoring ranges for their locally designed assessment methods. Students' numerical score on a standardized test in a major could serve as one way to interpret student achievement. Student's score on a portfolio ranked according to levels of expertise could serve as another way to interpret student achievement.

Establishing baseline data for entry-level students enables programs and an institution to chart how well students learn and develop over time. Column E (Figure 5.1), "Identify and Collect Baseline Information," lists some methods that an institution or program might use to chart students' chronological achievement. For example, using a case study when students enter a program, again at midpoint in students' careers, and then again at the end of their careers could reveal how well students develop disciplinary problem-solving abilities.

DETERMINING TIMING, IDENTIFYING COHORT(S), AND ASSIGNING RESPONSIBILITY

The next part of the Assessment Guide focuses on how and when institutions or programs within an institution decide to assess desired outcomes. The choices range from identifying cohorts of students based on institutional demographics to identifying appropriate times to assess students' level of achievement. Determining whom an institution will assess (see Column A, Figure 5.2) should also be incorporated into an institution's assessment plan. Institutions may choose to track all students or cohorts of students. Tracking may mean collecting the same examples of student performance or using the same instrument semester after semester. Student demographics at an institution or within a program become a way to track cohort performance. If an institution's profile consists of nontraditional-aged students and first-generation immigrant students, then tracking these cohorts' performance, and sampling representative diversity within those groups, would provide valuable information about how well each cohort and populations within each cohort achieve an institution's or a program's expectations. Results of cohort analysis bring focus to assessment interpretations and eventually to pedagogical or curricular changes. In addition, connecting other sources of data about cohorts, such as their enrollment patterns or their participation in support services, provides information that assists in interpreting assessment results. An institution might find, for example, that poor cohort performance may be affected by students' reluctance to seek assistance or their failure to enroll in certain kinds of courses.

Figure 5.2
Assessment Guide
(Part II: Determining Timing, Identifying Cohort(s), and Assigning Responsibility)

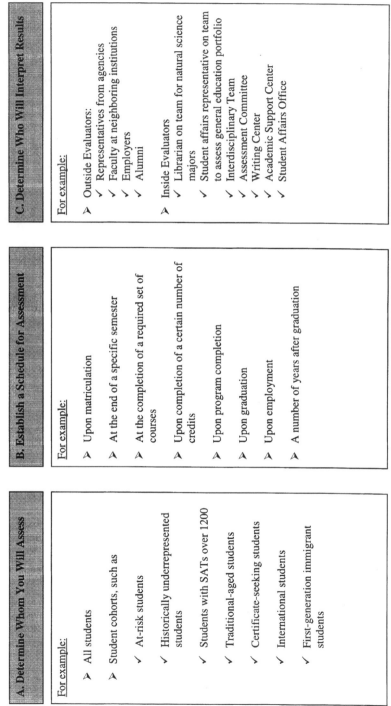

A. Determine Whom You Will Assess

For example:

- All students
- Student cohorts, such as
  - At-risk students
  - Historically underrepresented students
  - Students with SATs over 1200
  - Traditional-aged students
  - Certificate-seeking students
  - International students
  - First-generation immigrant students

B. Establish a Schedule for Assessment

For example:

- Upon matriculation
- At the end of a specific semester
- At the completion of a required set of courses
- Upon completion of a certain number of credits
- Upon program completion
- Upon graduation
- Upon employment
- A number of years after graduation

C. Determine Who Will Interpret Results

For example:

- Outside Evaluators:
  - Representatives from agencies
  - Faculty at neighboring institutions
  - Employers
  - Alumni
- Inside Evaluators
  - Librarian on team for natural science majors
  - Student affairs representative on team to assess general education portfolio
  - Interdisciplinary Team
  - Assessment Committee
  - Writing Center
  - Academic Support Center
  - Student Affairs Office

Column B focuses on the establishment of an assessment timetable. The assessment of some outcomes, such as students' moral or ethical behavior, for example, may stretch from matriculation to graduation to employment. Other outcomes, such as students' professional writing abilities, may be ones that a program wants to assure itself that its students have achieved by graduation because students' prospective employers expect that level of achievement. In either of these cases, however, institutions should develop a timetable that assesses students' development over time based on desired levels of achievement. For example, assessing students' professional or disciplinary writing abilities after a certain number of courses provides peers with an understanding of how well students are developing as professional writers. Interpretations of student achievement might cause faculty to integrate more writing into students' remaining courses. Assessing students' professional writing abilities in their senior year provides a "last look" at how well students have achieved a program's expected performance. However, that last look may be too late to address disappointing performance.

Assessing student learning over time—known as formative assessment—provides valuable information about how well students are progressing toward an institution's or program's expectations. In addition, interpretations of student achievement can be linked to the kinds of learning experiences that do or do not promote valued outcomes. Interpreting students' performance or achievement over time and sharing assessment results with students enable students to understand their strengths and weaknesses and to reflect on how they need to improve over the course of their remaining studies. Assessing student learning at the end of a program or course of study—known as summative assessment—provides information about patterns of student achievement without institutional or programmatic opportunity to improve students' achievement and without student opportunity to reflect on how to improve and demonstrate that improvement. Using both formative and summative assessment methods provides an institution or program with a rich understanding of how and what students learn. Results of these assessments may cause colleagues, for example, to introduce new pedagogies that more effectively address diverse learning styles or more effectively develop students' learning in a discipline. Results help answer questions about which kind of pedagogies or educational experiences foster disciplinary behaviors and modes of inquiry. When, for example, do students majoring in anthropology begin to behave and problem-solve like anthropologists?

For institution-wide outcomes, as well as those developed in programs and services, peers need to identify who will interpret students' work or performance. As Column C illustrates, the options are numerous, ranging from selecting individuals outside of a program or an institution to selecting those within an institution or program. Employers, neighboring faculty, community representatives, and alumni represent those from outside communities who may serve on assessment teams. For example, three external evaluators may review student portfolios or student performances in a major based on agreed-upon criteria for scoring. Members of educational centers within a college or university may assume the responsibility for assessing student work, such as members of a writing center or a support center. Emerging on campuses are cross-disciplinary teams of faculty and professional staff who score student work, such as students' solution to a problem or their writing samples in a portfolio.

INTERPRETING AND SHARING RESULTS TO ENHANCE INSTITUTIONAL EFFECTIVENESS

The third part of the Assessment Guide involves making decisions based on interpretations of assessment results and then establishing communication channels to share those interpretations so that an institution acts on and supports interpretations to improve student learning. The question underlying assessment results is "What has an institution or program learned about its students' learning?" Column A of Figure 5.3, "Interpret How Results Will Inform Teaching/Learning and Decision Making," provides some examples of how institutions or programs have interpreted results to change pedagogy, curricula, or practices. Interpretations of student performance might lead to innovations in teaching in general education courses or in redesigning the entire general education curriculum. For example, if an institution were to find that its students did not meet institutional expectations for quantitative reasoning, faculty and staff might conclude that they need to take two major steps—develop workshops to help faculty understand how to integrate quantitative reasoning into their courses and integrate quantitative reasoning across the curriculum.

These kinds of changes need to be recognized and addressed at an

Figure 5.3
Assessment Guide
(Part III: Interpreting and Sharing Results to Enhance Institutional Effectiveness)

A. Interpret How Results Will Inform Teaching/Learning and Decision Making	B. Determine How and with Whom You Will Share Interpretations	C. Decide How Your Institution Will Follow Up on Implemented Changes
For example:	For example:	Repeat the assessment cycle after changes have been implemented:
⋏ Revise pedagogy, curricula, and sequence of courses.	⋏ General Education Subcommittee of the Curriculum Committee through an annual report	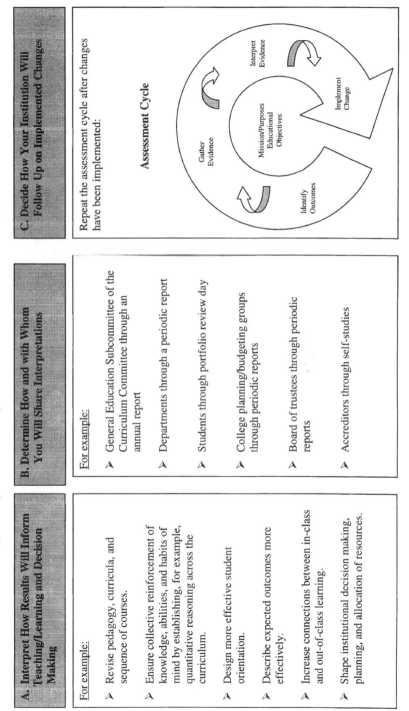
⋏ Ensure collective reinforcement of knowledge, abilities, and habits of mind by establishing, for example, quantitative reasoning across the curriculum.	⋏ Departments through a periodic report	
⋏ Design more effective student orientation.	⋏ Students through portfolio review day	
⋏ Describe expected outcomes more effectively.	⋏ College planning/budgeting groups through periodic reports	
⋏ Increase connections between in-class and out-of-class learning.	⋏ Board of trustees through periodic reports	
⋏ Shape institutional decision making, planning, and allocation of resources.	⋏ Accreditors through self-studies	

institution's highest decision-making levels to ensure that an institution commits the appropriate finances or resources to enact the kinds of changes or innovations that interpretations identify. As the examples in Column B illustrate, interpretations might be shared with program committees or subcommittees, such as a general education subcommittee of a curriculum committee. Boards of trustees should also receive interpretations to inform the institution's strategic planning and budgeting. Accreditors are increasingly interested in learning about what an institution has discovered about student learning and how it intends to improve student outcomes. In addition, students should receive assessment results so that they monitor and improve upon their learning.

If an institution aims to sustain its assessment efforts to improve the quality of education continually, it needs to develop channels of communication whereby it shares interpretations of students' results and incorporates recommended changes into its budgeting, decision making, and strategic planning as these processes will likely need to respond to and support proposed changes. Most institutions have not built into their assessment plans effective channels of communication that share interpretations of student achievement with faculty and staff, as well as with members of an institution's budgeting and planning bodies—including strategic planning bodies. Assessment is certain to fail if an institution does not develop channels that communicate assessment interpretations and proposed changes to its centers of institutional decision making, planning, and budgeting.

Once an institution or program makes changes to improve the quality of education, the assessment cycle begins anew to discover if proposed changes or innovations do improve student achievement. As Column C illustrates, the assessment cycle once again explores how well students are learning based on innovations or changes. Do changes in pedagogy or curricular design result in improved student learning?

Motivated by institutional curiosity, assessment will become, over time, an organic process of discovering how and what and which students learn. Launching a commitment to assessment works best when a group within a major or from across a campus, for example, plans how the process will actually work. Initially, limiting the number of outcomes colleagues will assess enables them to determine how an assessment cycle will operate based on existing structures and processes or proposed new ones. The weight of trying to assess too many learning outcomes as an institution is beginning its commitment may unduly tax faculty and professional staff who need to determine how their culture will integrate the process of learning about student learning into institutional rhythms and practices.

CONCLUSION

An institutional commitment to assessment reflects a curiosity about learning and will eventually transform institutions into learning communities raising questions about student learning and development. The results of this collaborative inquiry should inspire innovation and creativity in teaching and learning. Among those innovations might be:

- Fostering greater alignment between course or disciplinary content and pedagogy
- Encouraging pedagogical innovations that address differences in learning styles
- Encouraging greater collaboration between faculty and professional staff to develop or foster desired knowledge, abilities, or dispositions
- Providing increased opportunities for students to apply concepts, principles, and modes of inquiry that an institution and its programs value

CHAPTER 6

A Local Institutional Assessment Plan

Robert E. Dugan

Higher education institutions develop assessment plans as part of their accountability process for the purpose of demonstrating their institutional effectiveness to various stakeholders and constituencies. These plans are usually planned, created, and implemented at three levels: (1) institution, (2) academic departments, and (3) academic support departments such as the library. The plans created by academic departments and academic support departments are oftentimes initiated, and based upon, the mission statement that is the institution's declaration of educational goals, values, and basic principles. In turn, institutional assessment is usually a compilation of the reported findings of the broad educational objectives restated as measurable outcomes that academic and support departments implement, measure, and analyze. These objectives also are reflected by aggregated campuswide measures (e.g., retention, persistence, and graduation rates). Outcomes assessment places shared responsibility on all institutional units for providing evidence of how they contribute to desired educational outcomes and how they incorporate outcomes assessment into planning and improvement.[1]

INSTITUTIONAL ASSESSMENT PLANS

Through their review guidelines and standards, regional accrediting organizations, and some program accrediting organizations, require

higher education institutions to have institutional effectiveness programs. One organizing structure for the development of program assessment plans suggests that an institution:

- Determine its expectations
  - State expected outcomes
  - Identify where expected outcomes are addressed
  - Determine methods and criteria to assess outcomes
  - State institution's or program's level of expected performance
  - Identify and collect baseline information
- Determine timing, identify cohort(s), and assign responsibility
  - Determine whom the institution will assess
  - Establish a schedule for assessment
  - Determine who will interpret results
- Interpret and share results to enhance institutional effectiveness
  - Interpret how results will inform teaching/learning and decision making
  - Determine how and with whom the institution will share inter- pretations
  - Decide how the institution will follow-up on implemented changes.[2]

Additionally, several state government education commissions require
institutional effectiveness plans. One example is the Commonwealth of
Virginia. The State Council of Higher Education for Virginia (SCHEV)
explains the purpose of the reports of institutional effectiveness on its
Web site thusly:

> Welcome to the second edition of the Reports of Institutional Effect-
> iveness (ROIE)—annual reports intended to provide meaningful infor-
> mation on the academic quality and operational efficiency of Virginia's
> public institutions of higher education.
>
> SCHEV initiated and led in creating this new accountability tool. In
> 1999, SCHEV presented the concept of measures of institutional ef-
> fectiveness. In 2000, the Governor and the General Assembly agreed
> that this SCHEV initiative was a good idea and mandated by law ROIE's
> creation through the 2000–2002 Appropriation Act. (Item 162 #11c)

First published on July 2, 2001, the ROIE were developed to provide evidence of institutional effectiveness—the extent to which institutions accomplish their missions and students achieve their educational goals. In highlighting the institutions' accomplishments and demonstrating progress towards improvement, the reports give students, parents, policy makers, faculty and staff, employers, and the general public access to important information about each of Virginia's public four-year colleges and universities. . . .

Though not formally linked to any future funding model for higher education, the reports are intended to provide evidence of the value added by our colleges and universities to the Commonwealth of Virginia and its educational, economic, civic and cultural vitality.

Each institutional report is organized into five sections: institutional mission, college profile measures, system-wide measures, and institution-specific measures, and the core competencies.[3]

Either the institution or the university system sets institutional goals. For example, each institution of the University of Wisconsin System contributes to the systemwide "Core Mission of the University Cluster Institutions."[4] The University of Wisconsin–Whitewater (UW–W) has an additional mission that differentiates it from the other campuses in the system.[5] As part of its 1996 institutional plan, the "UW–Whitewater Vision Statement" states that:

As active partners in education, UW-Whitewater faculty, staff, and students will assume responsibility to ensure that its graduates fulfill the expectations of an educated person who possesses analytic, communication, and critical-thinking skills with the ability to integrate knowledge among diverse academic disciplines providing a basis for life-long learning.

That statement also explains that "the quality of UW-Whitewater programs will be maintained by rigorous processes of audit and review and assessment of student outcomes which utilize outside reviewers whenever possible."[6]

UW–W makes strategic planning assumptions, namely that "students must be life-long learners, prepared to live and work in an increasingly diverse, multicultural, and global society."[7] A priority among these assumptions is that the institution "will keep student learning as the paramount focus of its programs and services."[8] Some of the subgoals of this priority include:

> Student mastery of their disciplines that prepares them to flourish in a global environment. (GOAL 1.3)
>> Strategies
>> a. Monitor student learning through established outcomes assessment procedures to ensure high quality academic programs.
>
> Graduates who are broadly-educated, life-long learners. (GOAL 1.4)
>> Strategies
>> a. Integrate critical thinking, problem solving, collaborative learning, and creativity skills throughout the academic and non-academic programs;
>> b. Ensure that the goals of the general education program are widely disseminated and are being met by periodic program review and ongoing program assessment; and
>> c. Establish clear linkages between the general education program and each major, enhancing the major and reinforcing the general education program outcomes.[9]

The University of Wisconsin–Whitewater purposefully enhanced its mission and vision to include student learning outcomes by incorporating student learning priorities into its institutional strategic plan, well beyond the shared mission of the University of Wisconsin system. As of the fall of 2003, the University of Wisconsin–Whitewater community was engaged in revising its core values, mission, goals, and other institutional planning documents.[10]

While these examples highlight the effectiveness of institutional assessment plans for public universities, accrediting organizations and agencies, governing boards, and other institutional stakeholders also influence private universities as they meet the demands for increased accountability and demonstrate institutional effectiveness.

ASSESSMENT EFFORTS FOR ACADEMIC PROGRAMS

Aggregate outcomes, such as graduation and retention rates, are most often compiled and reported at the institution level. Student learning outcomes, seeking to determine if an individual's values and skills have been changed as a result of his or her contact with the methodologies and content of a course, are usually measured and reported at the classroom level. Student learning outcomes are directly, and indirectly, based on general educational objectives developed at the institution level and found in the institution's mission statement. These objectives state institutional expectations of what, and how, students will learn. The academic discipline, the program, and/or an instructor at the course level then refine and structure the objectives to be more specific and measurable. Oftentimes educational objectives and measurable learning outcomes are identified as such on an individual course syllabus. Educational outcomes are then implemented, and later measured and compiled, at the course level. The findings of those measurements are analyzed and used at the course and program levels to affect change—improve student learning by adjusting educational content, classroom pedagogies, and measurement instruments and processes. The findings are also reported through the academic program to the institutional level for compilation, analysis, and reporting to stakeholders. Regional accreditors expect that most, if not all, academic programs participate in the assessment process of identifying, developing, measuring, reporting, and analyzing learning outcomes to prove their effectiveness and to improve learning continuously.

Each institution's unique campus culture strongly influences the assessment process. For example, while general education objectives are oftentimes developed at the institutional level and included in the institutional mission statement as a statement of "what we value," the faculty through their strategic planning at the academic program level may have had an early influence on these educational objectives as later adapted and prioritized by the institution.

Institution/Academic Program Assessment Planning

This section offers examples of assessment planning at eight institutions.

Alverno College (Milwaukee, Wisconsin)

According to its mission statement, Alverno College educates women:

> The student—her learning and her personal and professional development—is the central focus of everyone associated with Alverno. Agree-

ment regarding this mission is evident throughout the college in its publications and operating philosophy. It is the recurring theme in messages of the Board of Trustees and the president of the college, in catalogs and educational publications, and in the daily approach of faculty and staff to their work. The college's accomplishments are measured by how well we carry out this central mission.[11]

Using the mission statement, the faculty develop and implement an "ability-based" undergraduate education, refining education in terms of the abilities needed by the student for work, family, and community.[12] The specific abilities that the faculty identified are:

- Communication: Make connections that create meaning between yourself and your audience. Learn to speak, read, write, and listen effectively, using graphics, electronic media, computers, and quantified data.
- Analysis: Think clearly and critically. Fuse experience, reason, and training into considered judgment.
- Problem Solving: Figure out what the problem is and what is causing it. With others or alone, form strategies that work in different situations. Then, get done what needs to be done, evaluating effectiveness.
- Valuing in Decision Making: Recognize different value systems while holding strongly to your own ethic. Recognize the moral dimensions of your decisions and accept responsibility for the consequences of your actions.
- Social Interaction: Know how to get things done in committees, task forces, team projects, and other group efforts. Elicit the views of others and help reach conclusions.
- Developing a Global Perspective: Act with an understanding of and respect for the economic, social, and biological interdependence of global life.
- Effective Citizenship: Be involved and responsible in the community. Act with an informed awareness of contemporary issues and their historical contexts. Develop leadership abilities.
- Aesthetic Engagement: Engage with various forms of art and in artistic processes. Take and defend positions regarding the mean-

ing and value of artistic expressions in the contexts from which they emerge.[13]

The faculty apply evaluative measures as course-based assessments and integrative assessments that measure learning collectively or from several courses. Students also routinely conduct self-assessment. This process of continuous assessment, which the faculty call "student assessment-as-learning,"[14] is used to improve learning.

King's College (Wilkes-Barre, Pennsylvania)

In the mid-1980s, King's College implemented its "CORE Curriculum" and initiated a comprehensive assessment program to improve student learning. This assessment program is faculty administered and evaluated, is course embedded, and provides students with clear expectations. Faculty members use the assessment findings to identify and respond to the strengths and weaknesses of individual students, of teaching/learning strategies, and of curricula.[15]

The CORE Curriculum has identified the following skills for liberal learning: critical thinking, effective writing, effective oral communication, information literacy, technology competence, quantitative reasoning, and moral reasoning. Liberal learning is defined by "A Statement of Purpose," which is based on the institutional mission statement:

> As affirmed in its Mission Statement, King's College is committed to offering its students an education which prepares them for a purposeful life, which makes explicit the human values inherent in a broadly based curriculum, and which actively encourages the religious and moral as well as the personal and social development of its students. More specifically, King's [College] seeks to:
> - Develop in students the fundamental thinking and communication skills required of every educated person;
> - Convey to students knowledge of the humanities, social sciences and natural sciences;
> - Give students an understanding of how the various disciplines differ, how they are related and how their distinct perspectives enrich our lives;
> - Endow students with a respect for their culture and the cultures of others;
> - Provide students with traditional academic and pre-professional

major programs of study that build upon the foundational courses of the CORE Curriculum;

- Engage students in the philosophical and theological dimensions of an examined life;
- Cultivate students' capacity and desire for independent and continuing learning;
- Lead students to recognize their personal worth and to develop a sense of purpose and willingness to assume responsibility for their own lives and decisions; and
- Encourage students to examine their own religious and moral convictions so that they may discover appropriate ways of attaining personal fulfillment and of improving the quality of life in society at large.[16]

Additionally, King's College identifies other institutional factors that directly support the above-mentioned educational goals:

- The explicit and implicit content of courses in many different disciplines
- The various teaching/learning strategies employed by instructors
- The effectiveness of advisement and counseling
- The impact of co-curricular activities
- The quality of facilities
- The intellectual, social, and spiritual atmosphere of the College[17]

The faculty, staff, and administration are charged with working together to ensure and enhance student learning.[18]

Roanoke College (Salem, Virginia)

Most efforts to demonstrate institutional effectiveness through implementation of the educational assessment program are delegated to academic programs. "In order to conduct a meaningful and systematic program of institutional effectiveness" at this level, all academic majors and programs complete three essential tasks:

1. The formulation of an assessment plan, including a mission statement, objectives, and assessment mechanisms
2. The conduct of an Annual Assessment Program

3. The integration of assessment activities within the college's planning and budget processes[19]

The assessment plan for each major and program

> includes articulation of a mission statement for the major/program, outcomes objectives for the major/program, and a brief description of assessment mechanisms that will be used to determine progress in meeting the objectives. A carefully written assessment plan serves as the foundation for all assessment activity. Nevertheless, it can be modified at any time as decisions are made to sharpen or extend the mission and/or as program objectives and assessment mechanisms are modified. A copy of the assessment plan for each academic major and program is kept on file in the appropriate Vice President's office and in the Office of Assessment.[20]

In addition, each academic program develops its own mission statement based upon three guidelines:

1. The mission statement should specify the purpose of the major/program within the overall college context; it should make clear the contribution of the major/program to the institution.

2. The mission statement should be an extension of the College Statement of Purpose, Institutional Standing Goals, and Curriculum Goals; it should make clear how the major/program contributes to the mission and goals of the college.

3. The mission statement should be succinct but should be sure to include the essential mission of the major or program (rather than the mission of any individual faculty member). Most statements are about 1–3 paragraphs in length.[21]

The institutional documents identified in number 2 above are clearly stated and grouped together by the college's assessment program for reference as the academic departments respond to the institutional mandate concerning institutional effectiveness.[22]

The academic major/program level develops outcomes and objectives, but the institution provides guidelines for their development.

1. The objectives should state the key standing (continuing) aims for the major/program. They should include the knowledge, skills, attitudes, behaviors, and achievements expected of students in the program. Appendix A, "A Classification of Outcomes Dimensions," should be helpful in consideration of possible outcomes.

2. The objectives should:

    a. Include an action verb and a statement of ability. Use meaningful verbs: better objectives use action verbs like "paraphrase," "compute," "describe," and "construct;" poorer objectives use verbs that are too general like "understand" and "appreciate."

    b. Involve objectives that can be operationalized and are empirically verifiable/directly observable.

    c. Be attainable or feasible given the resources of the major/program.

    c. Clarify or establish a link between what students accomplish in the program and what they do after they graduate.

    d. Permit multiple paths of demonstrating mastery of program objectives.

3. The objectives should be outcome- or result-oriented rather than statements of process, and they should be specific. This is contrary to the tradition of both administrative and academic departments which are more accustomed to identifying "what we will do." This model is based on identification of "what will occur" as a result of what we do. Thus, "offering sound courses in core areas of the discipline" is too process-focused. We should instead be thinking about what the objectives are. (In other words, why do we offer core courses? What are we trying to accomplish? How will students who take these courses be different?)

The presentation of objectives follows a singular format. Majors and programs "designate broadly stated learning goals, each of which is followed by two or more specific learning [outcomes] objectives."[23]

Roanoke College's academic programs have broad responsibility for the development and implementation of the learning outcomes assessment program, but that program is based on specific institutional guidelines. The learning outcomes adhere to the institution's Statement of Purpose, Standing Goals, and Curriculum Goals.

James Madison University (Harrisonburg, Virginia)

This public university's institutional mission statement, which states that "we are committed to preparing students to be educated and enlightened citizens who will live meaningful and productive lives,"[24] led to the development of institution-specific measures in the general education program. These measures reflect what the institution values:

> Every student . . . must complete two years in our General Education (http://www.jmu.edu/gened/) program, regardless of . . . [his or her] major. All eleven of our learning measures take place in the General Education program since this experience is common to all JMU students. We use these student learning data in three ways:
>
> 1. Competency: all . . . students must pass these measures before advancing to their sophomore year.
> 2. Value Added or "change over time:" these measure differences reported over two occasions: as entering first year students and after course completion.
> 3. Course versus No Course Comparison: sophomore-level students who have completed the required courses are compared to sophomores who have not yet completed the required General Education courses.[25]

Eleven measures are applied to every student:
Competency-based:

- Information-Seeking Skills
- Basic Technology
- Oral Communication
- Writing

For the other seven measures, student scores are reported on a common scale similar to the Scholastic Aptitude Test (SAT):

- American History and Government
- Critical Thinking
- Wellness and Human Development
- Arts and Humanities

- Quantitative Reasoning
- Natural World/Science
- Global Experience[26]

George Mason University (Fairfax, Virginia)

Each academic program supports the institutional mission statement through the development of its assessment plan. The planning efforts are initiated at the college or school level, and then focused at the department level. Student learning and other goals are then specified at the program level. Evaluation methods are identified at the program level; assessment and evaluation findings are accompanied by changes proposed or implemented to improve the academic program.[27]

Brenau University (Gainesville, Georgia)

According to its purpose statement,

> Brenau University is a private comprehensive university that includes the Women's College, the Evening and Weekend College, the Online College, and the Academy. These four divisions, distinct yet complementary, offer diverse educational opportunities founded in the liberal arts which lead to intellectual and professional development, foster personal growth, and encourage community responsibility and global understanding.[28]

"The Executive Council, led by the university president and consisting of all university vice presidents, develops and implements the annual institutional goals."[29] Despite the fact that the assessment efforts are initiated at the institutional level, the faculty play an active and positive role.

Ongoing assessment activities support the annual planning and budgeting processes, and provide continuous quality improvement for programs and services. University policy requires that all "academic majors, general education areas, and administrative and educational support services" create an assessment plan that outlines "their area mission related to Brenau's purpose." Those plans list expected outcomes and general means of assessment used, and they require the annual reporting of results.[30] At the same time, the plans support the institutional goals and strategic plan, and they

1. Describe the academic major, minor or general education area in the case of academic programs; in the case of administrative units there should be a description of the purpose of the unit. In both cases this description should be tied to the purpose of Brenau and the institutional goals.

2. List the expected educational outcomes of the educational program/course, or in the case of administrative units, list the major functions and goals of the unit.

3. Indicate general means by which, over time, the effectiveness of programs or units will be measured.[31]

Institutional guidelines for developing assessment plans indicate that these components of those plans, among others, must include:

- The mission statement of the program or general education area, and its relationship to the mission/purpose of Brenau. This section may include a program philosophy statement.

- A comprehensive list of the educational outcomes expected of all graduates of the program. All undergraduate academic majors should list as well the six cross-curricular outcomes that Brenau expects of graduates of all its undergraduate programs:

  Cross Curricular Outcome #1: Computer Competency
  Cross Curricular Outcome #2: Critical Thinking/Problem Solving
  Cross Curricular Outcome #3: Ethical Reflection/Values Awareness
  Cross Curricular Outcome #4: Cross Cultural Awareness and Global Perspective
  Cross Curricular Outcome #5: Oral Communication Skills
  Cross Curricular Outcome #6: Written Communication Skills[32]

- The various means of assessing expected program outcomes should be indicated in the "Plan." All measures are not necessarily expected to be utilized every year. Means of assessment may be listed globally in a separate section of the "Plan," or they may be indicated following each outcome listed in number 2 above. It is highly recommended that an external means of program assessment be incorporated at least once every 3–5 years. This may be a standardized field test, or an expert or working professional from the field or another university.[33]

Roles are assigned to the various academic participants:

- The Vice President for Academic Affairs: The VPAA will oversee the planning and evaluation processes of all academic programs. This will be accomplished via communication with the school deans and department chairs in the Academic Council, as well as in conjunction with the University Planning Committee, the University Assessment Committee, and the Executive Council. Assessment results will be utilized in planning and budgeting for academic programs.

- School Deans: Review with department chairs the assessment goals of departmental faculty for all

  - General education courses

  - Minors

  - Undergraduate or graduate majors taught within the department.

    - Review assessment goals before classes start in the fall and evaluate completed Assessment Reporting Forms in the spring when completed with "results" and "use of results." Lend special attention to cross-curricular goal setting and achievement in each area, as well as comparability studies when departmental courses are taught in more than one format or location.

    - Offer input at the Academic Council level and in budget planning and decision making, based on observed use of assessment results within departments.

    - Ensure completed Annual Assessment Reporting Forms have been forwarded by e-mail attachment to the Office of Institutional Effectiveness for posting on the Assessment Web site each spring before May 15.

- Department Chairs:

  - Ensure all faculty in department complete and finalize the reporting of assessment results in the spring post-planning period (May 1–15) and at the same time initiate assessment goal setting for the following academic year. Include summary of assessment results for year ending and assessment goals for coming year in departmental sections of annual reports to the VPAA.

  - Review faculty goals before the start of the academic year and ensure attention to the cross-curricular goals in some reasonable rotation.

- Emphasize to faculty the need for comparability studies and support data for any courses taught in more than one format (day, evening, online) or at more than one location. (Support from Office of Institutional Research and Planning on request.)
- Utilize assessment data to support budget requests for the department.
- Review departmental Assessment Reports with dean.
- Forward completed Assessment Reporting Forms by e-mail attachment each spring to the school dean and to the Office of Institutional Effectiveness for posting on the Web site.
- Faculty Members:
  - During May post planning, record "results" and "use of results" from annual assessments on the official Assessment Reporting Forms.
  - Submit forms to department chair for review and forwarding to school dean and the Office of Institutional Effectiveness.
  - During May post planning, initiate preparation of assessment goals for upcoming year, including any goals for improvement suggested by previous assessment results.[34]

Brenau University manages an ongoing assessment process, based upon its institutional statement of purpose. That process is directly linked to the annual planning and budgeting process. While the assessment process is initiated annually from the institutional level after the Executive Council sets the annual goals, the development of educational objectives and outcomes and the measurement and reporting of these objectives and outcomes are carried out in a continuous hierarchical loop involving the vice president for academic affairs, school deans, department chairs, and the faculty.

University of Washington (Seattle, Washington)

The University of Washington emphasizes the creation of Student Learning Outcomes (SLOs) to address the following questions:

- What do you want students to know by the time they finish a course or the major?
- What do you want students to be able to do with what they know by the time they finish a course or the major?[35]

Faculty are encouraged to work in small groups at the academic department level to create discipline-focused outcomes based upon the learning goals used in their individual courses. Course-based knowledge and performance values are compiled and discussed, and faculty reach consensus about which outcomes will be used with the academic majors.[36] Once departmental/academic major outcomes are made public, individual faculty members may decide to export them "as guides for articulating new or revised learning goals for their own courses."[37]

Faculty have wide latitude to access outcomes and may use a variety of direct and indirect measures for gathering evidence of student performance. However, the university stresses the need to incorporate "expert judgment of student products" in addition to depending upon student self-assessments of their own learning.[38]

California State University, Monterey Bay

While most programs at academic institutions require students to accumulate a specific number of credits from courses taken to graduate, California State University, Monterey Bay (CSUMB), lets each student demonstrate what he or she learned rather than which courses he or she took to graduate.[39]

CSUMB has seven general education Learning Goals:

1. Effective and ethical communication in at least two languages with widely diverse audiences

2. Cross-culturally competent citizenship in a pluralistic and global society

3. Technological, aural, and visual literacy

4. Creative expression in the service of transforming culture

5. Ethics, social justice, and care for one another

6. Scientific sophistication and value for the earth and earth systems

7. Holistic and creative sense of self[40]

The Learning Goals are, in turn, supported by thirteen University Learning Requirements (ULRs):

1. Community Participation

2. Creative and Artistic Expression

3. Culture and Equity

4. Democratic Participation

5. English Communication

6. Ethics

7. Language

8. Literature and Popular Culture

9. Mathematics Communication

10. Science

11. Technology Information

12. U.S. Histories

13. Vibrancy[41]

Student knowledge and skills to satisfy a ULR are evaluated through either course-based assessment or an independent assessment.[42] Each ULR is supported by specific, measurable learning objectives. For example, the "Technology Information" ULR specifies these requirements:

> Demonstrate comfort with technology and information search and discovery methods. Demonstrate the ability to use tools effectively for the discovery, acquisition, and evaluation of information as well as core computer tools for the manipulation and presentation of information in a creative and ethical manner.[43]

To satisfy these requirements, students will demonstrate the ability to:

- Use accepted word-processing techniques to produce a well-designed and esthetically pleasing formal document
- Use standard spreadsheet features to produce a representation and analysis of numerical data
- Identify and refine a topic and formulate a research question related to that topic
- Describe and categorize the basic types of information resources available for a single topic
- Locate, retrieve, and evaluate information relevant to the research question

- Organize and communicate research findings and conclusions to answer a research question
- Create an electronic document that discusses a single subject or conveys a message
- Create an original digital image
- Analyze and respond to an ethical issue related to computers and use of information using a variety of sources[44]

Courses teach students the knowledge and skills to meet these specific learning objectives.

CSUMB academics are arranged into colleges and then into academic program majors.[45] Each major identifies specific Major Learning Outcomes (MLOs) that guide students toward the acquisition of the knowledge and skills required for the major. Again, students must prove their mastery of expected knowledge and skills outcomes (the MLOs) through course-based or independent assessments. A senior-level capstone project in the major is required as a demonstration of cumulative learning of the Major Learning Outcomes.[46]

The Library as an Academic Support Department

In addition to the institutional and academic department levels, other sources of outcomes concerning institutional effectiveness and education quality include academic support departments. The academic library is an important and central academic support department in the higher education institution. Higher education administrator Kenneth R. Smith, in a paper prepared for the Association of Research Libraries, states that outcome assessment for the library should be treated like any other academic department: "Like the Physics Department, the Library should be able to contribute to the achievement of learning outcomes for various academic programs across the University."[47] As a contributor to the institution, the library must identify and be responsive to the following questions:

- What are the institutional goals?
- What do institutions think is important to learn or achieve?
- What does the library do/provide to support these goals?
- How does the library measure its contribution?
- How is that contribution reported?

- How does the library use the findings to improve its resources and services?

As such, library performance should be strongly influenced by the need to contribute to institutional goals and educational outcomes. While assessment efforts and results should focus on the primary role of the teaching-learning library, other performance indicators measure and document the library's impact on other identified campuswide outcomes.[48]

Library Measures

Academic libraries have been collecting operational data for decades. Inputs are the resources used to support the library's infrastructure: collections, staffing, the physical facility, and installed information technologies. They are often described in financial terms or quantities. Outputs measure the workload undertaken and/or completed, and the usage of resources and services provided. Both inputs and outputs are invaluable measures for making administrative and operational decisions concerning the provision of library services.[49]

As part of the effort to improve accountability, regional accrediting organizations increasingly focus on determining learning results rather than asking for a counting of the number of library books held or borrowed.[50] As a result, there are some problems in only applying inputs and outputs as library measures for accountability. Outputs are intended to measure the application of inputs. As such, outputs do not measure individual student learning outcomes because inputs and outputs are institutionally centered, not individually centered. Outputs do not measure changes in skills or attitudes of the individual as a result of that person's interactions with the library.

Furthermore, the measurement processes differ between outputs and outcomes. As outputs are not the same as outcomes, the evaluation and assessment processes are not synonymous. Evaluation measures whether or not a system does what it is designed to do in an efficient and effective manner. Examples include personnel evaluation (e.g., does the individual do what the job description calls for?) and systems evaluation (e.g., is the integrated library system doing what it was acquired to do?). The evaluation process is best applied to gauge inputs and outputs: did the outputs do what was wanted or planned with the inputs (resources) available and applied?

The outcomes-assessment process measures learner performance. As such, it is student oriented rather than institution centered. Outcomes assessment measures changes in library users as a result of their contact with an academic library's programs, resources, and services. As a result, such assessment addresses whether or not students know subject content, have developed skills and abilities, and have acquired positive learning attitudes and values. Assessment is composed of statements about what students will know, think, or be able to do as a result of their contact with library programs. Assessment does not revolve around statements about what the library should or could do to bring about desired outcomes.[51]

Librarians may misidentify outputs as outcomes, and an evaluation process as an assessment process.[52] As such, the current applications of input and output measures miss the point—if the mission of the university is teaching/learning, research, and services, how do these descriptive inputs and outputs measure the library's contributions? Because inputs and outputs are insufficient for assessing outcomes, assessment focuses on student learning outcomes.[53]

Information Competencies

Library and information resources and services support the quality of the institutional learning environment. To better meet the stakeholders' accountability needs concerning educational quality, librarians must "link enabling outputs and inputs to the desired outcome and . . . document the amount, quality, and effects of use of these outputs and inputs to the institutional goals and desired educational outcomes."[54] This effort should identify, measure, and report the library's contributions to supporting institutional educational goals, objectives, and outcomes (instructional roles), as well as the library's direct and indirect contributions to supporting other institutional objectives (e.g., the provision and usage of library information resources and services to faculty, students, and others).

Outcomes and outcomes-related statements that refer to libraries and information resources are most often located in the general education requirements section of the regional accrediting organizations' standards.[55] Furthermore, accrediting organizations have linked information literacy to student learning competencies in these standards, and have identified a direct role for academic libraries. The most direct contribution that the library makes to institutional educational goals and objectives is its role in developing clear student learning outcomes related to information literacy skills, assessing the progress and achievement of these outcomes, and showing how the outcomes are used to improve student learning.[56]

Responsibility for helping students meet information literacy competencies involves a collaborative effort between faculty members and librarians.[57] Smith suggests that both groups share a number of course objectives and outcomes, "especially where the expertise of the library complements the expertise of those in the academic programs." Librarians "must take the initiative in determining what the library has to offer that will help the department achieve greater success in achieving . . . [its] learning outcomes" because the faculty may not readily identify the library as a place to turn for help. An opportunity exists for the library to connect to academic programs by offering modules for incorporation into required courses that are specifically designed to meet identified learning objectives and outcomes.[58]

For years, academic libraries have measured their contribution to information literacy using inputs and outputs. For example, identified inputs often include the number of available librarian instructors. In turn, the number of instructors would directly influence the number of instruction classes that the library could conduct. Another input would be the number of available instruction rooms with the number of computers available in each room. This input would influence maximum instruction class size and the number of simultaneous instructions that could be conducted. Commonly reported outputs often include the total number of instruction sessions conducted and the total number of instruction attendees. Outputs may also consider demographic information (e.g., the number of instruction classes and attendees from each department).[59]

Again, in these examples, the compilation and reporting of these descriptive inputs and outputs miss the point concerning determining learning outcomes: what did students learn, and how is it known they learned it? Rather than solely employing inputs and outputs for accountability, academic libraries could apply learning outcomes that focus on information literacy. Differences exist among inputs, outputs, and outcomes by:

• Definitions: inputs and outputs quantify available resources (e.g., number of instructors and classrooms) and workload (e.g., number of instructions held). Outcomes measure what the student learned as skills acquired (e.g., Boolean operators, difference between scholarly and nonscholarly information sources, and evaluating Web sources) or attitudes reinforced (ethical uses of information, such as copyright compliance).

• Methodologies used to compile data: inputs and outputs are usually based on counts of tangibles, such as volumes and instructions held. Measuring outcomes applies both direct and indirect methodologies.

• Usage and analysis: How are the data compiled used? Library administrators use inputs and outputs to make adjustments—hours open, staffing levels and placement, and collection development (buy more or less of a subject area or format). Administrators also apply this information in arguments for changes to resource levels (more dollars) and resource allocations (how the levels of resources provided are applied—staff, collections, and so forth). Outcomes are used as feedback to identify necessary changes in library instruction in the ongoing effort to improve instruction methods and student learning results as a result of student receipt of library instruction.[60]

How may one differentiate between an output and an outcome? As an example, we can examine the objective "to reduce the number of retrievals (hits) per search on electronic aggregate and specialized databases." Outputs would include the number of instruction sessions given concerning this specific objective, the number of attendees, and class demographics if so compiled (e.g., 100 students received six instruction sessions in three classes of freshman English [sixty students] and three classes of junior transfer students [forty students]).[61] Outcomes might consider:

• Is the objective measurable? The number of retrievals can be compiled month to month from statistics supplied from many of the information vendors used by academic libraries.

• Can this objective be taught? One example is instructing students on the effective application of Boolean search operators applied during their information searches.

• Can one measure if anything was learned? One methodology would include pre- and posttests administered around a library instruction concerning the application of Boolean search operators. Another methodology would be to determine if the average number of retrievals per search decreased month to month (e.g., from September to December) during an academic semester. If a decrease is measured, it may be a result of the instruction.

- Can a change in the person be identified and/or measured? Apply posttests, self-assessment surveys, focus groups, and other methodologies.

- Can the results be used to improve instruction? The direct methodologies applied will indicate whether or not the instruction is effective in meeting the stated objective. If not, the instruction needs revision and reapplication to determine if its effectiveness increased.[62]

An Example of an Information Competency Program

The college library of the Minnesota Community and Technical College, which is a two-year institution located in Minneapolis, has created a comprehensive information literacy course based upon institutional mission, goals, and objectives. The mission statement emphasizes that the college "makes individual dreams achievable by offering high quality, lifelong learning opportunities within a student-centered environment."[63] Academic programs directly link to the mission statement and identify expected general education competencies:

Central to the mission . . . is the provision of general education as an integral part of all degree programs and programs of substantial length (two semesters or greater). General education refers to the measurable knowledge, intellectual concepts, and attitudes that serve as the foundation to success within all programs of study and throughout life.

The core general education competencies are a means to enhancing lifelong education by making it possible for students to:

- Communicate effectively;
- Think critically;
- Demonstrate social responsibility;
- Demonstrate effective life skills and personal responsibility; and
- Demonstrate computer literacy skills appropriate to their program of study.

Students completing programs resulting in two-year diplomas or degrees must complete all of the core general education competencies.[64]

One of the identified core general education competencies for the receipt of a degree relates to information literacy. The college defines a person who is information literate as understanding:

- The context in which knowledge is produced—including the so-cial, political, and economic conditions that shape the production of knowledge
- The context in which knowledge is organized—including catalog-ing and indexing systems and their biases and limitations
- How to develop information seeking strategies necessary to access information efficiently and effectively using a variety of sources
- How to evaluate information for accuracy, authenticity, and bias
- How to apply critical thinking skills to integrate new information into one's existing knowledge base
- The free and open communication of ideas is crucial to sustaining a democratic society[65]

Successful completion of Information Literacy & Research Skills (INFS 1000) fulfills this specific core education requirement.[66] This course, taught by library faculty, identifies course objectives that are measurable outcomes,[67] and it provides a Web-based tutorial should a class be missed.[68] The librarians have mapped the *Information Literacy Competency Standards for Higher Education* (Association of College and Research Libraries, ACRL)[69] and ACRL's *Objectives for Information Literacy Instruction: A Model Statement for Academic Librarians*[70] onto the:

- Syllabus (http://www.mctc.mnscu.edu/library/courses/infs1000/assessment/InfoLitSyllabus.pdf)
- Mid-term examination (http://www.mctc.mnscu.edu/library/courses/infs1000/assessment/MidTermExam.pdf)
- Final competency examination of INFS 1000 (http://www.mctc.mnscu.edu/library/courses/infs1000/assessment/FinalExam.pdf)

Supporting Other Institutional Learning Goals and Objectives

The academic library directly supports the institutional mission and goals, educational objectives and outcomes, and teaching and learning environments through its emphasis on teaching-learning outcomes[71] by providing students with the values and skills related to information ac-cess, retrieval, evaluation, and application processes. In addition, the library's information resources and services directly and indirectly con-tribute to other identified institutional goals and objectives, including:

- Supporting faculty teaching efforts
- Supporting faculty scholarly activity
- Supporting intrainstitutional services and activities such as committee work[72]
- Training staff, faculty, and students to appropriately apply technology
- Developing new knowledge or information-retrieval products[73]

Academic libraries must identify, measure, and report on their contributions and support for these five institutional goals and objectives. For example, an input would be the number of books in the library's collections. Circulation counts of use of the collection comprise an output measure. An outcome might be linked with the development and availability of the collection based upon recommendations from the faculty and collection development librarians, and faculty use of books in the classroom. An outcome might also relate to content and source material that students use to address specific course requirements, such as topic papers.

Not all course content comes from textbooks purchased from the campus bookstore. Reference services may also provide an outcome. Inputs would include the number of reference staff and hours worked at the reference desk, while outputs would include the number of questions to which reference staff responded. An outcome might focus on the library's provision of a direct service (library staff reference assistance) that is intended to add content to student efforts to meet course requirements (writing a paper), as well as the skills and values added from information skills instruction that the same reference librarians provide.

Bonnie Gratch-Lindauer, an academic librarian, describes five assessment domains for the teaching-learning library to connect the goals of the university with activities and measures within the library.[74] Library support for institutional objectives such as faculty scholarly activity might directly connect collection development efforts and indirectly link interlibrary loan services. Additionally, there may be an institutional goal concerning the building of community. Librarians may support these service efforts with membership on planning, curriculum, technology, effectiveness, and other institutional committees. Inputs would count the number of staff and hours of support; outputs would include the number of documents considered, developed, or revised. Outcomes would indirectly measure whether changes resulted in the revision of the core curriculum or whether a change in strategic direction led to initiatives to advance distance education offerings.

Completing the Assessment Cycle

Assessment requires the identification of objectives from the institution's stated mission and the development and implementation of a planned effort by the academic support department to contribute to the institutional goals and objectives. The assessment process requires that (1) this effort be measured, its findings reported in a form that all constituent and stakeholder groups might understand; and (2) the findings are applied to the continuous effort of improving student learning.

No single measure addresses the complexity of the library's contributions to the support of educational goals and other aspects of institutional effectiveness. There is a need for a multiplicity of measures (inputs, outputs, outcomes, and processes) to reveal all that a library contributes to support:

- Teaching (library resources used by the faculty in a classroom; assistance and guidance including library-developed help and subject guides; teaching faculty how to use technology and apply information policies)
- Learning (student learning, such as information process skills)
- Content (supporting content used in the classroom by students, developing collections, and providing reference assistance such as drop-in instruction sessions)
- Scholarly research (interlibrary loan and collection development)
- Service (participation in institutional governance structures)

After the measures are compiled and analyzed, the library must report the findings to demonstrate its contribution or support of the institution's mission and goals. Evidence may include the integration of library use or instruction into course syllabi, findings from librarians reviewing the bibliographic references in student papers to gauge impact of information skills instruction, or the acknowledgment by faculty that their research efforts were supported by the library's resources and services.[75] The evidence may appear in departmental, annual, or other progress reports that should be available for review by the institution's stakeholders.

The compiled and analyzed measures, and reported findings, are then applied to the library's planning process. What can the library do, or what does it need, in order to more effectively apply its resources and services to support the institution's mission and to improve the assessment results? If students do not understand the content presented, does the library decrease the number of students in its instruction sessions and increase the amount of attention given to each student? Does the library alter or revise the content presented because there was no measurable change in the student's measured skills? The assessment process is complete only when changes are implemented in the continuous effort to improve learning and other identified outcomes that support the institution's mission.

Learning outcome assessment observes, reports, or otherwise monitors quantified changes in attitudes or skills of students on an individual basis through their contact with library services, programs, or instruction. As such, learning outcome measures, which are intrainstitutional, are not intended to become benchmarks and used to compare learning with other institutions. However, these outcome measures can be used internally to discover whether or not continuous improvement concerning learning content and processes occurs.[76]

CONCLUSION

The key to setting meaningful and effective institutional outcomes is to ensure that all units of the institution derive a benefit; in effect, the end results can be linked to continuous improvement in student learning.[77] Although the institution may identify the desired outcomes, it is the academic programs, and the academic support units such as the library, that determine, develop, apply, measure, analyze, and report outcomes that are later conveyed to the institutional level where they are further compiled and aggregated, and reported to demonstrate institutional effectiveness to its stakeholders. Academic programs and departments are the most critical participants in the learning-outcomes assessment process. The library is also a participant because outcomes assessment measures the contributions that the library makes to the institution's educational mission as a whole.

Evaluating the process of conducting assessment on student learning outcomes is designed to improve library services through the application of the feedback loop within a systems planning model. The goal is to enable the library to participate formally in the learning process and to help ensure that instructional programs produce the intended learning changes in the individual.[78] Outputs demonstrate that the library meets stated standards efficiently and effectively, whereas outcomes demonstrate that the library is an institutional partner in the learning process.[79]

NOTES

1. Bonnie Gratch-Lindauer, "Defining and Measuring the Library's Impact on Campuswide Outcomes," *College & Research Libraries* 59 (November 1998): 548.

2. Peggy L. Maki, "Developing an Assessment Plan to Learn about Student Learning," *The Journal of Academic Librarianship* 28 (January–March 2002): 9, 11–12.

3. The State Council of Higher Education for Virginia, "Purpose of the Reports of Institutional Effectiveness," available at http://roie.schev.edu/ (accessed September 4, 2003).

4. University of Wisconsin–Whitewater, "Undergraduate Catalog, 2002–2004: Mission Statement," available at http://www.uww.edu/Catalog/02–04/Intro/4mission.html (accessed October 29, 2003).

5. University of Wisconsin–Whitewater, "Undergraduate Catalog, 2002–2004: Mission Statement."

6. University of Wisconsin–Whitewater, "UW-Whitewater Vision Statement," available at http://www.uww.edu/Admin/strplan/vision.htm (accessed September 4, 2003).

7. University of Wisconsin–Whitewater, "Strategic Planning Assumptions," available at http://www.uww.edu/Admin/strplan/assump.htm (accessed September 4, 2003).

8. University of Wisconsin–Whitewater, "The Six Priorities of the Strategic Plan," available at http://www.uww.edu/Admin/strplan/prior.htm (accessed September 4, 2003).

9. University of Wisconsin–Whitewater, "Strategic Plan: Priority 1," available at http://www.uww.edu/Admin/strplan/prior1.htm (accessed September 4, 2003).

10. University of Wisconsin–Whitewater, "Provost and Vice Chancellor for Academic Affairs: Values, Mission, Objectives, Goals," available at "http://acadaff.uww.edu/ValuesMissionObjectivesGoals.doc" from http://acadaff.uww.edu/index.htm (accessed October 29, 2003).

11. Alverno College, "Quick Facts about Alverno," available at http://

www.alverno.edu/about_alverno/quick_facts.html (accessed September 4, 2003).

12. Alverno College, "About Alverno: Ability-Based Curriculum," available at http://www.alverno.edu/about_alverno/ability_curriculum.html (accessed September 4, 2003).

13. Alverno College, "About Alverno: Alverno's Eight Abilities," available at http://www.alverno.edu/about_alverno/ability.html (accessed September 4, 2003).

14. Alverno College, "About Alverno: Ability-Based Curriculum."

15. King's College, "The Comprehensive Assessment Program," available at http://www.kings.edu/assessment/index.htm (accessed September 4, 2003).

16. King's College, "CORE Curriculum," available at http://www.kings.edu/academics/core.html (accessed September 4, 2003).

17. King's College, "CORE Curriculum."

18. King's College, "CORE Curriculum."

19. Roanoke College, "Institutional Effectiveness and Assessment for Academic Majors and Programs at Roanoke College: The Essential Components of Institutional Effectiveness in Academic Departments," available at http://www.roanoke.edu/inst-res/assessment/AcadMan.htm (accessed September 4, 2003).

20. Roanoke College, "Institutional Effectiveness and Assessment."

21. Roanoke College, "Institutional Effectiveness and Assessment."

22. Roanoke College, "Institutional Effectiveness Program," available at http://www.roanoke.edu/inst-res/assessment/ (accessed September 4, 2003).

23. Roanoke College, "Institutional Effectiveness and Assessment."

24. James Madison University, "Mission Statement," available at http://roie.schev.edu/four_year/JMU/body.asp?&m (accessed September 4, 2003).

25. James Madison University, "Institution-Specific Measures," available at http://roie.schev.edu/four_year/JMU/body.asp?&i (accessed September 4, 2003).

26. James Madison University, "Institution-Specific Measures."

27. George Mason University, "Assessment Plans: Listed by College/Department/Program," available at http://assessment.gmu.edu/programgoals/index.cfm (accessed September 4, 2003).

28. Brenau University, "Purpose Statement," available at http://intranet.brenau.edu/assessment/purpose.htm (accessed September 4, 2003).

29. Brenau University, "Assessment at Brenau: An Overview—Purpose and Planning," available at http://intranet.brenau.edu/assessment/Guide/guideframe.htm (accessed September 4, 2003).

30. Brenau University, "Assessment at Brenau: An Overview—Assessment and Planning," available at http://intranet.brenau.edu/assessment/Guide/guideframe.htm (accessed September 4, 2003).

31. Brenau University, "Assessment at Brenau: An Overview—Outcomes

Assessment Reporting Cycle at Brenau University," available at http://intranet.brenau.edu/assessment/Guide/guideframe.htm (accessed September 4, 2003).

32. Brenau University, "Assessment at Brenau: An Overview—Cross Curricular Goals: Criteria Statements and Support Documents," in A *Guide to Assessment*, available at http://intranet.brenau.edu/assessment/ccgoals.doc (accessed September 4, 2003).

33. Brenau University, "Assessment at Brenau: An Overview—Guidelines for Developing Assessment Plans in Educational Programs," available at http://intranet.brenau.edu/assessment/Guide/guideframe.htm (accessed September 4, 2003).

34. Brenau University, "Assessment at Brenau: An Overview—Assessment Roles, Responsibilities, and Time Frames: Educational Programs," available at http://intranet.brenau.edu/assessment/Guide/guideframe.htm (accessed September 4, 2003).

35. University of Washington, Accountability Board, "Student Learning Outcomes: A Faculty Resource on Development and Assessment," available at http://depts.washington.edu/grading/slo/SLO-Home.htm (accessed September 4, 2003).

36. University of Washington, Accountability Board, "Student Learning Outcomes: The Process of Designing Departmental Outcomes," available at http://depts.washington.edu/grading/slo/SLO-Issues.htm (accessed September 4, 2003).

37. University of Washington, "Student Learning Outcomes: A Faculty Resource on Development and Assessment," available at http://depts.washington.edu/grading/slo/SLO-Home.htm (accessed September 4, 2003).

38. University of Washington, UW Accountability Board, "Student Learning Outcomes: Assessing SLOs," available at http://depts.washington.edu/grading/slo/SLO-Assess.htm (accessed September 4, 2003).

39. California State University, Monterey Bay, "University Learning Requirements," available at http://csumb.edu/academic/ulr/ (accessed September 30, 2003).

40. California State University, Monterey Bay, "CSUMB Learning Goals," available at http://csumb.edu/info/academics/goals.html (accessed September 30, 2003).

41. California State University, Monterey Bay, "General Education/University Learning Requirements," available at http://csumb.edu/info/academics/freshman.html (accessed September 30, 2003).

42. California State University, Monterey Bay, "General Education/University Learning Requirements."

43. California State University, Monterey Bay, "Technology/Information," available at http://csumb.edu/academic/ulr/ulr/technology.html (accessed September 30, 2003).

44. California State University, Monterey Bay, "Technology/Information."

45. California State University, Monterey Bay, "Academic Information," available at http://csumb.edu/academic/colleges/index.html (accessed September 30, 2003).

46. California State University, Monterey Bay, "Academic Program Descriptions: Collaborative Health and Human Services (CHHS)," available at http://csumb.edu/academic/descriptions/chhs.html (accessed September 30, 2003).

47. Kenneth R. Smith, "New Roles and Responsibilities for the University Library: Advancing Student Learning through Outcomes Assessment," paper prepared for the Association of Research Libraries, May 4, 2000, available at http://www.arl.org/stats/newmeas/HEOSmith.html (accessed August 22, 2003).

48. Gratch-Lindauer, "Defining and Measuring the Library's Impact on Campuswide Outcomes," 547.

49. Robert E. Dugan and Peter Hernon, "Outcomes Assessment: Not Synonymous with Inputs and Outputs," *The Journal of Academic Librarianship* 28 (November 2002): 377.

50. Dugan and Hernon, "Outcomes Assessment," 378.

51. Dugan and Hernon, "Outcomes Assessment."

52. Dugan and Hernon, "Outcomes Assessment."

53. Dugan and Hernon, "Outcomes Assessment," 379.

54. Gratch-Lindauer, "Defining and Measuring the Library's Impact on Campuswide Outcomes," 559.

55. Bonnie Gratch-Lindauer, "Comparing the Regional Accreditation Standards: Outcomes Assessment and Other Trends," *The Journal of Academic Librarianship* 28 (January 2002): 18.

56. Gratch-Lindauer, "Comparing the Regional Accreditation Standards," 19.

57. Oswald M. T. Ratteray, "Information Literacy in Self-Study and Accreditation," *The Journal of Academic Librarianship* 28 (November 2002): 370.

58. Smith, "New Roles and Responsibilities for the University Library," 49; Dugan and Hernon, "Outcomes Assessment," 379.

59. Dugan and Hernon, "Outcomes Assessment," 379.

60. Dugan and Hernon, "Outcomes Assessment."

61. Dugan and Hernon, "Outcomes Assessment," 379–380.

62. Dugan and Hernon, "Outcomes Assessment."

63. Minneapolis Community and Technical College, "MCTC Strategic Plan: 1999–2004," available at http://www.minneapolis.edu/portfolio/planning/strategicPlan.htm (accessed September 4, 2003).

64. Minneapolis Community and Technical College, "Academic Programs," available at http://www.minneapolis.edu/academicAffairs/index.cfm (accessed September 4, 2003).

65. Minneapolis Community and Technical College, "Information Literacy

Tutorial," available at http://www.minneapolis.edu/library/tutorials/infolit/index.html (accessed September 4, 2003).

66. Minneapolis Community and Technical College, "Information Studies," available at http://www.minneapolis.edu/library/courses/infostudies.htm (accessed September 4, 2003).

67. Minneapolis Community and Technical College, "Syllabus: Information Literacy & Research Skills," available at http://www.minneapolis.edu/library/courses/infs1000/acrobat/Syllabi/Syllabus.pdf (accessed September 4, 2003).

68. Minneapolis Community and Technical College, "Tutorial: Introduction & Use Guides," available at http://www.minneapolis.edu/library/tutorials/infolit/tablesversion/home.htm (accessed September 4, 2003).

69. American Library Association, Association of College and Research Libraries, *Information Literacy Competency Standards for Higher Education* (Chicago: American Library Association, 2000), available at http://www.ala.org/Content/NavigationMenu/ACRL/Standards_and_Guidelines/_Information_Literacy_Competency_Standards_for_Higher_Education.htm (accessed September 28, 2003).

70. American Library Association, Association of College and Research Libraries, *Objectives for Information Literacy Instruction: A Model Statement for Academic Librarians* (Chicago: American Library Association, 2001), available at http://www.ala.org/Content/NavigationMenu/ACRL/Standards_and_Guidelines/Objectives_for_Information_Literacy_Instruction_A_Model_Statement_for_Academic_Librarians.html (accessed September 28, 2003).

71. Gratch-Lindauer, "Defining and Measuring the Library's Impact," 560.

72. Gratch-Lindauer, "Comparing the Regional Accreditation Standards," 21.

73. Gratch-Lindauer, "Defining and Measuring the Library's Impact," 560.

74. Gratch-Lindauer, "Defining and Measuring the Library's Impact," 557.

75. Gratch-Lindauer, "Comparing the Regional Accreditation Standards," 18.

76. Dugan and Hernon, "Outcomes Assessment," 379.

77. Bruce T. Fraser, Charles R. McClure, and Emily H. Leahy, "Toward a Framework for Assessing Library and Institutional Outcomes," *Portal: Libraries and the Academy* 2 (2002): 513.

78. Dugan and Hernon, "Outcomes Assessment," 378.

79. Dugan and Hernon, "Outcomes Assessment," 379.

CHAPTER 7

The Strategic Triad Supporting Information Literacy Assessment

Oswald M. T. Ratteray

Regional accreditation has long held that outcomes assessment is an important part of higher education. More recently, the focus on the assessment of student learning, one aspect of overall outcomes assessment, has intensified. Information literacy also has become more clearly defined as a critical student learning outcome. As colleges and universities begin to explore both assessment and information literacy in greater depth, motivated in part by the accreditation process, it is now appropriate to relate the widely accepted principles of assessment to the evolving field of information literacy. For this discussion, the essence of this relationship lies in the three concepts of planning, implementation, and improvement, which apply equally to assessment in general and to information literacy. They constitute what can be called the strategic triad that facilitates student learning and long-range institutional progress.

EVOLVING DEFINITIONS AND EMPHASES

Outcomes assessment is no stranger to regional accreditation. In fact, the Middle States Commission on Higher Education[1] has incor-

---

The views expressed in this chapter are those of the author and do not necessarily reflect the positions of the Middle States Commission on Higher Education.

porated outcomes assessment prominently in its standards for accreditation since 1953, and this chapter focuses on the specific standards and procedures of the Middle States region. However, even though each regional commission may have different standards and procedures, they are all grounded in the same underlying philosophy and general strategy that has evolved over more than 100 years. This philosophy and strategy for regional accreditation has been refined, especially since the 1970s, under the auspices of several national voluntary organizations that have been responsible for coordinating and/or providing official recognition of accrediting organizations.[2] In 2000, various commissions committed themselves to making a review of student learning outcomes in particular—one of the central factors in the accreditation process.[3] Three years later, the commissions endorsed principles that should govern the use of student learning data in the accreditation process.[4]

These principles indicate that an accrediting commission should expect institutions to:

- Define educational quality by how well it fulfills its declared learning mission
- Demonstrate that student learning occurs by setting clear learning goals, collecting evidence of goal attainment, applying collective judgment in interpreting the evidence, and using that information for program improvement
- Compile evidence from multiple sources
- Involve the collective participation of stakeholders who are concerned with defining educational quality
- Have broad participation in the process of reflecting on learning outcomes and improvement

In addition, the Middle States Commission on Higher Education has developed guidelines for the assessment of student learning.[5] This publication, *Student Learning Assessment: Options and Resources*, explains some of the many strategies that are available for effective assessment at colleges and universities, leading to improvement in individual learning and institutional effectiveness.

The term *information literacy* entered the standards of the Middle States Commission on Higher Education in 1994,[6] based on the definition promulgated by the library profession in 1989.[7] The librarians again took the lead in 2000 by publishing a relatively detailed definition of what should be expected of an information literate student in higher education.[8] Middle States incorporated elements of that new definition in its standards in 2002.[9] In 2003, the commission published *Developing Research & Communication Skills: Guidelines for Information Literacy in the Curriculum*, which further explains the concept and suggests options, based on best practices in the field, from which institutions might wish to glean fresh approaches.[10] These guidelines emphasize the need for a view of information literacy that broadly encompasses the entire learning process. They also illustrate the distinct and equally important roles of librarians and faculty in teaching information literacy skills.

After reviewing the literature and participating in a number of professional conferences, one could easily get the impression that the term *information literacy* begins and ends with issues that relate primarily to the role of the library in the life of the institution and in student learning. This is not surprising, because the concept emerged from the work of librarians in teaching library skills, even though the professional standards for information literacy recognize a role for faculty in the disciplines. As this author has noted in several speeches, "Information literacy instruction is a house that needs two foundations," meaning that more faculty should now follow the example of librarians and begin to articulate how their own existing pedagogical strategies fulfill the mission of graduating students who are information literate. In order to do this, it may be necessary for librarians and faculty "to engage in what will be for many either a new or a deeper level of collaboration."[11]

What is commonly referred to today as *information literacy instruction* is really only a part of what information literacy instruction really is. The current emphasis tends to be on teaching students to frame the research question, to gain access to information sources, to evaluate the sources, and to do all of these ethically and legally. It is critical, however, to recognize that what faculty in the disciplines are already doing (i.e., teaching students to evaluate content and to use information effectively in their work products) is also an integral part of information literacy instruction. For example, when a faculty member helps students to understand the significance of information the students have located, or to decide whether to incorporate that information into their knowledge base, or to consider whether they need to change their longstanding value system, or to construct a verbal, three-dimensional, or performance statement based on new information, those are all aspects of information literacy instruction. It is, and always has been, at the center of all effective teaching.

Information literacy instruction is not something that can be contained within a single course that is offered during the first two years at a college or university. It applies to every learning situation in the curriculum, whether the faculty member provides students with the information they need or whether the students are encouraged to discover information in or through a library or to take the initiative in seeking it from other sources. The status of being information literate may have its roots in the skills that students already have when they enroll at an institution, but it certainly applies from the beginning of a student's career at the institution to the end. The process of becoming information literate should be so indelible that it will sustain each individual throughout his or her lifetime and successive careers.

Faculty can help to ensure that techniques for information literacy instruction, and therefore the assessment of information literacy skills, are developed as part of a coherent, institution-wide design. They can do this by applying the label of *information literacy instruction* to their existing teaching practices. The Middle States accreditation standards explicitly refer to this coherence—not only in distinguishing undergraduate from graduate study but also in extending to co-curricular activities—as a criterion for promoting "synthesis of learning."[12]

Some regional commissions recently completed the revision of their standards, while others are engaged in or planning for the process. Middle States completed its review in 2002, and the revised standards applied to institutions that began their decennial self-study process in spring 2002 and are expecting to be visited by evaluation teams in academic year 2003–2004. Each year thereafter, a new cohort begins the process of discussing its learning outcomes, including information literacy, and determining how data can be provided to demonstrate that learning has occurred and that course and program improvements have taken place as a result of the evidence. It may even be necessary for an institution to consider developing new sets of assessment data, especially for the evolving field of information literacy. No one expects this process to occur overnight, but an institution should make a good-faith effort toward a long-range strategy with measurable milestones.

DEVELOPING THE STRATEGIC TRIAD

As noted in the Middle States publication *Developing Research & Communication Skills*, assessment is a "reflective, integrative, and iterative process."[13] It is reflective in that it enables faculty and students to reconsider their approaches to teaching and learning. It is integrative because it enables the institution to incorporate its goals for information literacy at the course level coherently across the curriculum. It is iterative in that once begun, the process can start anew.

Assessment, information literacy, and the assessment of information literacy all stand on three essential footings: planning, implementation, and improvement. The extent to which evidence of student learning enables an institution to achieve its mission reflects the institution's success in developing these foundations. Furthermore, if the planning is executed effectively, implementation and improvement should follow smoothly.

Planning

Effective planning is the key to success in implementing information literacy assessment and in subsequently improving student learning and teaching. It is a multistage process that includes defining objectives, reviewing what is currently taking place on campus and elsewhere, identifying gaps in the process, and then actually designing the plan.

Defining Objectives

The institution's mission provides explicit or implicit clues about the values that the institution wishes to promote, and these may be further explicated in accompanying statements of philosophy or vision. From these statements, the institution determines, on a macro level, what it wants students to know in order to fulfill the institutional mission. These institution-wide goals should then be linked in an unbroken chain to goals at the program and course levels. In other words, there should be no goals at the institutional level that are not implemented at the program and course levels; conversely, there should be no goals at the course level that cannot be traced to overarching goals at the program and institutional levels. This vertical coherence in programming would satisfy the spirit "or the letter, when applicable" of most of the standards in the Middle States publication *Characteristics of Excellence*. The standards also anticipate lateral coherence, in that an integrated set of learning goals, appropriate to higher education, should progress in their scope and complexity and culminate in the award of a recognized credential. Information literacy instruction, which is the basis for information literacy assessment, also should reflect this vertical and lateral coherence.

It is widely agreed in the higher education community that there are six basic elements of information literacy. These include the ability to (1) frame a research question, (2) gain access to the necessary information, (3) evaluate the sources, (4) evaluate the content, (5) use the information for a specific purpose, and (6) do all of these ethically and legally. Institutions are free to expand upon or add to any of these baseline characteristics. In *Developing Research & Communication Skills*, there are several examples of ways in which an institution can define the criteria for excellence in these skills, both vertically and laterally within the institution.

Looking Around

As in any area of endeavor, it is prudent first to take an inventory of what the institution currently is doing and, if necessary, what others outside the institution are doing. It is likely that there are several projects that are routinely conducted to assess various aspects of the total information literacy picture. These may be formal or informal evaluations, and as explained earlier, faculty are already collecting the necessary information, even if they do not yet associate what they are doing with the institution's information literacy initiatives. It is also not necessary to establish an entirely new assessment program labeled *information literacy assessment*. If it is determined that a new form of assessment should be developed for some aspect of information literacy, it is entirely possible that it could be linked to an existing assessment effort.

Taking inventory internally, therefore, requires that the institution step back and look at the big picture. There are many ways to accomplish this, depending on the investigator's research needs, learning style, or other preferences. I provide one example of how to track where in the institution one might find evidence of students' information literacy knowledge, skills, and competencies.[14] Other ways of identifying information literacy assessment activities that are scattered across the curriculum are illustrated here.

Figure 7.1 takes the macro approach to institution-wide activities. It

Figure 7.1
Mission-Critical Learning Goals

Goals	Quantitative Measures		Qualitative Measures	
	Direct	Indirect	Direct	Indirect
Goal 1: _____ **Role of Information Literacy:** _____				
Institutional Level				
Program Level				
Course Level				
Goal 2: _____ **Role of Information Literacy:** _____				
Institutional Level				
Program Level				
Course Level				
Goal etc.: _____ **Role of Information Literacy:** _____				
Institutional Level				
Program Level				
Course Level				

Note: Assessment can occur at any of the three levels, and different skills can be measured at different levels. In addition, the most appropriate measure for a particular skill may be quantitative or qualitative, and both are not required.

enables the investigator to pinpoint whether particular goals are defined and assessed at the institutional, program, or course level. Figure 7.2 offers a convenient way for individual faculty members to explain what they are already doing. Both figures enable a reviewer to determine if there is an overall balance between quantitative and qualitative measures and whether evaluations are based on direct or indirect evidence.

Figure 7.2
Course-Specific Information Literacy Goals

Department:_____ Course:_____		Year:_____		
Information Literacy Goals	Quantitative Measures		Qualitative Measures	
	Direct	Indirect	Direct	Indirect
Framing the Research Question				
Accessing Sources				
Evaluating Sources				
Evaluating Content				
Using Information for a Specific Purpose				
Ethical/Legal Issues, Laws, Regulations, and Policies				

Note: The most appropriate measure for a particular skill may be quantitative or qualitative, and both are not required.

It is important to note, however, that not all boxes need to be completed, because goals may be defined and assessed at different levels, and not all types of measures are relevant or meaningful for any particular goal.

Looking beyond the campus, institutions may find it useful to consider what other institutions are doing to assess information literacy skills. Although benchmarking per se is not required by the Middle States standards, an institution may already have determined which other institutions constitute a peer group for the purpose of making official comparisons. However, some of the institutions in that peer group may not have advanced very far in the particular field of information literacy assessment.

Designing the Plan

The next stage in planning is to outline, at the course level, which elements of information literacy assessment will be incorporated within the institution's overall plan for assessing student learning outcomes. It essentially revolves around answers to the following questions:

- What do we want students to know?
- What should students *do* to demonstrate their knowledge?
- What are the standards for excellence in performance?

The institution's standards for excellence in information literacy are best outlined in a rubric or chart that can provide uniformity of judgment over time and among different people who may be evaluating the work of students. It is also useful to specify whether a particular measure will be used for formative or summative evaluation, on what timetable this will occur, and to what extent sampling is considered more appropriate, more efficient, and cost-saving than evaluating the entire population.

Having identified the elements to be assessed, the institution should ensure that the measures selected are appropriate for the objective. There are circumstances when information literacy items can be incorporated within existing or planned comprehensive tests of multiple goals. Surveys of students and faculty, focus groups, and various methods for self-reflection provide indirect evidence of student learning, which may have limited value on their own but which can often be effectively compared with other direct evidence, such as grades in individual courses or in an overall review of transcripts. Student portfolios, if properly managed and evaluated, can provide powerful evidence of students' understanding, skills, and competencies. Peter Hernon and Robert E. Dugan discuss these and other options in some detail.[15]

Defining Resources

Finally, the institution needs to determine the answers to several key questions, including:

- Which materials are needed by each assessing unit
- Whether resources may need to be reallocated or derived from new sources

- Whether it is necessary to offer incentives for planning, implementation, or improvement
- Whether one person, a team assembled from across campus, or a single operating unit will be responsible for one or more aspects of the assessment process

IMPLEMENTATION

Each institution will have its own logistical approaches to implementing assessment, which will have been outlined in the previous planning stage; the significant issue here is what happens after the data are collected. During the planning process, the institution should have established the specific information literacy skills that are to be the targets of assessment. Determining if students have mastered these skills is the prism through which assessment data should be viewed.

The handbook *Developing Research & Communication Skills* identifies several questions to ask when reviewing data on information literacy.[16] Expanding upon this approach, the researcher should:

- Review the evaluation instrument to verify that the questions and instructions were clear and unambiguous
- Produce frequencies and other descriptive statistics as well as selected cross-tabulations
- Scan the data to determine if they appear to be reasonably distributed, to check for errors in data entry, and to identify possible associations that might require further exploration
- Examine the results to see if they make sense, and determine which data sets might be usefully illustrated with graphic presentations
- If random samples are used, check for associations using correlations, regression, or other tests
- Develop preliminary findings

A second review could involve disaggregating the data by type of student, learning environment, or other factors unique to the institution, its student population, its faculty, and the curriculum to identify other possible differences. This step could shed light on both teaching and learning, enhance or revise the preliminary findings, and reveal the need for further inquiry leading to greater improvement.

The next step is to develop a report of the preliminary findings in manuscript form. However, it is important to summarize this report, because the act of summarizing can highlight logical weaknesses and other possible flaws in interpretation. Distilling the essence of a report helps to pierce the veil of technical jargon that can sometimes be obfuscating for lay readers.

During the planning phase, the faculty members involved may have decided that the purpose of certain questions will be to elicit information about the student's mastery of course content. In some instances, it may be possible, based on the student's answers, to make inferences about some information literacy skills without directly measuring those skills.

Developing the raw data and the findings that state what the data mean are only the first phases of analysis. Next, it is important to identify the possible causes of student achievement (i.e., its rise, lack of change, or decline).

If the group is small, it also may be useful to examine the performance of individual students whom the faculty member or the administration may have reason to identify. Otherwise, there should be at least an overview of the entire population, and the collection and presentation of these data should be constructed in such a manner that they can lead to comparisons over time.

One important question that *Developing Research & Communication Skills* asks is "Do students have more difficulty with some areas of instruction than others?" For example, further exploration of the learning context may reveal that some students may have a personal reason for failing to understand, such as inadequate preparation, anxieties about any number of content or process issues, a learning style not accommodated by the type of instruction, family circumstances, or cultural background. Perhaps instruction could have been offered differently. Perhaps the institutional environment, such as campus or local area distractions, might have impeded understanding during the *learning moment* that may have been critical for particular students, given their learning style.

IMPROVEMENT

Improving student learning is a function of both internal and external communication at the institution. The stakeholders in information literacy instruction, which include the faculty members, librarians, and other administrators, should review the data from assessment to reach a consensus on what the data mean. They also should discuss those findings with peers at similar institutions or institutions with similar cohorts of students and faculty.

The objective of these discussions should be to help students find better ways of learning, to assist faculty in exploring more effective teaching methods, and to encourage administrators to take steps to improve the learning environments. The primary objective in each case should be to motivate students to learn and to encourage them to become more actively involved in the learning process. With reference specifically to information literacy, it should be noted that the commission's standards in *Characteristics of Excellence* identifies "programs that promote student use of information and learning resources" as a fundamental element that characterizes an accredited institution.[17] The uses to which information can be put are limited only by the individual creativity of all the stakeholders in the context of the institution's mission, goals, curriculum, and resources.

Frank discussions of assessment findings could prompt a review of the institution's internal processes, such as overly bureaucratic procedures that tend to increase student frustration with the institution as a user-friendly system, or the institution's schedules of activities that may coincide and unnecessarily compete for student attention. Sharing findings also can lead to strategic partnerships to maintain a supportive learning environment, help the institution to fulfill its mission and goals, and enable incoming students to understand their learning opportunities and their obligations while they are at the institution.

The cycle of information literacy assessment is complete when improvements are made. The institution may find that some changes can be funded with existing budgets, but it may be necessary to revise future budgets to accommodate long-range plans for information literacy.

CONCLUSION

Reaching the goal of facilitating student learning and long-range progress toward fulfilling the institution's mission and goals is a path that is strewn with experimentation as each institution explores the best ideas and informed judgments of its own community. Likewise, linking existing pedagogical strategies for content instruction to the elements of the information literacy paradigm may invoke the challenge of increased collaboration among faculty, librarians, and administrators, but it also should bring its own rewards in student learning and institutional effectiveness. In the strategic triad of planning, implementation, and improvement, the role of planning is of overwhelming importance. While planning may have value to some as a vehicle for reflection, it is generally meaningless unless there is a commitment to action and there is follow-through to improvement. Evidence of these improvements will be of great interest to peer evaluators and to an accrediting commission during the decennial accreditation process and any interim report in the accreditation cycle. Improvements in teaching, learning, and institutional effectiveness are, after all, signs of institutional vitality.

NOTES

1. The Middle States region, one of six regions (or eight regional commissions) in the United States, includes New York, New Jersey, Pennsylvania, Delaware, Maryland, the District of Columbia, Puerto Rico, and the U.S. Virgin Islands. The Commission on Higher Education also accredits some colleges and universities in locations abroad.

2. The organizations that have had a coordinating influence on regional accreditors were the Federation of Regional Accrediting Commissions of Higher Education (FRACHE) and its various successor organizations, including the Council on Postsecondary Accreditation (COPA), the Commission on Recognition of Postsecondary Accreditation (CORPA), and the contemporary Council for Higher Education Accreditation (CHEA).

3. B. McMurtrie, "Accreditors Revamp Policies to Stress Student Learning," *The Chronicle of Higher Education* (July 7, 2000): A29.

4. Council of Regional Accrediting Commissions, *Regional Accreditation and Student Learning: Principles of Good Practice* (May 2003). Each regional commission subsequently endorsed these principles. *Note:* The chair of the

council rotates among the executive directors of the eight regional commissions. The secretariat is located at that executive director's commission.

5. Middle States Commission on Higher Education, *Student Learning Assessment: Options and Resources* (Philadelphia: Middle States Commission on Higher Education, 2003).

6. Commission on Higher Education, Middle States Association of Colleges and Schools, *Characteristics of Excellence in Higher Education: Standards for Accreditation* (Philadelphia: Commission on Higher Education, Middle States Association of Colleges and Schools, 1994).

7. American Library Association, *American Library Association Presidential Committee on Information Literacy: Final Report* (Chicago: American Library Association, 1989).

8. Association of College and Research Libraries, *Information Literacy Competency Standards for Higher Education* (Chicago: Association of College and Research Libraries, 2000).

9. Middle States Commission on Higher Education, *Characteristics of Excellence in Higher Education: Eligibility Requirements and Standards for Accreditation* (Philadelphia: Middle States Commission on Higher Education, 2002).

10. Middle States Commission on Higher Education, *Developing Research & Communication Skills: Guidelines for Information Literacy in the Curriculum* (Philadelphia: Middle States Commission on Higher Education, 2003).

11. Oswald M. T. Ratteray, "Information Literacy in Self-Study and Accreditation," *The Journal of Academic Librarianship* 28 (November 2002): 368–375.

12. Commission on Higher Education, *Characteristics of Excellence*, Standard 11, 31–36.

13. Middle States Commission on Higher Education, *Developing Research & Communication Skills*, 39.

14. Ratteray, "Information Literacy in Self-Study and Accreditation."

15. Peter Hernon and Robert E. Dugan, *An Action Plan for Outcomes Assessment in Your Library* (Chicago: American Library Association, 2002).

16. Middle States Commission on Higher Education, *Developing Research & Communication Skills*.

17. Middle States Commission on Higher Education, *Characteristics of Excellence in Higher Education*, 34.

CHAPTER 8

Selecting from the Assessment Tool Chest

Peter Hernon

Assessment for excellence engages "a campus community collectively in a systematic and continuous process to create shared learning goals and to enhance learning."[1] That process focuses on an organization/institution actively seeking to improve student learning and the environment in which learning occurs. Within this context, it is important to select appropriate methods for gathering evidence about the success of the institution and its various programs in meeting those student learning outcomes specified in the assessment plan. Success is viewed in the context of using the evidence gathered for the purpose of continuous quality improvement in teaching and learning.

Methods for gathering evidence can be characterized as *direct* and *indirect*, and both types apply to student learning outcomes at the course, program, or institutional level. As explained in *Student Learning Assessment*,

Direct and indirect methods of evaluating learning relate to whether or not the method provides evidence in the form of student products or performances. Such evidence demonstrates that *actual learning* has occurred relating to a specific content or skill. Indirect methods reveal characteristics associated with learning, but they only imply that learning has occurred. These characteristics may relate to the student, such as perceptions of student learning, or they may relate to the institution, such as graduation rates.

When a student completes a calculus problem correctly and shows her work, learning is demonstrated *directly*. When the same student describes her own calculus abilities as excellent, she is demonstrating *indirectly* that she has learned calculus. Both of these pieces of information about the student's performance are important. For example, a student's perception that she is doing poorly in calculus when she is actually doing well would provide important information to both the student and the professor. However, indirect evidence—in this case, a perception—is less meaningful without the associated direct and tangible evidence of learning.[2]

"The institutional context is grounded in the institution's mission, and it is shaped by the institutional culture."[3] Naturally, regional accrediting organizations focus on the institutional level, but there are also national accrediting organizations for programs of study (e.g., in education, accounting, and library and information science). As well, faculty should be encouraged to engage in outcomes assessment at the course level to ensure that progress toward meeting any learning outcomes that an institution or program uses actually occurs.

Most likely, departments, programs, and institutions select multiple methods of gathering evidence, some of which rely on direct evidence and others on indirect evidence, perhaps even anecdotal evidence. Following the example of Truman University, direct and indirect methods might be applied by class level, program, and discipline.[4] The point is that there are choices and that triangulation, the use of multiple methods, provides a richer portrayal of student learning, especially when some of the methods selected rely on direct evidence.

DIRECT METHODS OF EVALUATING STUDENT LEARNING

Direct methods "are those that provide evidence of whether or not a student has command of a specific subject or content area, can perform a certain task, exhibits a particular skill, demonstrates a certain quality in his or her work (e.g., creativity . . .), or holds a particular value."[5] They directly show that any outcomes related to problem solving, critical thinking, knowledge acquisition, and communication and presentation skills have been achieved and that the change specified in an outcome occurred. Such methods are either quantitative—data are represented numerically—or qualitative, which is often expressed in general categories, prose, or narrative form and not numerically.

As noted in *Student Learning Assessment*, direct methods provide "evidence of *what* the student has learned" but not why the student has or has not learned. "The 'why' of student learning is especially important when students have not learned, because one of the primary goals of assessment is to make learning experiences more effective."[6] As well, indirect methods such as the degree of satisfaction with a program or instructor, or ambient conditions of a class, may influence performance as assessed by direct methods. Thus, there are limitations to the use of direct methods and the interpretation that can be attached to any evidence gathered. Still, it is important to ensure that data collection instruments are reliable (accurate and consistent) and valid (measure what is intended—learning over time). "In and of themselves . . . grades are not direct evidence of student learning. That is, a numeric or a letter grade alone does not express the content of what students have learned; it reflects only the degree to which the student is perceived to have learned in a specific context."[7] For this reason, grades should not be confused with outcomes assessment; each provides different insights and can be used for different purposes.

Embedded Course Assessment

Such assessment reflects student performance on given instruction (projects, assignments, or examination questions) and the extent to which course content as reflected in program outcomes was mastered. It indicates the extent to which students gained higher-order skills, including critical thinking, problem solving, and decision making. The *capstone* course or culminating experience is a type of embedded assessment. It provides a venue for students to apply the knowledge and skills that they have acquired during the program. It also reflects the extent to which one course builds on another, thus enabling students to gain a comprehensive understanding of a discipline and the institution's general education goals. Such a course or culminating experience might also prepare students for life after graduation.

A capstone experience might consist of a course taken prior to graduation in which students integrate and synthesize principles, concepts, and abilities stressed throughout their program of study. As an alternative to a formal course, the capstone experience might consist of a project (e.g., senior or master's paper) or a short-term get-together (e.g., weekend or weeklong) in which students demonstrate their written and presentation skills on a selected topic, perhaps one chosen from their portfolio (see below).

The minute paper, which provides written feedback on what students learned in class that day, is one form of embedded course assessment. A few minutes before the end of a class, the instructor asks students to answer two questions: "What was the most important thing you learned during this class?" and "What important question remains unanswered for you?" The written answers reflect "more than mere recall. To select the most important or significant information, learners must evaluate what they recall. Repeated use of minute papers helps students learn to focus more effectively during lectures." Variations of the minute paper call for students to direct their responses to someone who was absent that day or to describe what they found to be most confusing about the subject matter presented.[8] Another option is to ask them to reflect on the subject matter and to prepare a short paper, perhaps one not exceeding one page.

Portfolios

A print or digital portfolio is a "purposeful collection of student work that exhibits the student's efforts, progress, and achievements [and intellectual growth]." The collection must let students participate "in selecting contents, the criteria for selection, the criteria for judging merit, and evidence of student self-reflection."[9] To provide longitudinal evidence of student learning and development, portfolios must be developed with a clear vision of the desired learning outcome (e.g., one related to the ability to understand issues, evaluate conflicting arguments, use appropriate evidence and reach a reasoned conclusion, and demonstrate overall writing ability). Some of the advantages of using a portfolio include the review of multiple samples of student work over time; gaining a broader, more in-depth examination of student knowledge and communication and technological skills; showing the development or mastery of learning; and offering those who rate performance with an opportunity to base their assessment on work that truly reflects students' progress, achievements, and efforts. On the other hand, there can be disadvantages, such as the challenge of establishing reliable and valid rating criteria; a concern of faculty that there is a hidden agenda, one intended to validate their grading or the effectiveness of their teaching; and maintaining proper security over student work.

Turning to two examples, Alverno College uses the Diagnostic Digital Portfolio (DDP), a Web-based system, to monitor progress in student learning through a program of study. The DDP provides students with feedback from instructors, external assessors, and peers; enables them to reflect on that feedback; and generates performance data with which students can create an electronic resume for job seeking or as part of the application process for applying to graduate schools.[10] The Rose-Hulman Institute of Technology, on the other hand, uses the RoseE-Portfolio, a Web-based system that enables students to gain access to their portfolios through a secure network username and password.

Instead of using either of these electronic portfolios, institutions and programs might adopt, for instance, the iWebfolio, "a Web based tool that gives individuals a personalized, flexible online portfolio" applicable to institutional assessment. TracDat, another option, "is a software package that assists with the management of the assessment-based portion of undergraduate academic program review."[11] However, before examining any package, it might be useful for those unfamiliar with e-portfolios to see the "E-portfolio Collaboration Project," which shows that faculty maintenance of the portfolios can be minimal.[12] For faculty and outside assessors, it is important to know that the assessment itself, not the compilation of that portfolio, could be somewhat time-consuming. Finally, a good way to introduce e-portfolios is by selecting the desired outcomes, showing how portfolio content can meet those outcomes, and encouraging students to share their portfolios—in their entirety or parts of them—with potential employers as evidence of their learning and skills.

Figure 8.1 illustrates that a jury or panel might rate student portfolios according to the written or oral communication skills displayed. When students give oral presentations, the results of those assessments might be included in the portfolio, or an electronic portfolio might even contain the digitized presentation itself. A panel could review the digital presentation outside of the original setting. Because the purpose of portfolio assessment is to view student development over time, portfolios, in fact, are *developmental portfolios*. As a consequence, the assessment scale used might be broad (five, seven, or ten points) to document incremental changes over time. The more points in the scale, the more likely the intent is for assessment to occur at regular intervals.

Figure 8.1
Sample Portfolio Scoring Guide

Outcome

Demonstrate an ability to explain ideas, express feelings, or support a conclusion in an understandable and well-organized fashion (*written form*).

Scoring (Written Communication Skills)*

Read through the items selected from the course portfolio and rate the extent to which each criterion related to writing is addressed. The scale ranges as follows:

1 = poor, 2 = fair, 3 = satisfactory, 4 = good, 5 = excellent

Criteria	1	2	3	4	5	Comments
Develops a clear, significant, and complete thesis statement						
Moves the essay or narrative toward a clear conclusion						
Supports claims by presenting credible and persuasive evidence						
Develops and explains points in clear, specific, lively language, providing concrete referents for key concepts that the audience can easily understand						
Diagnoses errors in spelling, usage, and grammar, correcting most independently and seeking aid in correcting others						

Outcome

Demonstrate an ability to express one's ideas or feelings, or support a conclusion in a clear, understandable, and organized fashion (*oral communication*).

Scoring (Oral Communication Skills)

Four broad criteria (organization, eye contact, delivery, and the use of technology) guide the rating of a successful oral performance. The scale ranges as follows:

1 = the point is poorly addressed
2 = the point is satisfactorily addressed
3 = the point is well addressed

Criteria	1	2	3	Comments
Organization • There is a logical sequence of ideas • Presenter provides ample explanations/elaboration when necessary				
Eye Contact • Presenter makes eye contact with audience • Presenter does not read entire paper				

Figure 8.1 (continued)

Delivery
• Presenter speaks clearly
———————————
 	
• Presenter can be heard by all in the
    audience
———————————
 	
• Presenter does not make grammatical
    errors
———————————
 	
• Presenter does not mispronounce some
    terms
———————————
 	
• Presenter is not "wooden"—stands stiff
    in one place
———————————
 	
• The presentation ends on time
———————————
 	
• The presenter can handle questions well				

Use of Technology
• The content of PowerPoint slides is
    appropriate
———————————
 	
• The slides contain no misspellings
———————————
 	
• The presenter knows how to use the
    technology and can handle problems if
    any occur
———————————
 	
• The presenter does not merely read
    content from the PowerPoint slides				

*See also Middle States Commission on Higher Education, *Student Learning Assessment: Options and Resources* (Philadelphia: Middle States Commission on Higher Education, 2003), 44.

Performance

Performance, in the context of task completion or a demonstration of problem-solving or critical-thinking skills, might be evaluated by means of internships, a practicum, or student teaching. Evaluation might come from work or faculty supervisors or from student participants themselves. When students work cooperatively in groups, the group project, as well as group interaction, might be evaluated. Intercollegiate competitions comprise a form of assessment in which students demonstrate knowledge or skills that are linked to the expected learning outcomes associated with their program of study. An alternative way to examine performance is simulated task performance whereby students identify and solve problems within a specified context. Independent assessors might directly observe student performance (even their participation in teams and any collaborative problem solving), or students might write an essay or participate in an oral debriefing.

Kathleen Dunn, chair of the California State University Information Competence Assessment Task Force and an assistant university librarian at California State Polytechnic University, Pomona, identifies six "core information competencies" and "corresponding scenarios." "These scenarios were constructed to elicit evidence of information competence when applied to general knowledge, rather than discipline-based knowledge." Each scenario was constructed "around real life/workplace information needs . . . to see if students could make the connections between theoretical knowledge learned in school and every day life/workplace tasks."[13] Students could be tested by means of performance tests, including the use of think-aloud protocols whereby they verbalize their thoughts as they complete the task. Those verbal reports can be compared with "think afters," or the verbal reports provided after completion of the tasks. Perhaps students might be videotaped, and the think-after protocol lets them comment on their performance.[14] However, some individuals or groups might not be able to verbalize their thoughts well.

Students in a course might complete a test of their subject knowledge and skills at the beginning and end of the school term. Pretesting and posttesting might go beyond a course and look at students at the start and end of their program of study. As part of a longitudinal study, students might be tested midway (or more often) through the program to monitor the extent of their progress. Such formative assessment enables the faculty to take corrective action as necessary. At the program and institutional levels, test participants could be selected on the basis of probability sampling (see section later in this chapter). To prevent instrument bias as a threat to internal validity, alternate forms of the test might be developed, and no statistically significant differences between (or among) the alternate versions documented. A caution is that the use of experimental designs requires knowledge and the application of hypothesis testing and inferential statistics.

Most interesting is a story that appeared in the *St. Petersburg Times* mentioning that the state of Florida is considering "requiring students at . . . [the state's] public universities to take a standardized test when they enter school and another before they graduate to determine whether they learned anything while there." The proposal "would not affect a student's ability to graduate. But it would tie a significant portion of each university's funding to the test results." In addition to the use of a standardized test, the state is considering other measures: perceptions of employers and peer reviews conducted by faculty at out-of-state universities.[15]

Graduating students might participate in structured interviews that test their knowledge of discipline-specific terminology and issues. Student performance, as reflected in student teaching or making class presentations in which they construct an oral argument, might be videotaped. Students might be asked to critique their performance, and outside assessors, following a predetermined set of guidelines, could review that performance and the accuracy of the self-assessment.

Another way to analyze performance is by viewing performance on licensure and qualifying examinations for professional or graduate school. The percentage that passed is an output measure and does not relate to program improvement, which focuses on the failures, the reasons for those failures, and the steps taken to correct any problems identified. Still, such tests provide evidence of student achievement based on norms established external to an institution.

Professional Jurors or Evaluators

Outside examiners from business, industry, and the professions (e.g., librarians) might provide feedback on student projects, papers, portfolios, performances, recitals, essays, or exhibits. However, there should be a scoring guide or criteria for them to use in rating the ability of students to engage in problem solving and critical thinking, and to present ideas effectively in an oral or written form (see Figure 8.1). These examiners should also receive some training to ensure the likelihood that their analysis matches the purpose of the intended learning outcome. Appendix I of *Developing Research & Communication Skills* identifies "criteria for information literacy competency."[16] Assessment criteria are delineated for each competency, and the information-literate student is judged as "novice," "developing," "proficient," or "accomplished." Because the goal, over time, is to move students from the first to the last category, the examiners should participate in a pretest to ensure (interscore) reliability—the extent of consistency among them in their scoring.

Testing

The degree to which students have achieved an overall understanding of their major field might be tested during the senior year. The test might take such forms as a senior seminar requiring the application of knowledge and skills acquired through the major; a senior thesis or paper indicating mastery of the knowledge and skills taught in the major and demonstrating independent study; or a comprehensive examination, written and/or oral. The examination might even rely on the use of a standardized or locally developed test.

As discussed in the section on "Performance," a locally developed test might be administered as a pretest and posttest. There might even be oral-proficiency examinations. Students might be tested about their knowledge and understanding of general concepts in their subject major. That test might be given in their junior and senior years, and the results compared. Master-level students might be tested at the beginning and conclusion of their program of study and the results compared. Locally developed tests indicate how well student achievement matches program or institutional expectations.

An example of a nationally normed, general education test is the College BASE Exam, a criterion-referenced academic achievement examination produced by the University of Missouri that evaluates knowledge and skills in English, mathematics, science, and social studies. It provides evidence useful for examining the goals and outcomes of a general education program.[17]

Furthermore, end-of-major examinations (major field assessment tests, or MFATs) exist for disciplines such as biology, business, chemistry, computer science, economics, education, English literature, history, mathematics, music theory and history, physics, political science, psychology, and sociology. Such examinations "assess the mastery of concepts, principles, and knowledge expected of students at the conclusion of an [undergraduate] major."[18]

Other tests cover student writing and quantitative skills. For relevant information, see the University of Washington's "Student Writing and Quantitative Skills."[19] The ACT Assessment, for instance, examines the general education development of high school students and their ability to complete college-level work related to reading, English, mathematics, and science reasoning.[20] The Collegiate Assessment of Academic Proficiency (CAAP) measures student achievement in six areas: reading, writing skill, writing essay, mathematics, science reasoning, and critical thinking.[21]

Theses/Senior Papers

Culminating research or honors projects might require an oral defense or interview. A panel or jury might review such projects, or the content of these projects might be subjected to content analysis to determine the extent to which predetermined knowledge and skills (e.g., critical thinking or written communication skills) have been obtained.

INDIRECT METHODS OF EVALUATING STUDENT LEARNING

Such methods involve evidence that is "related to the act of learning, such as factors that predict or mediate learning or perceptions about learning but do not reflect learning itself."[22] The evidence is gathered from students or alumni as they reflect on what they think they learned, or from employers as they reflect on their employees. Any connection about change is therefore inferred. Indirect evidence also includes " 'demographic' statistics about the student population of an institution, such as overall GPA [grade point average], student retention rates, graduation rates, and job placement rates."[23] Similar to direct methods, indirect ones rely on qualitative methods and quantitative methods of data collection and interpretation.

Surveys

There might be nationally developed surveys such as the National Survey of Student Engagement or the College Student Experiences

Questionnaire. The former, developed by the Carnegie Foundation for the Advancement of Teaching and the Pew Forum on Undergraduate Learning, enables students to reflect on and assess their undergraduate education, whereas the latter, developed at Indiana University, examines "how students spend their time in course work, in the library, in contacts with faculty, in extracurricular activities, and other areas of college life."[24] The Community College Survey of Student Engagement is a project of the Community College Leadership Program at the University of Texas at Austin. The survey instrument, known as the Community College Student Report, provides "information on learning-centered indicators of quality for community colleges," and it "asks students about their college experiences—how they spend their time; what they feel they have gained from their classes; how they assess the quality of their interactions with faculty, counselors, and peers; what kinds of work they are challenged to do; how the college supports their learning; and so on."[25] (A search on Google or other general search engines would reveal the availability and use of other freshman and senior experience surveys.)

Locally developed surveys might be administered to students in a program (*general education assessment*), those about to graduate from the institution (*exit survey*), alumni (*general education assessment*), or employers (*perceptions of the graduates they hire*). Such surveys might ask students to assess their gain in knowledge, changes in skill levels, and levels of involvement in the learning process.

Surveys of alumni ask questions related to program objectives and the outcomes studied. The purpose is to use the evidence gathered for curricular improvement. Anyone conducting these surveys must recognize that the longer the period of time since graduation and the less contact the former student has with the program, the less useful is the information gathered. Given these circumstances, surveys might probe the person's perceptions one year after graduation. Surveys of employers of alumni, on the other hand, focus on general information about the graduates of the program or specific information about a particular graduate. These surveys might be handled via focus group interviews (see below).

Some colleges have an "assessment day" during the fall and spring school terms, when graduating students, and perhaps others, participate in different assessment activities. Among these activities might be an opportunity for them to rate the services they used and to provide faculty and program administrators with written comments about their overall experiences.[26]

Through its Office of Academic Assessment, Virginia Polytechnic Institute and State University has two online surveys, a senior survey and a survey of student perceptions of writing-intensive courses.[27] Students might also engage in self-reflection about their program of study and the results compared with their responses on direct methods. Self-reflection might also occur at different stages of the program, and the completed survey(s) could be placed in their portfolio.[28]

Another type of survey is the focus group interview in which students who are about to graduate or recent graduates of a program come together in groups of six to ten and interact as they answer five to seven general questions. Such interviews might also be conducted with area employers or students at different stages of program completion. One focus group interview might be held with students who have just completed the set of required courses in their major. A second interview might involve the same students during their elective program, and a third might occur at the time of graduation. The purpose of these interviews is to gain perceptions about student learning.

Tracking Student Data

Under this category are graduation and retention rates, and employment statistics. A group of students might be monitored over time to determine term-to-term persistence program completion, and time completion (e.g., the extent to which students completed the undergraduate program in four years) rates; course passage rates; and grade point averages. For instance, the percentage of students who go on to attend graduate school indicates how well an institution prepared students for advanced work, whereas an analysis of which programs they enrolled in, and the national reputation of those programs, provides a general indication of quality or prestige. Retention rate is an indicator of institutional success, and job placement statistics indicate how well an institution prepared students for entry into the workforce.

OTHER

The Commission on Assessment for Student Development, together with the American College Personnel Association and Indiana University, operates a clearinghouse of assessment instruments that describes various ones, provides information about how to acquire them, and offers reviews of them.[29] For examples of a "suggested outline for assessment plan" and different samples of evidence gathering, see the Program Assessment of the California State Polytechnic University, Pomona.[30] As well, the Middle States Commission on Higher Education maintains a Web site, http://www.msache.org/mainstudents.html, which identifies institutions involved with student learning outcomes and presents exercises, assessment practices, and guidelines.

CRITICAL THINKING

The Critical Thinking Assessment Project (http://www.csuchico.edu/phi/ct/ct_assess.htm) of the Department of Philosophy, California State University, Chico, identifies instruments that use either direct or indirect methods. Most helpful is the list of critical thinking competencies, such as the ability to "evaluate credibility of sources of information and opinion," "identify relevant and irrelevant claims in a given context," and "determine when additional information is needed for a given purpose." For each competency, the project covers "instruction practices" and "assessment techniques." Such competencies might be presented in the context of direct or indirect methods.

The Critical Thinking Consortium (http://www.criticalthinking.org/) identifies resources including conferences and books. It also covers research, standards, and testing. The Watson-Glaser Critical Thinking Appraisal assesses critical thinking skills (inference, recognition of assumptions, deduction, interpretation, and evaluation of arguments) by asking the examinee "to evaluate reading passages that include problems, statements, arguments, and interpretations." This tool comes in two alternate versions (each has eighty items that can be completed in sixty minutes) as well as in a short form (forty items that can be completed in forty-five minutes).[31] However, before exploring this test, see Figure 12 in *Student Learning Assessment* first, which defines critical thinking and reports on its subscales, design, and intended audience. Most importantly, the figure also lists other "commonly-administered measures of critical thinking" and key readings.[32]

Figure 8.2
Institutional Effectiveness (The Learning Organization)*

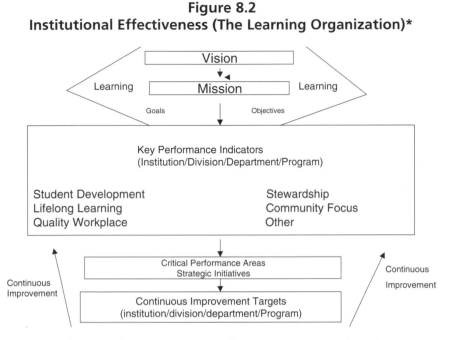

*Adapted from Sinclair Community College, "Assessment of Student Learning: Program Outcomes Reports" (Dayton, OH, 2002), http://www.sinclair.edu/about/assessment/reports/index.cfm (accessed March 2, 2004).

AN EXAMPLE OF THE USE OF BOTH DIRECT AND INDIRECT METHODS: SINCLAIR COMMUNITY COLLEGE

Sinclair Community College's home page provides excellent coverage of the institution's commitment to learning outcomes and the assessment of student learning. As Figure 8.2 and the Web site explain:

An institution of higher education should express clearly to students their expectations of student performance. These statements of expected student outcomes should be described in terms of knowledge, intellectual capacity, and skills.

The learning outcomes for students' achievement in each program are published in departmental brochures and identify specific courses that are related to preparing students to attain each outcome in the program.

All degree-seeking students are required to complete a core of general education courses. These courses relate directly to the general education learning outcomes identified as important for all students regardless of their major.[33]

The following ten principles guide the college's assessment program:

1. The primary reason for assessment is to improve student learning and development.
2. The development of an effective, valid assessment program is a long-term dynamic process.
3. The priorities of the assessment program should be founded in the core goals of . . . [the college's] mission statement.
4. Assessment must involve a multimethod approach.
5. Assessment of student learning and development is a process that is separate from faculty evaluation.
6. The assessment program is most beneficial when used primarily for making internal decisions that seek to improve programs, instruction, and related services.
7. Assessment program initiatives must include training and related support for faculty and staff who are responsible for assessment activities.
8. Assessment results are not intended to be used punitively against students.
9. The assessment program will seek to use the most reliable, valid methods and instruments of assessment.
10. Assessment objectives/goals should be stated in terms of observable student outcomes, and are generally categorized into one of the following areas: basic college readiness, general education, major areas of study, career preparation, and personal growth and development.[34]

Against the above framework, the home page offers departmental reports and shows how multiple methods of data collection fit together for the purpose of assessing and improving the learning experience. There is a reminder that institutional effectiveness is

the process of articulating the mission of the college, setting goals emanating from that mission, defining how the college and the community will know when goals are being met, and using the data from assessment in an ongoing cycle of goal-setting and planning. . . . Putting it another way, effectiveness suggests that a college has a discernable mission, is producing outcomes that meet constituency needs, and can conclusively document the outcomes it is producing as a reflection of the mission.[35]

Finally, as the college notes, "A basic element of an effective assessment program is the identification of 'critical success factors' and the design of appropriate tools to collect data which documents that the College and departments are achieving their mission and goals linked to student academic achievement." The ten "critical success factors" that the college selected include *direct methods* to assess "basic skills, general education skills, learning outcomes in the major," and licensing/accreditation; and *indirect methods* to examine "student satisfaction, transfer success, student goal attainment, graduate placement, employer satisfaction, [and] graduate success/satisfaction."[36]

TAKING A CENSUS OR A SAMPLE

When assessment goes beyond the course level, there may be too many students involved to examine each one, especially on a recurring basis. Furthermore, tools such as portfolios may contain too much source material to enable reviewers to examine each item. Thus, at the program or institutional level, the decision must be made to examine the *universe* (take a census) or a *sample* of the students and their work.

A sample is a portion of a universe, and sampling refers to the methods for selecting that portion. When the intent is to generalize findings from a sample to a given universe, that sample should be representative of the universe. Those engaged in assessment must define the universe, or population, and take a reasonably complete and accurate representation of it. That representation should have some degree of measurement precision. Those doing the assessment can determine the amount of error that arises because a sample does not correspond exactly to the universe. This is an important feature of statistical sampling because assessors can be precise about the error introduced by the sampling process. They can then decide whether the amount of error is tolerable when weighted against trade-off factors such as the cost of obtaining a larger sample that has less error.

Probability Sampling

Probability sampling enhances the likelihood that the sample accurately represents the total population from which that sample is drawn. Random sampling is the simplest and most common method of drawing a probability sample. It involves the selection of cases or subjects so that each one has an equal and known chance of inclusion, and the selection of one case or subject does not influence the selection of another. Simple random sampling does not attempt to separate any portion of the population into distinct groups before the sample is selected. Therefore, if students compile portfolios, a simple random sample would be a portion of the student body or of the entire contents of those portfolios.

Systematic sampling does not choose each member of the population independently. Once the first member of the population has been selected, other members of the sample are automatically determined. Using the *nth* procedure (e.g., determination that each tenth item selected will be included in the sample), the assessors can go through the population taking all of the tenth items as the sample.

Another sampling procedure is the systematic random sample in which items are categorized into discrete groups, and those doing the assessment could use simple random sampling to select the sample items from each group. In other words, assume that the contents of the portfolio could be classified as term papers, completed self-assessment surveys, book reviews, and examination results. The sample would be drawn from the four groups so that it reflects the contents of each group. On the other hand, use of a simple random sample does not permit the comparison by these groups.

Example

As explained in *Student Learning Assessment*:

Plunging immediately into assessing a large number of students on a full range of learning outcomes will overwhelm faculty members and institutional resources. It will produce an overwhelming amount of information that may be impossible to interpret or to use in enhancing a program. It makes more sense to begin with a more limited approach. For example, faculty members assessing student writing skills might gain more from a thorough analysis of a sample of 30 papers than from a more perfunctory review of 300, as well as by assessing only a few key goals.[37]

How is the sample size determined, and how is that sample of thirty papers drawn—with which type of probability sampling? If on the other hand, the assessors use a nonprobability sample, they cannot generalize from a sample to a population because there is no assurance that the sample indeed represents the population. Thus, the thirty papers do not represent the 300; instead, generalization is only to the thirty.

CONCLUSION

Multiple assessments contribute to a comprehensive understanding of how well and under what pedagogies or educational experiences students learn those outcomes that an institution values. Drawing evidence and interpretations from different sources provides richer insights into why, how, and which students learn. As Peggy Maki, then director of assessment, American Association for Higher Education, explains, "Information [gathered] through multiple lenses contributes to developing a narrative that tells the story about student learning so that institutions can identify successful learning experiences, as well as improve upon learning experiences to enhance student learning."[38]

Direct methods provide stronger evidence about the knowledge and skills that students in their major have learned, value, and are able to demonstrate upon graduation. Indirect methods support the desired educational outcomes to a lesser degree. For the most complete picture of the learning experiences and strategies that students have mastered, it is best to select a combination of methods from the tool chest discussed in this chapter; however, those methods should not be solely indirect ones. Once the evidence is gathered, what patterns emerge? How is that information linked to the assessment plan and used for program review and revision? A related question is "What changes are made to the assessment plan as a result of collecting evidence and using that evidence to improve the quality of learning?" However, before making decisions about what to select from the tool chest, it is best to develop an assessment plan, determine which methods best address spe-

Figure 8.3
Principles of Good Practice for Assessing Student Learning*

1. **The assessment of student learning begins with educational values.** Assessment is not an end in itself but a vehicle for educational improvement. Its effective practice, then, begins with and enacts a vision of the kinds of learning . . . [that are most valuable] for students and strive[s] to help them achieve. Educational values should drive not only *what* we choose to assess but also *how* we do so. Where questions about educational mission and values are skipped over, assessment threatens to be an exercise in measuring what's easy, rather than a process of improving what we really care about.

2. **Assessment is most effective when it reflects an understanding of learning as multidimensional, integrated, and revealed in performance over time.** Learning is a complex process. It entails not only what students know but what they can do with what they know; it involves not only knowledge and abilities but values, attitudes, and habits of mind that affect both academic success and performance beyond the classroom. Assessment should reflect these understandings by employing a diverse array of methods, including those that call for actual performance, using them over time so as to reveal change, growth, and increasing degrees of integration. Such an approach aims for a more complete and accurate picture of learning, and therefore firmer bases for improving our students' educational experience.

3. **Assessment works best when the program it seeks to improve has clear, explicitly stated purposes.** Assessment is a goal-oriented process. It entails comparing educational performance with educational purposes and expectations—those derived from the institution's mission, from faculty intentions in program and course design, and from knowledge of students' own goals. Where program purposes lack specificity or agreement, assessment as a process pushes a campus toward clarity about where to aim and what standards to apply; assessment also prompts attention to where and how program goals will be taught and learned. Clear, shared, implementable goals are the cornerstone for assessment that is focused and useful.

4. **Assessment requires attention to outcomes but also and equally to the experiences that lead to those outcomes.** Information about outcomes is of high importance; where students "end up" matters greatly. But to improve outcomes, we need to know about student experience along the way—about the curricula, teaching, and kind of student effort that lead to particular outcomes. Assessment can help us understand which students learn best under what conditions; with such knowledge comes the capacity to improve the whole of their learning.

5. **Assessment works best when it is ongoing, not episodic.** Assessment is a process whose power is cumulative. Though isolated, "one shot" assessment can be better than none; improvement is best fostered when assessment entails a linked series of activities undertaken over time. This may mean tracking the process of individual students, or of cohorts or students; it may mean collecting the same examples of student performance or using the same instrument semester after semester. The point is to monitor progress toward intended goals in a spirit of continuous improvement. Along the way, the assessment process itself should be evaluated and refined in light of emerging insights.

Figure 8.3 (continued)

6. **Assessment fosters wider improvement when representatives from across the educational community are involved**. Student learning is a campus-wide responsibility, and assessment is a way of enacting that responsibility. Thus, while assessment efforts may start small, the aim over time is to involve people from across the educational community. Faculty play an especially important role, but assessment's questions cannot be fully addressed without participation by student-affairs educators, librarians, administrators, and students. Assessment may also involve individuals from beyond the campus (alumni/ae, trustees, employers) whose experience can enrich the sense of appropriate aims and standards for learning. Thus understood, assessment is not a task for small groups of experts but a collaborative activity; its aim is wider, better-informed attention to student learning by all parties with a stake in its improvement.

7. **Assessment makes a difference when it begins with issues of use and illuminates questions that people really care about**. Assessment recognizes the value of information in the process of improvement. But to be useful, information must be connected to issues or questions that people really care about. This implies assessment approaches that produce evidence that relevant parties will find credible, suggestive, and applicable to decisions that need to be made. It means thinking in advance about how the information will be used, and by whom. The point of assessment is not to gather data and return "results"; it is a process that starts with the questions of decision-makers, that involves them in the gathering and interpreting of data, and that informs and helps guide continuous improvement.

8. **Assessment is most likely to lead to improvement when it is part of a larger set of conditions that promote change**. Assessment alone changes little. Its greatest contribution comes on campuses where the quality of teaching and learning is visibly valued and worked at. On such campuses, the push to improve educational performance is a visible and primary goal of leadership; improving the quality of undergraduate education is central to the institution's planning, budgeting, and personnel decisions. On such campuses, information about learning outcomes is seen as an integral part of decision making, and avidly sought.

9. **Through assessment, educators meet responsibilities to students and to the public**. There is a compelling public stake in education. As educators, we have a responsibility to the publics that support or depend on us to provide information about the ways in which our students meet goals and expectations. But that responsibility goes beyond the reporting of such information; our deeper obligation—to ourselves, our students, and society—is to improve. Those to whom educators are accountable have a corresponding obligation to support such attempts at improvement.

*American Association for Higher Education, "9 Principles of Good Practice for Assessing Student Learning" (n.d.), http://www.aahe.org/assessment/principl.htm (accessed March 2, 2004). This document was developed under the auspices of the AAHE Assessment Forum with support from the Fund for the Improvement of Postsecondary Education with additional support for publication and dissemination from the Exxon Education Foundation.

cific learning outcomes, and review the nine "Principles of Good Practice for Assessing Student Learning" (see Figure 8.3).[39]

Any report of student learning should not be a mere recounting of the extent to which student learning outcomes have been met and how the evidence gathered results in program improvement. That report should also reflect on the richness of the curriculum, the extent to which undergraduates can complete programs within four years of full-time study, the extent to which the curriculum is reviewed and revised, the level and type of classroom support (e.g., for those with disabilities), the modernization of classrooms (e.g., the extent to which they are electronic classrooms and use furniture that supports—does not detract from—learning),[40] the accessibility and modernization of laboratories (language, science, and computer), the number of the students in the classroom compared to determinations of comfort levels (at what point does class size detract from learning), and the measures of faculty productivity. Clearly, learning is multifaceted, and some of the above-mentioned variables may contribute indirectly to student learning. Still, the ten critical success factors selected by Sinclair Community College provide an excellent starting point. As the college home page reminds us, whatever evidence is gathered must come from the use of reliable and valid data-collection processes. Such evidence enables the institution to state "with confidence that, upon gradation, students have achieved the institution's standards for clearly stated and measurable learning outcomes."[41]

NOTES

1. Middle States Commission on Higher Education, *Student Learning Assessment: Options and Resources* (Philadelphia: Middle States Commission on Higher Education, 2003), 5.

2. Middle States Commission on Higher Education, *Student Learning Assessment*, 28.

3. Middle States Commission on Higher Education, *Student Learning Assessment*, 8.

4. See Truman University, "Assessment: Components of the Program" (Kirksville, Mo.: Truman University, n.d.), available at http://www.truman.edu/pages/150.asp (accessed February 28, 2004).

5. Middle States Commission on Higher Education, *Student Learning Assessment*, 30.

6. Middle States Commission on Higher Education, *Student Learning Assessment*, 31.

7. Middle States Commission on Higher Education, *Student Learning Assessment*, 37.

8. Diane M. Enerson, Kathryn M. Plank, and R. Neill Johnson, "An Introduction to Classroom Assessment Techniques" (University Park: Pennsylvania State University, Center for Excellence in Learning & Teaching, n.d.), 3, 4, available at http://www.psu.edu/celt/CATs.html (accessed February 28, 2004).

9. L. F. Paulson, P. R. Paulson, and C. Meyer, "What Makes a Portfolio a Portfolio," *Educational Leadership* 48, no. 5 (1991): 60–63.

10. Alverno College, "AC*CEL: The Diagnostic Digital Portfolio" (Milwaukee, Wisc.: Alverno College, 2002), available at http://ddp.alverno.edu/ (accessed February 28, 2004); and see *Student Learning Assessment*, 53, for a list of questions to consider "when deciding to use portfolios." For an overview of the "major features of the digital portfolio," see http://ddp.alverno.edu/ddpsamp/index.html (accessed February 28, 2004). Alverno's students must demonstrate their competency in eight ability areas, and the college approaches student performance from the perspective of "student assessment-as-learning." See Alverno College, "About Alverno" (Milwaukee, Wisc.: Alverno College, n.d.), available at http://www.alverno.edu/about_alverno/ability_curriculum.html (accessed February 28, 2004).

11. For information about iWebfolio and TracDat, including a demonstration of each, see http://www.nuventive.com/html/products.htm (accessed February 28, 2004); see also http://www.sct.com/Education/Products/Connected_Learning/TracDat.html (accessed February 28, 2004).

12. See Connecticut College, "E-portfolio Collaboration Project" (New London, Conn.: Connecticut College, 2003), available at http://www.conncoll.edu/admissions/admitted/eportdemo/ (accessed February 28, 2004).

13. Kathleen Dunn, "Assessing Information Literacy Skills in the California State University: A Progress Report," *The Journal of Academic Librarianship* 28 (2002): 29. These scenarios might even be judged according to Wiggins and McTighe's "Six Facets of Understanding"; see G. Wiggins and J. McTighe, *Understanding by Design* (Alexandria, Va.: Association for Supervision and Curriculum Development, 1998).

14. See Peter Hernon and Robert E. Dugan, *An Action Plan for Outcomes Assessment* (Chicago: American Library Association, 2002), 105–106.

15. Anita Kumar, "College FCAT? Failure Could Hurt Alma Mater," *St. Petersburg Times* (May 1, 2003), available at http://www.sptimes.com/2003/05/01/State/College_FCAT_Failure_.shtml (accessed May 3, 2003).

16. Middle States Commission on Higher Education, *Developing Research & Communication Skills: Guidelines for Information Literacy in the Curriculum* (Philadelphia: Middle States Commission on Higher Education, 2003), 68–71.

17. A perusal of "College BASE Exam" on Google and other search engines

will disclose a number of colleges and universities that use such an examination.

18. MFAT (Major Field Assessment Test) (Rolla: University of Missouri, Office of Institutional Research and Assessment, n.d.), available at http://web.umr.edu/~assess/instrumt/mfat.html (accessed February 28, 2004).

19. See "Student Assessment" (Montgomery: University of Alabama, College of Business Administration, 2003), available at http://www.cobanetwork.com/soap.htm (accessed February 28, 2004).

20. See "Act Assessment" (Iowa City, Iowa: ACT, 2004), available at http://www.act.org/aap/ (accessed February 28, 2004).

21. See "CAAP (Collegiate Assessment of Academic Proficiency)" (Iowa City, Iowa: ACT, 2004), available at http://www.act.org/caap/ (accessed February 28, 2004).

22. Middle States Commission on Higher Education, *Student Learning Assessment*, 32.

23. Middle States Commission on Higher Education, *Student Learning Assessment*.

24. For the National Survey of Student Engagement (Bloomington: Indiana University, Center for Postsecondary Research, 2004), see http://www.indiana.edu/nsse/ (accessed February 28, 2004); for the College Student Experience Questionnaire (Hanover, N.H.: Dartmouth College, 1999), see http://www.dartmouth.edu/evalres/experiences.shmtl (accessed February 28, 2004); also see University of Washington, Office of Educational Assessment, "Student Writing and Quantitative Skills" (Seattle: University of Washington, 1998), available at http://www.washington.edu/oea/rptsqsr.htm (accessed February 28, 2004).

25. See Community College Survey of Student Engagement (Austin: University of Texas, 2003), available at http://www.ccsse.org/ (accessed February 28, 2004).

26. For instance, see Davis & Elkins College, "Assessment at Davis & Elkins College" (Elkins, W.Va.: Davis & Elkins College, n.d.), available at http://www.davisandelkins.edu/academics/assessment.htm (accessed February 28, 2004).

27. See Virginia Tech University, Office of Academic Assessment (Blacksburg: Virginia Tech University, 2003), available at http://aappc.aap.vt.edu/ (accessed February 28, 2004).

28. See Middle States Commission on Higher Education, *Student Learning Assessment*, 49, for an example of a self-reflection survey.

29. See Commission on Assessment for Student Development, Clearinghouse on Environmental and Student Development Assessment Instruments (Raleigh: North Carolina State University, Dept. of Educational Research and Leadership and Counselor Education, 2004), available at http://www.acpa.nche.edu/comms/comm09/dragon/dragon-index.html (accessed February 28, 2004).

30. See California State Polytechnic University, Pomona, "Program Assessment: Assessment Tools. . . ." (Pomona: California State Polytechnic University, n.d.), available at http://www.csupomona.edu/~academic/programs/assessment/tools_assess.htm (accessed November 11, 2003); see also the General Program Assessment Home Page (Pomona: California State Polytechnic University, n.d.), available at http://www.csupomona.edu/~academic/programs/assessment/body.htm (accessed November 11, 2003).

31. Harcourt Assessment, "Watson-Glaser Critical Thinking Appraisal" (San Antonio, Tex.: Harcourt Assessment, 2004), available at http://market place.psychcorp.com/PsychCorp.com/Cultures/en-US/dotCom/Assessment+Center/SubPages/Watson-Glaser+Critical+Thinking+Appraisal+(WGCTA)+Forms+A+and+B.htm (accessed February 28, 2004).

32. See Middle States Commission on Higher Education, *Student Learning Assessment*, 52; also see Figure 9 of that work, which is an "example of a holistic scoring guide (for critical thinking)."

33. Sinclair Community College, "Assessment of Student Learning" (Dayton, Ohio: Sinclair Community College, n.d.), available at http://www.sinclair.edu/about/assessment/outcomes/index.cfm (accessed February 28, 2004).

34. Sinclair Community College, "Guiding Principles" (Dayton, Ohio: Sinclair Community College, n.d.), available at http://www.sinclair.edu/about/assessment/principles/index.cfm (accessed February 28, 2004).

35. Sinclair Community College, "Program Outcomes Reports" (Dayton, Ohio: Sinclair Community College, n.d.), 2, available at http://www.sinclair.edu/about/assessment/reports/index.cfm (accessed February 28, 2004).

36. Sinclair Community College, "Program Outcomes Reports."

37. Middle States Commission on Higher Education, *Student Learning Assessment*, 41.

38. Peggy Maki, "Using Multiple Assessment Methods to Explore Student Learning and Development Inside and Outside of the Classroom," *NetResults* [National Association of Student Affairs Professionals] (January 15, 2002), 3, available at http://www.naspa.org/netresults/article.cfm?ID=558&category=assessment%20/%20Research (accessed November 10, 2003).

39. See L. Pausch and Mary P. Popp, "Assessment of Information Literacy: Lessons from the Higher Education Assessment Movement," unpublished (Chicago: American Library Association, Association of College and Research Libraries, 1997). According to them, there is a tenth principle: "Assessment is most effective when undertaken in an environment that is receptive, supportive, and enabling" (1).

40. See Thomas Bartlett, "Take My Chair (Please)," *The Chronicle of Higher Education* (March 7, 2003): A36–A38.

41. Middle States Commission on Higher Education, *Developing Research & Communication Skills*, 55.

CHAPTER 9

Evolving an Assessment of the Impact on Pedagogy, Learning, and Library Support of Teaching with Digital Images

Danuta A. Nitecki and William Rando

The quest to gauge the value of libraries to education presupposes a benefit of using information to advance teaching and learning. A formula for such a measurement might relate benefits to students and teachers of using information, and to library efforts required to facilitate such use. To understand these benefits and efforts, librarians are challenged to assess the impact of teaching with information resources on pedagogy, learning, and library support. Assessing student learning outcomes, or the impact of teaching, is not simple. Librarians often measure service inputs and, at times, outputs, but they have little evidence on how to assess the outcomes, let alone the impact over time, of teaching evidence-based inquiry. Libraries have not typically engaged in seeking such evidence, but in partnership with others, some are beginning to provide insights on how this might be done.

Libraries are increasingly finding that collaborations with other offices on campus with complementary expertise allow them to maximize the effectiveness of the library in support of teaching. The project described in this chapter presents such collaboration, between a library, a teaching and learning center, and an office of information technology. Working together in consulting teams, we developed a new mode of service delivery to faculty, which includes information management, technological training, and pedagogical consultation. In each of these areas, we were also able to provide assessment services that generated data for faculty on the impact of their teaching, and data for the library teams on the efficiency and efficacy of their service.

Digital images present a powerful format for the presentation of visual information, while emerging software technologies are introducing robust new methods for their organization, retrieval, and display. Many faculty members are eager to apply this power to their teaching, but are stymied logistically by a lack of technical expertise and scarce digital image content offered through library collections, and are limited pedagogically by a lack of understanding about the impact of using images in education. In addition, many faculty members are unable to demonstrate the success of their innovative endeavors because they are unfamiliar with basic strategies for formal testing and learning outcomes assessment.

At Yale University, this situation provided an ideal opportunity for formal collaboration among the library, the Graduate School Teaching Center, and Academic Media & Technology (AMT) to bring technical and pedagogical support to faculty members in the service of enhanced undergraduate education. We have embarked on a three-year, grant-supported project to formally assess the impact of digital images on teaching, learning, and service support. The two authors, from the library and the teaching center, bring different perspectives to their stimulating partnership that has been formed for the assessment focus of this project.[1]

This chapter describes the project and how we have organized our effort to address its deliverables; discusses the methodology used to gather data about teaching, learning, and service support; and illustrates initial results developed to support faculty teaching. The chapter also presents three preliminary rubrics that are designed to understand the progress of teaching, learning, and service support from traditional modes of using images to innovated levels of activities in the educational process. We have completed only the first year of the project and so our results are preliminary tests of the action research methods we have introduced to gather data. This chapter shares our design and structure but is not intended to be a definitive summary of the project's work. (We expect to complete the work in 2005.)

PROJECT OVERVIEW

A $250,000 grant has allowed us to explore the impact of digital images on teaching and learning American studies. This project is the first within the Electronic Library Initiatives (ELI) program within the Yale University Library, intended to highlight collaborative efforts to integrate new technologies and collections of information resources in the support of teaching and learning at Yale. Although improving technologies, building digital collections of images, and devising instruction tools are important components of the project, the emphasis on systematic assessment provides the setting for this chapter's interest. During the three years of funding, we are using a case-study method, working with at least fourteen faculty members at different times to gather data through interviews and course exercises.

We have identified six critical elements of delivering support for the management and effective educational use of digitized images:

- Design improvements for an image management platform
- Integration with other software used for in-class presentation and out-of-class study
- Building and indexing digital image collections
- Instructional guidance
- Clarification of copyright and intellectual property rights
- Assessment of the impact of digitized images on pedagogy and library services

These elements reflect the project deliverables and provide evidence for further insights about the problems facing libraries trying to support this form of information, and the possibilities created by this new technology.

These topics also became the focus of the project's six Working Groups,[2] each composed of two to five staff members who explore specific problems and develop solutions that also are leveraged for applications elsewhere in the campus services. In addition, a team of directed experts consisting of staff from across the campus is convened to provide assistance specifically for each individual faculty member who is participating in the project and preparing for a course related to American studies. The project is introducing a new, directed support team approach to providing customized service, and the benefits and difficulties for sustaining such a model will be among the elements for the project assessment. These Working Groups and Support Teams relate to each other through some overlap in membership, through the coaching of a project manager, and through the discussions of the ELI Steering Committee. The conveners of each faculty support team is an ex-officio member of the Steering Committee, which consists of other administrative stakeholders including the university librarian, director of AMT, director of the Graduate Teaching Center, an associate university librarian who is the principle investigator for the grant, and other library managers and staff with programmatic interest in the project. The Steering Committee meets irregularly, but a couple of times each term; the Working Groups meet as their charge requires; and the Support Teams' efforts vary by the demands of the faculty member each supports.

LITERATURE REVIEW

We examined published information about projects and services that we identified as providing course support for faculty and students using digital images or textual materials. A cursory review of this material confirmed our impression that although there is a growing number of institutions engaged in providing digitized information for classroom applications and some projects have undertaken assessments of issues related to performance of enabling technologies, relevance of metadata structures, and collection implications, none has explored the impact of utilizing digital images on the pedagogy, the behavior of faculty and students, and learning as we are attempting to do. For example, the cross-disciplinary Visual Image User Study at Pennsylvania State University is assessing the needs of three core groups—teachers, students, and information management staff—regarding developing and testing a delivery system for digital images.[3] The posted preliminary findings focus on student and faculty behavior, expectations, demands, fears and hopes, and desirability in using digital information. Other studies of classroom applications include the librarian and faculty collaborations at Vassar College's Media Cloister[4] or the emerging new service support offered at Cornell Library.[5] The study reported here is unique among assessments of using digital images in its focus on pedagogy.

METHODOLOGY

In keeping with the highly exploratory and service orientation of the ELI project, we chose an action research[6] methodology that would allow us to:

- Involve all of our collaborators (faculty members, teaching fellows, library and systems staff) as learning investigators in the research process. That is, we needed a methodology that would allow us to explore with our partners, not to investigate them.
- Explore open-ended questions about our project, with flexibility to adjust our methodology in response to preliminary findings and insights.
- Derive qualitative, descriptive results that speak to the process as well as the impact of this type of collaboration. Such results are appropriate at this stage of this work, and will be useful and informative to faculty members, consultants, and library staff members.

Combining rigorous standards of qualitative research, as cited above, with practice-based action research strategies, we developed a series of methodological strategies to address the following core research questions:

- How does the use of digital images change the way faculty members teach?
- How do these images change the way students learn, what they learn, or how much they learn?
- What role(s) can libraries play in support of teaching with digital images, and what are the effects of this support?

We have undertaken the following three approaches for the ELI Project:

1. Collect and cross-validate data through structured interviews, in-class observations, surveys, pre- and posttests.

2. Analyze data through qualitative methods, grounded theory, and cross validation involving our research partners.

3. Express results in qualitative rubrics.

We applied specific methodologies to address each of our research questions in the following ways.

Digital Images and Teaching

The research into this question begins with an induction interview with our faculty partners. During these structured, audiotaped interviews, we asked faculty members a series of questions regarding their teaching history and goals, particularly as they pertain to using images (digital or analog) in teaching. During these interviews, we also asked them to articulate specific aspects of their teaching that they would like to change or improve by "going digital."

During the semester, we acted as pedagogical consultants to help faculty members make the pedagogical changes they identified in the induction interview. These consultations included discussions of changes to lectures, assignments, papers, work of teaching fellows, and tests and exams. Some of these interviews were also taped and analyzed. We followed our consultations with in-class observations of lectures. Each observation included two researchers whose notes were included in the data pool.

At the end of the semester, we audiotaped structured debriefing interviews with our faculty partners. In these interviews, we collected faculty members' reflections on the experience of teaching with digital images, use of technology, and their impressions of how students and teaching fellows responded to the new format. At this juncture, we have analyzed some of the data we collected and developed preliminary rubrics that we will present to the faculty for validation.

Digital Images and Student Learning

As with our research into digital pedagogy, our research process into student learning began with the induction interview. We asked faculty members to reflect on the learning goals they have for students, specifically as they relate to students' abilities to work with images. In addition to gathering data on faculty members' goals and attitudes about student learning, we asked them to identify one or two specific changes they hoped to see in students' performance that were the result of teaching with digital images. We then worked with them to fashion these hopes into research questions. Once the questions were developed, we collaborated with faculty to develop methods for collecting data.

Faculty members were interested in the relationship between the use of images in lectures and assignments, and the skills students develop in the use of images as items for intellectual consideration. We settled on a simple pre- and posttest design to assess these changes. Faculty members asked students to write about an image at the beginning of the course, and then repeated the request at the end of the course. These data were added to our data pool.

In the analysis, we combined these data from students with data from our in-class observations, interviews with teaching fellows, and survey responses from students. At this junction we have developed our first rubric describing the elements of image analysis and levels at which students perform. We have begun validation of our initial results with faculty members and teaching fellows.

Service Support

Designing and establishing a service support model for the project took the better part of the first year of the project. Our goal to assess this component of the project is twofold: to identify the expectations for service support faculty have of the library, and to project the costs, staffing requirements, and issues involved in providing a sustainable and responsive library support service. We have begun three approaches to gather data about this part of the assessment. Through the interview process described above, we solicited faculty opinions about the type of assistance library staff might best provide them in preparing courses and teaching students, and the value they found in the support teams we introduced. We also asked teaching fellows and students but have only obtained a few anecdotal comments, planning this next year to obtain more. We also calculated costs for scanning and processing a digital image, including indexing it at levels appropriate for a library collection. Because much time this year was spent organizing our effort, we are not confident that our initial calculations reflect production costs once a service is established. Finally, we also held a focus group interview, followed by a confidential survey that used a brief questionnaire e-mailed to staff participants from the support teams to gather data on their perspective of what services the library offered, what problems were experienced, and what is valued assistance to provide in the future. We have comments to begin to form insights about the success of cross-organizational support teams, the challenges of classroom facilities and faculty equipment required to utilize digital images in teaching, and the expectations for metadata indexing provided by the library compared to self-service cataloging.

EARLY FINDINGS

Using these three data sources, we developed three descriptive rubrics. One describes layers and qualities of image analysis, another did the same for image-based pedagogy, and a third proposes levels of library service support and their associated requirements of staff, collections, and infrastructure.

Teaching with Images

This first rubric (see Figure 9.1) was derived from the descriptions of teaching with images provided by our faculty partners. The rubric illustrates the role that images play in the central mission of the course (columns A, B, C, going across) in terms of four elements of teaching with images (rows across): Image Standards, Student Interfaces, Intellectual Goals, and Motivational Goals. Each cell provides a description of choices faculty members make at each level, and for each element. The elements of teaching with images are as follows:

• Image Standards (1): Every faculty member (FM) makes choices about the types of images or objects students will see. Image standards include such notions as authenticity, importance, temporal accuracy, and even the quality of the metadata that accompanies the image. For our purposes, image standards do not refer to the quality of the visual, although for certain types of analysis, this may be an issue. Our meaning of "image standards" refers to the intellectual coherence between the image and the subject being studied.

• Student Interfaces (2): Faculty members must decide how, when, and why students will interact with images. This refers to such things as how much time students will spend with images, in what settings they will study them, and under what kind of pedagogical conditions.

Figure 9.1
Teaching Rubric

Faculty Use Image as →	Visual Illustration	Secondary Evidence	Primary Evidence
	A	B	C
Elements of Teaching with Images ↓			
Image Standards	FM chooses a combination of images, some anachronistic, some original. FM uses images to illustrate a point in history. Lots and lots of images create a picture book of history.	FM uses actual images from the time to illustrate history. Any image that accurately portrays a moment in time will suffice.	Students study bodies of images (including originals) created during a specific period or by a certain image-maker over time.
Student Interfaces: How Students Encounter Images	Students see images in lecture, and may have access to the same images outside of class through Web site or printed format. Images are only loosely tied to texts.	Students see images in lecture complete with citation. Images are linked to other documents in texts or Web sites. Images are used on occasion during discussion. Students are expected to be familiar with images for tests and may use them as examples in papers.	Faculty member models image analyzed during lecture, and images are then discussed extensively in section. Students work on images in specific visual-literacy assignments outside of class. Students construct media combining text and image. Images are a major part of exams and papers. Students take images seriously.
Intellectual Goals	Image as illustration. FM uses images as visual support for text, without supporting their ability to critique the image or its context. Little is expected of students' use of images in tests and papers. In a worst-case scenario, images hypnotize students and undermine their critical faculties.	FM uses images as supporting evidence, combining with textual analysis, but not always successfully. Images are still secondary to text as evidence, though more than illustration. FM uses images to confirm or dispute text, but not as content in their own right.	FM uses images as content, teaching students all the skills of visual literacy in historical argument. FM focuses on images as historical objects and attempts to instill historical sensitivity and knowledge through the critique of images and image-makers.
Motivational Goals	FM uses images to break up the lecture and keep students paying attention. Images meet students' expectations for "edutainment."	FM picks images that heighten emotions and increase interest and the impact of lectures and texts. FM designs image assignments that are fun for students and allow them to feel closer to the material.	FM relies on the power of images as evidence. Motivation is derived from critical examination and the development of new critical faculties. FM helps students mediate the interplay between emotional/aesthetic response and intellect.

The "student interface" element also refers to the degree to which images are integrated into the daily life of the class and experienced through lectures, discussions, assignments, and grading.

• Intellectual Goals (3): Faculty members make choices about the centrality of images to the core intellectual work of the class. "Intellectual goals" refers to how images are dealt with in lectures, how prominently they figure into class discussions, and how central they are to the successful completion of assignments. It also refers to how a faculty member uses images as evidence.

• Motivational Goals (4): When deciding to introduce images in the classroom, faculty members consider the fact that images, while typically powerful in enhancing students' attention and motivation, can also undermine or distort more critical understandings of a topic or issue. Still, many faculty members choose to introduce an image, film, or audio clip for the purpose of enhancing students' interest by bringing written material to visual life.

Learning with Images

This second rubric (see Figure 9.2) is our most fully developed. Derived from interviews with faculty and the results of the pre- and posttests of students' performance, it represents how students learn to use images (columns A, B, C, going across) in terms of three elements of the image: the depiction, the depicted, and the depicter. This rubric contains numbers and letters below each of the cells. These reference examples of the statements we have taken from student data to provide illustrations of each cell. We have listed some of those examples along with the cells in the rubric with which they correspond (see Figure 9.3). This small sample illustrates how these rubrics function as a qualitative research tool. This level of detail is proving to be extremely valuable as we validate our findings with our faculty partners.

Support Use of Images

The rubric designed to explain the services evolving to support the use of digital images was drawn first by this chapter's authoring librarian, but then clarified through discussion with the coauthor. Figure 9.4 summarizes the three distinctive levels of service and five elements of analysis that we propose. The levels of service (organized by columns) are characterized as Collection Building, Information Consulting, and Knowledge Transformation, and evolve along a continuum that reflects a historic progression of library services, where the later levels build upon the prior ones. The five elements of analysis (presented by rows)— service role of librarian, collections, organizational norms, infrastructural requirements, and client expectations—will serve here as the perspectives by which to describe these levels of service.

Figure 9.2
Learning Rubric

Level of Analysis →	Factual	Interpretative	Evidential
	A	**B**	**C**
Element of Analysis ↓			
The Depiction 1	Student knows enough to accurately identify the basic elements of the image. Student can identify image by type (painting, photograph, and household object), by constitution (ink, wood, stone), or by genre (impressionist, documentary photo, advertisement). Student can describe the emotional or aesthetic impact of the image.	Student uses historical knowledge to explain or explore elements in the image, including those that are characteristic or novel. Student can explain the significance of the image's construction and features, including significant omissions, relationships, and visual emphasis in terms of other images created before or since. Student can describe visual impact in terms of how the image would have been viewed at given time.	Detailed knowledge of the physical construction, including analysis of technological shifts and their relationship to the evidentiary value of the image. Image type analyzed in relation to historical elements and their impact at the time or over time. Awareness of image construction as an historical event, with precedence and effects both technical and aesthetic.
The Depicted 2	Student has enough knowledge to identify the name of who or what is depicted, and when and where the subject lived or occurred.	Student uses knowledge of the person or object depicted to speculate about their relationship to other elements in the image, as well as with the image-maker. Student describes the depicted's iconic status or social importance as it relates to our understanding of a time, place, or set of events.	Student uses knowledge of history and of things depicted as evidence for or against a particular perspective. Student may describe the depicted subject's participation in the creation of the image itself as well as history's hand in the selection of the depicted. Student analyzes the depicted as actors (willing or otherwise) in the unfolding of history.
The Depicter 3	Student has enough knowledge to identify the name of the image-maker, a timeline of works produced, relevant locations (birth, death, artistic venue, etc.), and a description of work (genre, media, style, etc.).	Student can discuss the image in terms of decisions made by the image-maker, including composition, subjects and their relationship to other elements in the image, and the physical construction of the image: choice of media, etc.	Student uses knowledge of history and that of the image-maker to use an image in an historical argument. Analysis reflects image-maker as both creator of and created by history. Student advances an argument drawing on the image-maker's experience, perspectives, limitations, intentions, and goals.

Figure 9.3
Sample Quotes from Student Work (Pre- and Posttests) Used to Develop the Learning Rubric

1-A
This image of homesteaders in Nebraska by Soloman Butcher dates back to the 1880's. The settler family is proudly standing in front of their own house.

1-B
Looking at this photograph, one feels that these are good, honest people, proud of what they have and have worked for.

1-C
Since owning a house and land were essential goals for [Americans?], homestead photographs helped document efforts to settle on the plains and build a place to live and to work.

1-C
Paintings, for instance, of wealthy English landowners on their property with a view of their estate, are deeply a part of our visual culture. The advent of photography democratized this genre of representation, allowing even those who have very little to brag about have a picture of their family with their home and land.

2-A
Soddies, houses made out of sod, dominated the American homestead tradition in the 1880's. Made famous in Laura Ingalls Wilder's *On the Banks of Plum Creek*, the soddy was the cheapest homestead. Made out of sod, the house often leaked in rainstorms, and dirt often fell from the roof. This soddy looks better built than others. The soddy has two doors and a chimney. The doors are supported by a wooden structure—high class for this era. The soddy is bigger to accommodate this family of eight. The house seems situate in an unpopulated landscape.
The family probably sees little human interaction.

2-B
Racial prejudice was extremely prevalent, and though this family might not have meant any harm to their farmhand, by placing him in the background they are giving him less importance.
Butcher was fascinated by these families along the plains, and took many pictures of them in this position.

2-B
During this time period, pictures of homesteads were very popular because families were proud of their land and possessions.

Figure 9.3 (continued)

2-C

The family in the picture is having the picture taken for a reason; to show the audience, whether they be their family back East or students of History 140b, what they have and that they are making it, surviving on their own. It was this kind of attitude that fostered manifest destiny and allowed American settlers to carve a place for themselves in this nation; from sea to shining sea.

2-C

The family that Butcher photographed using a glass-plate was positioning themselves outside of their soddy in a very unnatural, posed way. This family would like for history to see that on their claim in (most likely) Nebraska, they had 5 (or 6—hard to see in copy) horses, a well-constructed soddy, 5 children, and what appear to be two farm and/or house hands.

3-A

The photograph, done in the tradition of Solomon Butcher, relates a variety of information concerning housing, property, and people during this time period.

3-B

Butcher chronicled the pioneers of the west and the homesteaders through his photos.

3-B

Why would someone want to record this photograph? The land, the house, and the people tell a story of survival. They are surviving the American West; in fact, they define the spirit of the west. They are probably homesteaders working the land for five years until they can own it. They are hard working, ambitious, and persevering. They are trying to conquer the frontier. They represent the American spirit—the ideals preached by Jefferson, where every man lives off the land in a democratic fashion. Why photograph them? Because . . .

3-B

By placing him in the picture, yet far off in the background, Butcher is using him as an example of the race relations during the late 1800's.

3-C

The family portrait, popularized by influential photographer Solmon D. Butcher, exemplifies American pride in survival and success.

Figure 9.4
Service Rubric

Levels of Service → →	COLLECTION BUILDING	INFORMATION CONSULTING	KNOWLEDGE TRANSFORMATION
SERVICE ROLE OF LIBRARIAN	Librarian uses knowledge of scholarship and bibliographic organization in order to acquire, organize, and preserve information resources within a clearly defined scope to meet institutional mission. Librarian responds to clients' requests by describing the organizational structure of the collections. Success is the comprehensive application of knowledge of scholarship and accurate application of bibliographic controls.	Librarian combines bibliographic expertise with skills in interviewing, interpreting, and building relationships with clients in order to interpret client needs and provide guidance to locate and access information to meet individual requirements for information. Designs customized search strategies and system interfaces to facilitate client search for information. Success is defined by client satisfaction and service quality.	Librarian draws upon bibliographic and consultative expertise, as well as understanding of the academic enterprise, in order to build partnerships with clients and colleagues throughout the academe that maximize the institution's ability to create and share knowledge in the service of research, teaching, and growth. Success is measured by changes in institutional norms regarding relationships between people, information, and the core mission of the institution.
Self-definition	Collectors	Responsive consultant	Leader
Derived satisfaction	Build comprehensive collections	Satisfy clients and provide service quality	Affect change
COLLECTIONS	Library collections address subject areas of institution's focus and strengths. They are described through standard methods of cataloging and by use of authoritative entries for consistent and related organization.	In addition to collections built for institutional purpose, library ensures access to material regardless of location to meet individual's needs. Provide tools and guidance for clients to organize personal sources of information.	Library joins others to create methods by which individuals' collections of resources are preserved and accessed in an integrated fashion with those collections provided by the library. Metadata allow for seamless searching of multiple files.
ORGANIZATIONAL NORMS	Value is placed on "more is better." Information is acquired for "just in case" use. Knowledge of how information is organized is a prerequisite to its use.	Greater value is placed on "access" over ownership with intent to provide information "just in time." Teaching skills in locating and evaluating information sources is fundamental to self-sufficiency and personal success.	Recognition that no institution or unit within it can provide all resources needed to meet requirements for information in teaching, learning, or research. Expertise is drawn from multiple sources.
INFRASTRUCTURAL REQUIREMENTS	Space is essential for collections as well as records describing information with user accessibility.	Delivery and access networks and systems are critical to success. These include both reliable and adequate systems for communication both between institutions as well as within teaching and research facilities.	Social networks provide needed communications for understanding of pedagogical goals, technological potentials, and content availability.
CLIENT EXPECTATIONS	Information resources are available to them in the library.	Access to informational materials is convenient [e.g., fast and effortless].	Partners are easily identified and made accessible to use information to create new knowledge for teaching research and professional promotion and to collaboratively provide evidence of the value of such knowledge.

Service Role of Librarian

In the Collection Building level of service, the librarian uses knowledge of scholarship and bibliographic organization in order to acquire, organize, and preserve information resources within a clearly defined scope to meet institutional missions. The librarian responds to client requests by describing the organizational structure of the collections. Success is a comprehensive application of the knowledge of publishing and the accurate application of bibliographic organization. In the Information Consulting level of service, the librarian combines bibliographic expertise with skills in interviewing, interpreting, and building relationships with clients in order to interpret client needs and provide guidance to locate and access information to meet individual requirements for information. At this level, librarians design customized search strategies and system interfaces to facilitate client searches for information. Success is defined by client satisfaction and service quality. At the Knowledge Transformation level of service, the librarian draws upon bibliographic and consultative expertise, as well as an understanding of the academic enterprise in order to build partnerships with clients and colleagues throughout the academe that maximize the institution's ability to create and share knowledge in service of research, teaching, and growth. Success is measured by changes in institutional norms regarding relationships between people, information, and the core mission of the institution. The progression across the three levels of service reflects a shift in the librarian's self-definition from collector, through responsive consultant, to leader. Satisfaction is derived from building comprehensive collections, to satisfying clients and providing service quality, and ultimately to affect change.

Collections

The customization and organization of collections also shift across these three levels of service. In the Collection Building level of service, library collections address subject areas that reflect the institution's focus and strengths. They are described through standard methods of cataloging and by use of authoritative entries for consistent and content-related organization. In the Information Consulting level of service, in addition to collections built for institutional purposes, the library ensures access to material regardless of location to meet individual client needs. It provides tools and guidance for clients to organize their personal sources of information. In the Knowledge Transformation level of service, the library joins others to create methods by which individuals' collections of resources are preserved and accessed in an integrated fashion with those collections provided by the Library. Metadata and search engines allow for seamless searching of multiple files.

Organizational Norms

The three levels of service function under different institutional attitudes and values. In the Collection Building level, value is placed on "more is better," as reflected by long traditions of research library success measured by size of collection. Information is acquired for "just in case" use. Knowledge of how information is organized is a prerequisite for its use. In the Information Consulting level of service, greater value is placed on access over ownership, with an organizational intent to provide information "just in time." Teaching the skills to locate and evaluate information sources is fundamental to self-sufficiency and personal success. In the Knowledge Transformation level of service, recognition is given that no institution or unit within it can provide all resources needed to meet the requirements for information in teaching, learning, or research. Expertise about the organization, the delivery, and the use of information is drawn from multiple sources. The shift in organizational norms across the three levels of service emphasizes a vision of the library in relation to information and the client as the gatekeeper, the enabler, and the collaborator.

Infrastructural Requirements

Each level of service has different demands on an institution for facility and technological support. In the Collection Building level of service, space is essential to house collections in environments that support their long-term preservation, to continually store records describing their information content, and to allow, comfortably, user accessibility to both. In the Information Consulting level of service, delivery and access networks that are critical to success complement these requirements. These include reliable and adequate systems for communication both between institutions (e.g., resource sharing libraries or information providers) as well as within teaching and research facilities (e.g., classrooms, offices, and dorms). In the Knowledge Transformation level of service, social networks provide the needed communications for understanding pedagogical goals, technological potentials, and content availability, and extend the infrastructural requirements necessary to provide the other levels of services.

Client Expectations

The perspective of the client, the person who interacts with the library and its services, also evolves across the three levels of service. In the Collection Building level, clients expect that information resources are available to them in the library. In the Information Consulting level of service, the client expectation increases to also include convenient— fast and effortless—access to informational materials. A more dramatic shift evolves when a client expects the Knowledge Transformation level of service, through which partners are easily identified and made accessible who will use information to create new knowledge for teaching, research, and professional promotion. As partners, they are expected also to collaboratively provide evidence of the value of such knowledge to the academic enterprise.

Most of the evidence we have gathered thus far in our project supports the descriptions of the first two levels of service support. Not surprisingly, these reflect the traditions of library services familiar to most contemporary clients of academic library services. We have, however, uncovered several statements that imply the need for the third level of service and a couple that suggest recognition of its value as initially explored through the cross-organizational support teams provided in the ELI project. Figure 9.5 provides a sample of statements from the faculty interviews that illustrate the different levels of service.

From staff serving on the support teams, we consistently heard the enthusiasm and value experienced in working with other experts to provide negotiated deliverables to help a faculty member prepare and deliver their teaching. The next challenge is to determine how such a new model of service support may be sustained and with what levels of resource.

WHAT REMAINS TO DO?

There is considerable more data to analyze from the first round, and we are about to embark with five new faculty as the new semester and our second year of work begin. We will further analyze the pre- and posttest data to understand better change in student learning and to integrate additional student data into the "learning rubric." More attention will focus on gathering and analyzing support team survey data as well as costs of resource production and participation; we have not yet identified much data on what it will take to provide the new model of service support. Finally, we look forward to the validation and adoption of rubrics with other faculty members and service staff in the library and elsewhere on campus.

CONCLUSION

This study offers several core contributions through practical insights into the role of digital images in teaching, learning, and service

Figure 9.5
Sample Comments from Faculty That Illustrate the Service Rubric

From faculty interviews, the following statements illustrate the orientation toward a Collection Building level of service:

> *Some instructors—and I didn't think this was such a great idea—told students to go in the library and pick any picture they want in the library and into the museums, pick any picture you want. I think that's really daunting.* [BS: Debriefing: 189]

> *If you go in [for images] through the library, you know you have to get into it from the library website and there are a lot of steps to get there, and at first the students found that—you know this is the beginning of their first semester for one thing, and I think it's important to remember because maybe it made it harder that way than it would have been. There are a lot of steps to just to get to it.* [F3: Debriefing: 200]

Similarly, it wasn't difficult to find comments from the faculty that reflect the Information Consulting level of service, as the following illustrate:

> *They were . . . so well organized, everything was prepared. I mean, it was pedagogically, it was practically perfect, you know. They had all the sites ready, they could just go right to them, it was all prepared and organized so that the students understood exactly what they needed to do. It was spectacular. . . . It was very creative, and that whole creative aspect of it was, well, I mean I know I sound sort of stupid about it—it was just fun. It was—it made all of what they were doing that was, in my mind, academically so important, it was just—made it fun.* [BS: Debriefing: 78 & 97]

> *These students who go through the more traditional Sterling Library sessions, you know, none of them will ask, will have a research idea and ask for specific help which I think is great. . . . I go to all of them. I know I learned something new, and I always learn more than the students do anyway. I didn't know you could do that now, well I just had forgotten about those. And at the end of the term as they start to panic, inevitably someone says, . . . this is a lot harder than I thought. There's so much information we've been warning you all semester. So much information of this stuff. And there's in a sense that the only way to discover that when they stumble into the stacks, right before break to get the research so they can write you know something during break, and also they panic. So if there's a way to force them in there earlier, get them motivated to . . . go there themselves.* [JH: Initial: 148]

> *The team basically has recreated the Filemaker Pro template in the digital library in sort of a faculty access space which makes . . . the cataloging immediate, you can see if you made a mistake and go back and fix it, it makes things significantly easier. . . . If I get an image in a book I can just catalog it immediately, and to my*

Figure 9.5 (continued)

specifications using the library formula. I mean that makes it dramatically easier, and it releases the library staff from having . . . [to] translate it. [F2: Debriefing: 23]

You know who would really benefit . . . in addition to faculty, at the beginning of the school year to introduce this database to all of the TA's who are teaching in the department to say, you know you're running a discussion on it, you know you want to use images, that would be unbelievable. [F2: Debriefing: 105]

I think it's extending what the library's already doing as far as research of the written word is concerned, to helping students to understand how they might conduct research in images. And that, you know, it quickly becomes an instructional issue, not just a reference issue, because one has to know what one's looking for, and the kinds of questions that one is asking, and you know, as I said . . . I've been very impressed with the library's ability to square that circle in regard to research instruction, and this would be extending that. [F2: Debriefing: 172]

The evolution to our third level of service, Knowledge Transformation, is illustrated by a comment such as the following, in which the faculty member starts with a clear role of the librarian as that of consultant to help clients navigate systems to find information, but progresses to describe the role of one who facilitates the client's use of information found.

I'm a big supporter of what the library has done . . . as far as the electronic classroom is concerned, and assistance for history seminars, giving students the tools they need to do research. . . . If I can imagine what might have happened different this time that would have been good, it would have been that we would have been able to have that kind of a session about using images in historical research. And how to get them and how to find them, and . . . what the cataloguing system is like, and how to get into that, how to do research with the database . . . how to work the software, how to use it, what you could use it for, what can you do with it, how can you find things with it, and that would have started off with a session for the TA's to get that up and running. . . . As it was, G came in and did a half of a class period, which I think was good, but only a bare introduction for students. They need to be able to sit at a terminal with the keyboard with themselves, have somebody look over their shoulder and give them help, just the way the library does . . . currently with other kind of research. So that's the support that would have made a big difference. [F1: Debriefing: 107]

Several faculty comments, such as the following, imply or seek a notion of a Knowledge Transformation level of service:

So for me this is the next step as far as the technology is concerned is moving beyond that sort of haphazard way of collecting material [I do] and presenting it to a much more systematic scholarly citation-mode manner of doing this. [F1: Initial: 9]

Figure 9.5 (continued)

I don't know where the library draws the line on its responsibility, it becomes fuzzy because that so much of it's instructional. You know, and I mean aside from the hardware problem and what are just the inadequacies of the software itself and the design of the software—where there was the possibility of real support that wasn't there, and I'm not saying this as criticism—is you know the outfitting of the classrooms, the training of my TA's. [Debriefing: 101]

[It] would be really interesting to figure out how we as librarians and instructors set the assignment that then leads them [students] down that path. And I think that that could be really exciting in the context of a seminar. I mean it could be exciting in the context of the lecture. [F2: Initial: 147]

There was the messy shoebox that I'd brought to the library, of data—sort of "the everything." Then there was the digital library that was created with ELI with support, and then there is the Luna Insight taken from the digital library, and a few things that aren't in the digital library that I—that they will be part of it but they aren't presently, things I came across during the fall term that will be ideal I thought for the Luna part of the project. So the Luna part was really 30 images and sound files that, let's say 25 of them came from the digital library, and the digital library I thought was everything in my shoebox only organized. But I'm now pretty certain that there are a number of images that never got translated over just because of the mess that my shoebox was in and because of a range of factors. (By the way, there's somebody now trying to sort out the mess. Everything in my shoebox will be in the digital library, and if they aren't there already, they're going to be there.) [JH: Debriefing: 9]

Well I don't know how you could improve it to be honest. I think it worked great for me because, for these kinds of things: When you're working cross-disciplines you're bringing together different kind of expertise for the outsider who's being serviced. That could be profoundly confusing in terms of trying to figure out who to go to for what issue. As I was pointing out yesterday there is one person for me to go to and it is G. I said G I don't get this . . . —help me. And you know, without exception, I can't think of any exception, I got the answer back real fast. And it wasn't like you needed to go contact PM about this, it's like this is what the answer is. So for me the team was transparent, or is invisible . . . for me was perfect. In fact, probably because I don't remember names that well, I can only think of a few people from the team. But I think that's a good thing from a service recipient's point of view. [F2: Debriefing: 92]

You need—we need to plan technical support so that it comes in just as they're confused but before they're so confused that they can't go ahead or they panic. [F3: Debriefing: 43] support, as well as to evolving a model of discovery and expression of an assessment project results. The new paradigm for service support involves cross-divisional expertise brought together to maximize knowledge transformation in support of teaching and learning. Such a paradigm evolves within a new model for collaborative organizational change. The new environment requires and achieves high levels of faculty engagement. Although the study's scope has been limited to teaching of American studies and using digital images, the insights gained thus far will have far reaching applications to the way that information is discovered, organized, and utilized for teaching, as well as the ways that librarians will assume leadership roles as partners with faculty and colleagues elsewhere on campus to transform information they have traditionally preserved through collection building into knowledge that shapes learning.

NOTES

This chapter expands a presentation on the topic published in summary form in the Proceedings of the Fifth Northumbria International Conference on Performance Measurement in Libraries and Information Services, July 28–31, 2003, Collingwood College, Durham, England.

1. We appreciate the assistance provided by the project's research assistant, Janice Weynart, in transcribing and categorizing extensive data gathered in our efforts.

2. The Working Groups are more fully described on the project Web site, http://www.library.yale.edu/eli. These include technical system staff who have analyzed the effectiveness of the Insight software and its various releases. We expected to use this system from Luna Inc., but soon discovered that not all participants found it adequate for their teaching needs. So, the Platform Working Group is also modifying and testing the "Digital Library" software developed for order handling in the Beinecke Rare Book and Manuscripts Library at Yale, and faculty members are finding both helpful. The Integration Working Group also includes technical experts who have addressed questions of linking one of these image asset management software programs with other tools used for teaching and study such as a campus-developed courseware [http://www.classes.yale.edu] and PowerPoint. The third Working Group aims to understand requirements for building collections of digital images while ensuring that access to over 100,000 digital images will be possible. It also is tackling the question of how much indexing is enough for resources that begin life as an object used in teaching and may not need to be fully cataloged for long-term inclusion in a preserved library collection. The Instruction Group frequently is

called upon to develop or update instructions on how to use the technologies and how to locate and evaluate digital images, whether available through electronic sources or not. The Copyright Group has drafted guidelines written in practical terms for a faculty member to check legitimacy of using image sources found through the Web, through publications, or in licensed collections. Finally, the Assessment Working Group consists of the authors of this chapter, working with the help of a research assistant, and aims to address the issues reported in this chapter.

3. For more information on the Penn State study, see "Visual Image User Study (2003)," http://www.libraries.psu.edu/vius/ (accessed February 28, 2004).

4. For more information on the Media Cloisters at Vassar College, see "Media Cloisters," http://mediacloisters.vassar.edu/flash/ (accessed February 28, 2004).

5. For more information on the Cornell project, see "Office of Distributed Learning," http://www.library.cornell.edu/dl/aboutus.htm (accessed February 28, 2004).

6. The field of action research is "intentionally idiosyncratic, personalized, and contextual," referring to the many foci that people have brought under the heading of action research. For our purposes, we rely on the more "British" view of action research with its attention to collaborative methods of data gathering and validation for the purpose of solving practical problems and enhancing organizational effectiveness. See D. W. Kyle and R. A. Hovda, "Action Research: Comments on Current Trends and Future Possibilities," *Peabody Journal of Education* 64 (1989): 170–175.

CHAPTER 10

Outcomes Assessment in a College Library: An Instructional Case Study

Elizabeth W. Carter

The faculty of the Daniel Library at the Citadel, Charleston, South Carolina, are involved in several ongoing assessment projects that evaluate nearly every aspect of the library, including satisfaction with services and facilities, satisfaction with the adequacy of collections, and the effectiveness of instruction programs. Data acquired from these assessment efforts influence purchasing of library resources, physical arrangement of the library, plans for library expansion, the nature and focus of services offered, teaching methods and content of library research instruction, and relationships with faculty colleagues and college administrators.

The Daniel Library is currently engaged in five assessment projects. First, first-year students are pretested and posttested for their abilities to describe how they would accomplish a research task, and they are also asked to respond to a series of attitudinal and usage questions. Second, sophomore history majors enrolled in a historiography class participate in end-of-term focus group sessions sharing information about their research experiences. Third, students from a cadet living group are taking part in a four-year study to examine if and how student research needs, information-seeking behaviors, and library use change and evolve from freshman to senior years. Fourth, upper-level biology majors enrolled in a genetics course in which science literature is used to enhance student understanding of the scientific method are assessed at the end of the course about the success of this method. And fifth, the most recent assessment project is the Daniel Library's participation in the spring 2003 *LibQUAL+* survey of library service quality, which examines the gap between community expectations and their perceptions of library service.

Internal and external needs at the Citadel Library drive assessment. Within the library, there is a need and desire to identify whether goals of effectively providing research instruction to undergraduate and graduate students are being met. To colleagues in other academic departments it is vital to provide feedback about validity of research instruction provided for their students. Furthermore, program assessment data must be provided to the institution as well as to governing agencies and accrediting organizations.

The purpose of the library's multifaceted assessment plan is to contribute to the change that takes place in college students through academic processes. Library faculty undertook a study of the genesis of each component of the assessment program, how it has evolved, how and why changes were made throughout, what was learned from each effort, and changes that were made based on that information. Additionally, they are examining the management of the process, the program's effects within the library and on the college at large, and next steps and strategies.

DEVELOPING AN ASSESSMENT CULTURE

What is now an extensive and multifaceted program of assessment began on a very small scale with the simple goal of determining the effectiveness of library instruction provided to students in one course, a core curriculum psychology course. The success of this project and the ease with which it was accomplished led to other assessment efforts and collaborations.

Support of the library director was a crucial factor in developing the program. Initial support took the form of time: time to devote to a nascent library instruction program and develop collaborative efforts with other faculty. Support later included direct funding to buy equipment, assignment of two additional faculty positions for instruction, and construction of a state-of-the-art instruction laboratory.

The library director provided initial support to encourage growth of the instructional program. Credibility and growth of the program developed from collaborations with faculty colleagues. This bottom-up approach spread from faculty member to faculty member. Working relationships established through instruction and assessment of the core psychology course grew throughout that department, and help given to a history professor to introduce his graduate students to online searches back in the early days of end-user database searching laid groundwork for extensive instruction and assessment in a required history course. When colleagues of a biology professor who was using literature searches as a teaching tool in her genetics classes saw success in that approach, they incorporated similar methods in their own courses.

These "victories" and others like them eventually caught the attention of the college administration. They saw that the library was involved in much of the academic assessment. This recognition brought additional support, both administrative and financial, including services of the Office for Institutional Research that were made available to enter and analyze data, school time provided to meet with focus group subjects, and funding provided to facilitate the project. Most recently, the college provided funding to participate in the 2003 *LibQUAL*+ survey of the Association of Research Libraries and Texas A&M University.

BACKGROUND ON ASSESSMENT PROJECTS

The library's assessment program began very simply as collaboration between the author and a psychology professor in the mid-1990s as both wanted to determine if research instruction for numerous sections of a core course, Psychology 209, "Psychology of Individual Behavior," was effective. In the course, offered to nonmajors as fulfillment of the core curriculum social science requirement, students developed a hypothesis about an aspect of human behavior, collected statistics from a database of student surveys, and reviewed psychology literature to test their hypothesis. During research instruction classes, students learned about resources and strategies for searching the psychology literature.

A pretest/posttest assessment utilizing a free-response-key-concept methodology along with attitudinal and usage measures was used to measure effectiveness of instruction. A rating system describing an ideal response was developed, and students received one point for each correct step in their answers. Two librarians not connected with the study rated responses, each rating a full set of answers without knowing respondents or whether they were scoring pretests or posttests. Ratings

Figure 10.1
Psychology Pretest/Posttest and Survey

Clearly list all of the steps you would go through in order to perform the following task:
Obtain an article published in a psychology journal concerning the relationship between *stress*
and *health*.

How many times LAST SEMESTER did you . . .

        visit the Daniel Library?   _____

        check out books from the library?   _____

        use a computer database in the library?   _____

        obtain a copy of an article from the library?   _____

        attend library instruction with a class?   _____

        complete assignments that required library research?   _____

Indicate how much each of the following statements is true for you . . .

	Not True				Very True
I feel comfortable in libraries	1	2	3	4	5
I am good with computers	1	2	3	4	5
I enjoy reading	1	2	3	4	5
I can usually find what I need at the library	1	2	3	4	5
I like puzzles and brain teasers	1	2	3	4	5
I prefer Macintosh computers	1	2	3	4	5
I probably don't spend enough time at the library	1	2	3	4	5
I like to do my studying at the library	1	2	3	4	5
I usually get the help I need at the library	1	2	3	4	5
I have learned a lot about research from libraries	1	2	3	4	5

were combined to give each subject a presemester score and postsemester score. Items on the usage and attitude questionnaire were summed and pre- and postsemester ratios were calculated for each subject.[1]

This assessment method concept originated from Donald Barclay's 1993 article as he both decried the dearth of effective assessment in libraries and provided a remedy.[2] Barclay, coordinator of instruction at the New Mexico State University Library, hypothesized that most libraries do not assess the effectiveness of instruction due to a lack of institutional support, a perceived difficulty of the process, and time constraints.[3] He further contended that careful, effective, and meaningful evaluation of instruction programs is possible despite the existence of constraints. He also identified and described a scalable methodology that can be as small or large, as simple or elaborate, as allowed by the resources of the evaluator.[4]

Using Barclay's methodology, the researchers developed a similar instrument to determine if psychology students could search psychology literature and locate an acceptable article supporting their hypothesis and whether their attitude toward research and their library use changed over the semester (see Figure 10.1). Results showed that

> outcome-focused library instruction in psychology appears to lead to skill development, improved efficiency, and positive attitude change. Participating students showed evidence of change across the semester during which the instruction was offered. It appears that co-development (between course and library faculty) with a focus on outcomes may be an effective approach to library instruction.[5]

The key component of his methodology is the free-response-key-concept method of testing. After conducting research he concluded that "testing is the only practical way for instruction librarians to collect hard evaluation data," and he determined that a free-response question elicits the best indication of student knowledge because "the act of writing an answer to a free-response question . . . has more in common with the unstructured act of library research and so may be a better test of a student's ability to use a library."[6] Scoring answers against a key or ideal response provided a layer of objectivity in the scoring. Barclay's methodology has now been effectively used in additional iterations of the library's assessment of instruction, including Freshmen Library Instruction and First Year Seminar.

ASSESSING RESEARCH INSTRUCTION

This section discusses the assessment of first-year students and the other assessment programs of the library.

Freshmen Library Instruction

Concurrent with assessing effects of library research instruction in psychology, library faculty also taught an instruction program for first-year students. The primary goal of this one-time, two-hour class was to introduce new college students to college-level library research. Librarians met with students in groups of 25–30, engaging them in class discussions and hands-on searching in learning to discern scholarly from popular sources, evaluate information, and search for information on assigned topics in catalogs, indexes, and databases related to their major field of study.

Figure 10.2
Freshmen Library Instruction Pretest/Posttest and Survey

Clearly list all of the steps you would go through in order to perform the following tasks:
1. Find a book in The Citadel Library on the subject of *earthquakes*.
2. Find a journal or magazine article on the subject of *earthquakes*.

How many times LAST SEMESTER did you . . .

        visit your high school library? _____

        check out books from that library? _____

        use a computer database in that library? _____

        obtain a copy of an article from that library? _____

        attend library instruction with a class? _____

        complete assignments that required library research? _____

Indicate how much each of the following statements is true for you . . .

	Not True				Very True
I feel comfortable in libraries	1	2	3	4	5
I am good with computers	1	2	3	4	5
I enjoy reading	1	2	3	4	5
I can usually find what I need at the library	1	2	3	4	5
I like puzzles and brain teasers	1	2	3	4	5
I prefer Macintosh computers	1	2	3	4	5
I probably don't spend enough time at the library	1	2	3	4	5
I like to do my studying at the library	1	2	3	4	5
I usually get the help I need at the library	1	2	3	4	5
I have learned a lot about research from libraries	1	2	3	4	5

The psychology pretest/posttest and attitudinal and usage measures methodology were modified to assess program effectiveness. The free-response question was changed to include two questions asking students to describe steps they would take to find a book and a journal article on a designated topic (see Figure 10.2), and the pretest attitudinal and usage measurement asked students about their library experiences in high school, whereas the posttest measurement queried students about their first-semester library experiences. The pretest was administered during Freshman Academic Orientation, and student academic leaders within student residences administered the posttest at semester's end.

Adapting Barclay's methodology to the assessment of freshmen library instruction illustrates the simplicity and elegance of his process. Collaborating with a psychology professor versed in statistics produced results that could be evaluated using t tests and ratios. For assessment of freshmen instruction, a simple method of scoring responses and averaging scores was employed. While less elegant, the manual method was just as effective.

Results from 1999, the final year of the Freshmen Library Instruction Program, showed an average pretest score of 2.15 and an average posttest score of 5.23. Similarly, responses to the attitude and usage scale were tallied and averaged. During the just-completed semester, students reported on average that they visited the Daniel Library 40.6 times, checked out books 4.7 times, used a computer database 31 times, obtained a copy of an article from the library 3.5 times, attended library instruction with a class 2.5 times, and completed assignments that required library research 3.1 times. Furthermore, students rated their success in finding what they needed at the library as 4.0, and in getting the help they needed as 4.1, both on a Likert scale of 1 to 5.

First Year Experience

In fall 2000, Freshmen Library Instruction was integrated into a newly formed course, Citadel 101: A First Year Experience, to achieve a major course goal of developing library research skills. Within this required, one-semester, one-credit-hour course, first-year students participate in two class periods of library instruction. Library faculty work closely with Citadel 101 faculty to develop a unit that is integral to the class and teaches students to narrow topics; develop search strategies; utilize a variety of sources; evaluate sources for accuracy, relevance, and appropriateness; and document references to complete a graded assignment. Assessment of Freshmen Library Instruction provided visibility and credibility for the program and library faculty, thus ensuring a major role in Citadel 101 for library research instruction.

Library faculty continued to assess the effectiveness of instruction for first-year students using a version of Barclay's methodology of a free response test with attitude and usage survey. However, the attitude and usage scale was revised. In previous pre- and posttest iterations, open-ended response options of "how many" often elicited vague responses such as "a lot" or "every day." Therefore, response options were tightened from "how many" and "how true" to "how many times" and "do you agree" and a scale of "strongly agree" through "strongly disagree." Also, three questions designed to study student understanding of the Internet as a research tool were added (see Figure 10.3). Pretests continued to be administered during Freshmen Academic Orientation; however, Citadel 101 faculty, within their classes, gave posttests at the end of the semester.

Responses continued to be scored against a "perfect" answer, and recent test results showed an average pretest score of 1.80 and an average posttest score of 5.18. The rubric for assessing Freshmen Library

Figure 10.3
Citadel 101: First-Year Seminar Pretest/Posttest

Clearly list all of the steps you would go through in order to perform the following tasks:
1. Find a book in The Citadel Library on the subject of *earthquakes*.
2. Find a journal or magazine article on the subject of *earthquakes*.

During the fall 2000 semester:
Did you receive instruction on how to use the Daniel Library?
      Never   Once   2–5 times   More than 5 times
Did you use the Daniel Library to use or check out books, articles, or other material for your classes?
      Never   Once   2–5 times   More than 5 times
Did you use resources from the Daniel Library to prepare a research paper or bibliography?
      Never   Once   2–5 times   More than 5 times
Did you use the Internet or World Wide Web to prepare a research paper or bibliography?
      Never   Once   2–5 times   More than 5 times
Did you use the library as a quiet place to read or study?
      Never   Once   2–5 times   More than 5 times
Did you ask a librarian or a staff member for help in finding information on a topic?
      Never   Once   2–5 times   More than 5 times
Did you use a computerized index or database (of journal articles or books) to find information on a topic?
      Never   Once   2–5 times   More than 5 times

Do you agree?
Do you agree with the statement, "Everything is on the Web"?
      Strongly Agree   Agree   Disagree   Strongly Disagree   Don't Know
A step in using Web-based materials for research is to examine the Web page for information about its author's qualifications and affiliation.
      Strongly Agree   Agree   Disagree   Strongly Disagree   Don't Know
You must always document information found on the Internet.
      Strongly Agree   Agree   Disagree   Strongly Disagree   Don't Know

Instruction and Citadel 101 scores is as follows. A score of 5 indicates an adequate understanding of the research process. Through their answers, respondents showed that they:

- Know to use the catalog to find books and databases to find articles
- Understand the need to search by topic or keywords
- Indicate that they should choose the item that best suits their information needs
- Know information needed to locate the item (call number or citation)

A score of 6 to 7 indicates more advanced proficiency in the research process. These students, in addition to skills listed above, can usually list appropriate databases and display higher order thinking skills. A score of 8 or higher indicates an outstanding understanding of the research process.

The attitude and usage scale showed that in the just-completed semester 96.3 percent of first-year students participated in library instruction classes, with a majority (70.5 percent) participating two to five times; 74 percent had used or checked out library resources at least once (50 percent two or more times, but 22 percent never); 78.3 percent had used library resources to prepare a research project (40.7 percent more than once); 82.7 percent use the library to read or study; 74.2 percent have asked for help in finding information in the library; and 83.7 percent have used library databases. Ninety-two percent of first-year students have their own computers, while 95.9 percent found library computer services to be very satisfactory or satisfactory.

Three new questions related to Internet research were:

- "Do you agree with the statement, 'Everything is on the Web'?" The results showed that 8 percent strongly agree, 53 percent agree, 31 percent disagree, and 3 percent do not know.
- "A step in using Web-based materials for research is to examine the Web page for information about its author's qualifications and affiliation." More than 84 percent either strongly agreed or agreed; the rest disagreed, did not know, or did not respond.
- "You must always document information found on the Internet." To this question, 90 percent either agreed or strongly agreed; the rest disagreed, did not know, or did not respond.

The unknown variable in these responses is the student's ability to distinguish between Web sites and subscription-based scholarly sources accessed via the Internet, such as full-text journal databases. This variable needs to be addressed through further study and revision of the instrument.

History Majors Focus Groups

Borrowing from a method advanced by Peggy Seiden of Skidmore College, Citadel Library faculty embarked on using focus groups to discover students' information-seeking behaviors. Speaking as part of an Association of College and Research Libraries panel program on understanding digital library users during the 1999 American Library Association Annual Conference, Seiden described a project where librarians used focus groups conducted in dormitories to discover students' information-seeking behaviors. She and colleagues met with student volunteers and queried them on their selection of sources, searching techniques, and influence of faculty in their selections.[7]

The library adapted Seiden's methodology to assess the effectiveness of extensive instruction taught in a required historiography course for undergraduate history majors. As with the psychology classes that were the origin of instruction assessment at the Citadel, library and history faculty wanted to measure the effectiveness of their efforts. Students enrolled in History 203, "Introduction to the Discipline of History," required of all history majors, spent two class periods in the library learning research techniques and resources essential for the course's research paper.

Course professors provide a class period at the end of the term for librarians to meet informally with the students and discuss their research experiences. The meeting provides an opportunity to evaluate the information-seeking behaviors of history majors and determine the effectiveness of library research instruction. Librarians are interested in learning what strategies and sources students actually used, what was successful, what was not, and problems and barriers students encountered. Students are first engaged in open-ended discussions about their experiences and then they complete a questionnaire allowing for individual responses.

Not only does outcomes-based assessment benefit this particular class, but information gleaned from these students affects resources and services for all. From focus groups it was learned that sophomore- and junior-level students need upper-level research instruction and feel that an intense research-level class is worth the time. Students found instructional sessions helpful in making it possible for them to locate and use research collections and acquire important works through interlibrary loan. Students reported that they want full-text journal articles, they use interlibrary loan extensively, and they prefer to do research from their rooms. Students found that the library's book collection, supplemented by interlibrary loan, was, for the most part, adequate for their research needs; however, journal collections were deficient in their topic areas.

Based on student feedback that was gathered longitudinally, the library and history faculty have modified library instruction sessions (e.g., included hands-on exploration of library collections, and spent more time on some issues and less on others), purchased databases (e.g., *JSTOR*), and offered or changed library services (a scanner in the instruction lab, designating sections of books stacks for library use only).

In years one and two of the History Focus Groups, the instrument was not changed; however, in year three (2002) a free-response question asking students to describe how they conducted research (similar to that in the Citadel 101 pretest and posttest) was added (see Figure 10.4). Responses indicated that they understood and incorporated search strategies such as narrowing topics, identifying keywords and concepts, and employing Boolean operators. Students knew to use catalogs and databases; could name important sources such as *WorldCat*, *JSTOR*, and *Historical Abstracts*; and knew to utilize bibliographies, book reviews, and interlibrary loan.

Alpha Company Focus Groups

Focus group methodology can provide a valuable source of information on student information needs and information-seeking behaviors, and the library and college administration have used it in decision making. With statistical support from the Office of Planning and Assessment, and funds from the provost to facilitate the project, in 2002 library faculty embarked on a four-year project of conducting annual focus group sessions involving a cadet living group to track a large, diverse set of undergraduates with the intent of gaining insights into how students' research needs, information-seeking behaviors, and library usage change and evolve from freshman to senior years. This group, Alpha Company, consists of about 100 students, first years through seniors, representing all academic majors. The focus group process is similar to that of the history majors; however, data collection takes place over lunch.

From the 2003 Focus Groups (year two; see Figure 10.5), it was learned that:

- 92.2 percent of students had at least one assignment requiring information gathering. Of these, 58.4 percent had two to five such assignments and 18.2 percent had more than five. (Q2)
- 77.9 percent of these students used material from the Daniel Library (e.g., books and journal articles) for projects. (Q3)
- 64 percent got information from the Internet (Q7). It is unclear if

Figure 10.4
History 203 Focus Group Student Research Survey
(December 9, 2002)

1. What did you learn in the library research instruction classes that you did not previously know?
2. What was **not** covered in the library research instruction classes that you wish had been covered?
3. What was most helpful about the library research instruction classes?
4. What was least helpful?
5. Were the two class periods devoted to library research instruction adequate time to cover what you needed to know?

   Adequate_____   Too much_____   Too little_____
6. Describe the steps you used to find books for your paper:
7. Describe the steps you used to find journal articles for your paper:
8. What sources did you use to find research material (e.g., books and journal articles) for your paper? Check all that apply.

   Daniel Library catalog _____
   C of C catalog _____
   Historical Abstracts _____
   America: History & Life _____
   Expanded Academic Index _____
   WorldCat _____
   JSTOR _____
   Project Muse _____
   Bibliographies in books _____
   Bibliographies in articles _____
   Internet Web sites _____
   Other (please explain):
9. Did you use materials (books, journal articles, etc.) from the Daniel Library?

   Yes_____   No_____
10. If you answered **NO** to # 9, or if you also used materials from other sources, where and how did you get the needed information for your paper?

    Other libraries _____
    Interlibrary loan _____
    Your professor's collection _____
    Other (please explain) _____
11. Was the Daniel Library's collection (books, indexes and databases, journals) adequate for your research needs?

    Yes_____   No_____
12. If you answered **NO** to # 11, what did the Daniel Library not have that you needed?
13. Did you get materials (books, journal articles, etc.) from interlibrary loan?

    Yes_____   No_____
14. If you answered **YES** to #13, approximately how many items did you get?
15. Assuming you did not wait until the last minute, did the interlibrary loan material arrive in time to use in your paper?

    Yes_____   No_____
16. Where did you do most of your research?

    In the Daniel Library _____
    Your own computer _____
    ITS labs _____
    Other _____
17. When/if you sought individual research help in the Daniel Library, did you receive adequate assistance? Please explain.
18. What we most want to know is if the Daniel Library is meeting your research needs in terms of research instruction, reference help, and library materials. Please tell us about your research experience—what worked and what didn't, successes, problems, or anything else that may help us to help you and future history students.

they meant Web sites, Internet-based library resources, or both. This needs to be better defined next year.

- A majority of students could identify a source for the information they retrieved—a database, a search engine, or type of material. (Q12, Q17)
- 43.4 percent learned about sources from a librarian (in a class or one-on-one), 28 percent learned from a professor, 12 percent from a classmate, and 15 percent found it themselves. (Q13)
- 69 percent of students participated in a library research instruction session in the past year. Of that group, 27 percent attended one class, 36 percent attended two to five classes, and 5 percent attended more than five. (Q15)
- 76 percent of Alpha Company students reported that they study in their room, and 40 percent of those state that they do not study in the library because of the requirement of wearing the regulation uniform in the library. Only 8 percent report that they study in the library. (Q20 and Q21)

Data from this survey, along with results from the 2003 *LibQUAL+ Survey of Library Quality*, formed the backbone of the library's component of the College's Quality Enhancement Plan for the 2004 Southern Association of Colleges and Schools (SACS) reaffirmation.

Literature Searches in Biology

In an attempt to take biology students beyond the textbook and into primary science literature, a literature search exercise was designed collaboratively between library faculty and a biology faculty member as a teaching method in an upper-level genetics course. Integral to the project was a library instruction session designed to teach students about appropriate databases, search methodologies, and evaluation of materials. Instrumental in breaking down barriers to student research are the increasing numbers of scholarly databases available to students throughout the last five years and the ease with which these are searched. The goal of this research project continues to be the exposure of students to the primary science literature via use of article abstracts. However, advances in technology and growing numbers of scholarly journals available electronically enable high-quality information to

Figure 10.5
Alpha Company Focus Group Survey of Student
Information-Seeking Behaviors
A Company
(April 2003)

Please circle one:
Freshman   Sophomore   Junior   Senior

Research patterns:
1. What is your major?
2. Approximately how many class assignments did you have this year that required some kind of information gathering (research papers, reports, book reports, etc.)?
    None   One   2–5   More than 5
3. Did you use material (books, journal articles, etc.) from the Daniel Library for this project?
4. Was the Daniel Library's book collection adequate for your research needs? Please explain why or why not.
5. Were the Daniel Library's indexes and databases adequate for your research needs? Please explain why or why not.
6. Was the Daniel Library's journal collection adequate for your research needs? Please explain why or why not.
7. If you answered **NO to question #3**, where and how did you get the needed information for your research project?
    Other libraries _____
    Interlibrary loan _____
    Your professor's collection _____
    The Internet _____
    Other (please explain) _____
8. If you answered **NO to question #3,** what did the Daniel Library not have that you needed?
9. Did you get material (books, journal articles, etc.) from interlibrary loan?
10. If you answered **YES to question #9**, approximately how many items did you get?
    One   2–5 items   More than 5 items
11. Assuming you did not wait until the last minute, did the interlibrary loan material arrive in time to use in your research project?

Research strategies:
12. What database(s) do you use for research in your major?
13. How did you learn about this (these) database(s)? Please check all that apply.
    Professor recommended _____
    Librarian recommended _____
    Learned about it in a research instruction class _____
    Classmate recommended _____
    Found it yourself _____
    Other (please specify) _____
14. Does this database (or databases) generally supply the information you need?
15. Approximately how many times in the past year have you received library research instruction, taught by librarians, in your academic classes?
    Never   Once   2–5 times   More than 5 times
16. What was the topic of your most recent research project?

Figure 10.5 (continued)

17. Describe how you found journal articles for that project.
    - What resources did you use?
    - Did you use indexes and databases?
    - Which ones?
    - What other resources did you use?
    - What key words did you use to search for articles on your topic?
    - **Approximately** what percent of the journal articles you found on your topic were full text? _____
    - **Approximately** what percent of the journal articles you found on your topic were in paper format? _____
    - **Approximately** what percent of the journal articles you found on your topic were on microfilm or microfiche? _____
    - **Approximately** what percent of the journal articles you found on your topic were not available in the Daniel Library? _____
18. What would you do if your search retrieved too many hits?
19. What would you do if your search retrieved too few hits?

Study Patterns:

20. Where do you do most of your studying?
    Own room _____
    Classroom _____
    Library _____
    Other (please describe) _____
21. Why do you study there?
22. What time of day (or night) do you do most of your studying?
23. If you study in the library, where do you work?
24. If you do not study in the library, why not?
    Noise _____
    Lack of study space _____
    Hours don't fit my schedule _____
    Have to wear uniform _____
    No snacks _____
    Other (please describe) _____
25. How do you use the library? (Please check all that apply.)
    Study _____
    Research _____
    Get help for papers and projects _____
    Use the computers for research _____
    Write papers _____
    Check out books _____
    Photocopy class material _____
    Check e-mail _____
    Read magazines/newspapers _____
    Other (please specify) _____
26. The Daniel Library is scheduled for a major renovation in the next two years. What suggestions do you have for making the library a more conducive place for study and research?

Figure 10.5 (continued)

Computer Experience and Use

27. Do you have a computer in your room?
28. If yes, what kind?
   PC ____
   Macintosh _____
29. Is it a desktop or a laptop?
30. What operating system do you use?
   Windows 9x ____
   Windows ME ____
   Windows XP ____
   Windows 2000____
   Linux ____
   Mac OS ____
31. Which of the following Internet browsers do you prefer?
   Internet Explorer ____
   Netscape Navigator ____
32. If the library provided network connections, would you bring your laptop to work in the library?
33. If the library provided Internet-accessible and Microsoft Office–equipped laptops for check out for library use only, would you take advantage of this service?
34. If you could add one computer-related service to the library, what would it be?
Final question:
35. As a college senior, what do you know now about research that you wish you had known three or four years ago when you were starting your college career? For example, what is the most significant research trick or technique you have learned and how did you learn it?

reach students quickly. Therefore the focus of student instruction is twofold: to develop (1) gatherers of information and (2) evaluators or discerners of information.

Throughout the semester, students repeatedly searched science literature on a variety of different subjects, and were assessed on their abilities to complete the task and thereby demonstrate abilities to use skills. Literature searches were worth 12.5 percent of a student's final grade. Students demonstrated they could successfully retrieve information on a variety of topics using scientific bibliographic databases. In addition, students indicated that this was an enjoyable learning activity.

At semester's end, after completing four literature searches, students were asked to evaluate the activity. Overwhelmingly they felt that literature searches helped them during the course by assisting them in understanding textbook material (85 percent), learning vocabulary (98 percent), improving problem solving (66 percent), and developing a better appreciation for the field of genetics (100 percent). Students also

Figure 10.6
Evaluation of Literature Search Activity by Students

Yes   No
1. Did the literature searches help you to understand textbook material?
2. Did the literature searches help you learn and understand vocabulary words?
3. Did the literature searches help with your problem solving?
4. Did the literature searches give you a better appreciation for the field of genetics?
5. The four searches combined were worth 100 points (12.5 percent) of your total 800 points.
6. Do you feel that you got adequate credit for the work that you put in?
7. Would you prefer to do four literature searches rather than one research paper during one semester?
8. Were the directions clear as to what was expected from you?
9. We spent one 2-hour lab period learning how to do the literature searches. Was this adequate training?
10. Was the training period necessary or not (because you already knew how to search databases)?

felt that they received adequate credit for their work (83 percent), and they preferred conducting four literature searches rather than writing one research paper (98 percent). They also felt that the directions and expectations were very clear (98 percent), and a two-hour lab period provided adequate training time (98 percent) (see Figure 10.6).

In 1998, when researchers first collaborated on ways to connect genetics students with primary science literature, online, end-user-focused databases of scientific literature were not as readily available as they are today. Additionally, students, while already quite computer savvy, were not so familiar with scholarly, scientific resources and methods of searching and evaluating results. Possibly for these reasons, early student assessment of the activity was usually positive as students found the research instruction valuable and enlightening.

Since 1998–1999, the research universe has changed dramatically. Scholarly, full-text databases are available in nearly every school, public, and academic library, and students develop and hone searching and evaluative skills at younger ages. In the 2003 assessment, fewer students reported that extensive research instruction was useful, and many felt they had already learned what they needed during Biology 101 (where they also learn to review biology literature) and in Citadel 101 (a first-year experience that devotes considerable time to research instruction).

Overall, assessment is worth the time and effort if and only if results are analyzed and used to improve what is evaluated. Upon reviewing student responses from the latest assessment, the two collaborating faculty members deliberated on what had caused the change. It was speculated that this particular group of students were more advanced researchers than previous classes, or that they did not like literature searches and were unhappy with any aspect of them, or that they really were already information literate.

In considering research experiences that could be available to students today, it is entirely plausible that they could enter a course conversant with identifying and searching science databases, evaluating results, and using information effectively. Externally, many students have grown up online and have been exposed to quality material from numerous sources. Internally, at least at the Citadel, research and writing are components of many courses taken. By the time students reach an upper-level genetics class they have done biology field research and searched science literature to support their findings, and they have participated in extensive research instruction through their first-year experience course and other core curriculum and major courses.

To test this belief, the library and biology faculty members are revising the instruction for next semester. Instead of teaching students to conduct literature reviews, they will be given a directed task. The instructors will be present to observe what students are able to do, and where, or if, they need guidance.

LibQUAL+

In the spring of 2003 the Citadel Library participated in *LibQUAL+ Survey of Library Quality*.[8] The abundance of information provided by this instrument will continue to be analyzed for some time, but results have been utilized in both the library's annual report and the college's 2004 reaffirmation document for the Southern Association of Colleges and Schools (SACS). In addition, the library is using students' responses about access to information, effect of service, library as place, and personal control as supporting documentation for its part in the college's Quality Enhancement Plan in the SACS reaffirmation process.

MANAGING THE PROCESS

If there are key components of the Citadel Library's program of assessment, these may best be described as bottom-up, based on collaborations with other faculty in the college, methodologies that are as simple as possible, and results that are measurable and used to improve what is being measured. All assessment efforts were initiated by librarians collaborating with faculty colleagues rather than mandated from above by administrators and, with the exception of *LibQUAL+*, were developed in-house. Starting with the simple goal of measuring what students are learning in one aspect of one course, seeking a methodology within one's capabilities, and gathering solid data are admirable goals for assessment. Indeed, as Barclay writes, librarians should not be stymied by perceived difficulties and roadblocks associated with effective assessment (e.g., lack of institutional support, perceived difficulty of the evaluation process, and time constraints). Instead, librarians should move past these hurdles to meaningful assessment and perform the best evaluation possible with the skills and resources at hand.[9] Barclay is by no means advocating careless research. An issue as vital as this to the library profession demands the best research possible; however, "some hard evaluation data, even if the data may be less than perfect, are better than either no data at all or soft data obtained from anecdotal observation and surveys of student satisfaction."[10] Elaborate statistical support for data collection and evaluation is great; however, pencil and paper pre- and posttesting of student learning are equally meaningful. Insights into how well student needs are met can be accomplished through a debriefing upon completion of research papers.

Gathering data is not the end of the assessment process. There must be a willingness and commitment to study data. If one asks the question, one must be prepared to hear the answer, which is sometimes a painful exercise. Each time we assess something, we should be prepared to try and do it better the next time. This requires taking hard looks at results and making changes. For example, through various assessment instruments, Citadel students have said the library did not have the journals needed for their research, they did not study in the library because it was too noisy, and there were not enough group and individual study areas. However, students also demonstrated through pre- and posttesting that they were able to find books and articles on given topics.

A varied and sustained program of outcomes assessment has enabled us to define what we are trying to do in our instruction program and why we are doing it, examine why we do it the way we do, and determine if it is working. Outcomes assessment alerts us to what students know and do not know about library research, thus allowing librarians to adapt instruction to the needs of students. It also helps us to determine what we are doing right and what we are doing wrong, what needs more emphasis, and what students already "get." In short, our instruction is better because we know how we are doing.

Perseverance in measuring the success of what one does, and the collection and analysis of useful data, can develop into greater support from administrators as they report college-wide assessment to governing and accreditation agencies. Such support may aid in continuing and expanding assessment efforts and to correcting problems exposed by assessment. Information gained from the Citadel Library's assessment projects has resulted in additional funding for more full-text databases and the creation of more and better-quality study areas. The assessment circle is closed when information is acted upon.

CONCLUSION: NEXT STEPS

Outcomes assessment is vital to the library both internally and externally. It is also essential to know when enough information has been gathered. Thus, assessment projects have a life span. The work begun ten years ago of evaluating research skills of first-year students is evolving toward an information literacy standard as a requirement for graduation. The multiyear focus group study of the research practices of history majors is now focusing on political science majors. Instead of teaching biology majors to conduct literature searches, they will now be required to demonstrate research skills required for the course. Two years remain in the four-year study of the information seeking behaviors of a diverse group of undergraduates. Finally, the library plans to again participate in *LibQUAL+* in 2006 when those who participated as freshmen are seniors.

NOTES

1. See Peter Hernon and Robert E. Dugan, *An Action Plan for Outcomes Assessment* (Chicago: American Library Association, 2002); and Timothy K. Daugherty and Elizabeth W. Carter, "Assessment of Outcome-Focused Library Instruction in Psychology," *Journal of Instructional Psychology* 24 (1997): 32, for a fuller discussion of the pretest/posttest.

2. Donald Barclay, "Evaluating Library Instruction: Doing the Best You Can with What You Have," *RQ* 33 (Winter 1993): 195.

3. Barclay, "Evaluating Library Instruction," 196.

4. Barclay, "Evaluating Library Instruction," 197–198.

5. Daugherty and Carter, "Assessment of Outcome-Focused Library Instruction," 32.

6. Barclay, "Evaluating Library Instruction," 197.

7. For a complete treatment of Seiden's research, see Peggy Seiden, Kris Szmborski, and Barbara Norelli, "Undergraduate Students in the Digital Library: Information Seeking Behavior in a Heterogeneous Environment" (Chicago: American Library Association, 1997), available at http://www.ala.org/Content/ContentGroups/ACRL1/Nashville_1997_Papers/Seiden,_Szymborski,_and_Norelli.htm (accessed September 21, 2003).

8. *LibQUAL+* (Washington, D.C.: Association of Research Libraries, 2003), available at http://www.libqual.org/index.cfm (accessed September 21, 2003).

9. Barclay, "Evaluating Library Instruction," 196.

10. Barclay, "Evaluating Library Instruction," 196.

CHAPTER 11

Four Perspectives on Assessment and Evaluation

Peter Hernon and Robert E. Dugan

For years, different literatures have provided extensive coverage of measures (e.g., input, output, performance, efficiency, and productivity), and, more recently, discussion, for instance, has extended to customer-related, outcome, effectiveness, and impact measures. The definition of terms such as *performance measures* has shifted over time, and in some respects *performance measures* is an all-encompassing term or type of measure that even includes indicators of effectiveness and impact. However, in the case of team-based organizations, J. Richard Hackman, professor of social and organizational psychology at Harvard University, sees effectiveness as multidimensional and not confined to organizational outputs or results. It may include the degree to which people work together (*a social aspect*) and grow professionally (*a personal aspect*).[1]

New perspectives on different measures will continue to emerge and incorporate a broader array of issues and variables. As well, disciplines and stakeholders, which serve as a source of funding and/or accountability (e.g., U.S. federal and state governments and U.S. higher education associations), may have their own views about what is important

---

This chapter is adapted from a paper, "Different Perspectives on Assessment and Evaluation: The Need to Refine and Link Them," which was presented at "Library Measures to Fill the Void: Assessing Outcomes," Fifth Northumbria International Conference on Performance Measurement, Collingwood College, University of Durham, Durham City, England, July 28–31, 2003.

to ascertain, relevant measures, and the tool chest of critical methods for gathering evidence that their constituencies should use.

The purpose of this chapter is to:

- Offer a framework to guide future discussion of measures and to demonstrate that currently existing measures have not gained universal acceptance
- Demonstrate that terminology varies across (and even within the perspectives discussed below)
- Place outcomes assessment within a broader assessment and evaluation context

The chapter also illustrates the ability of stakeholders to reshape the discussion of assessment priorities and foci, interpretative measures of "success," and the tool chest of methodologies that reflect their expectations for documenting evidence that demonstrates accountability for excellence. Clearly, outcomes assessment enables educational institutions and their various units to focus on their mission and the extent to which reality matches the aspirations expressed therein.

FOUR PERSPECTIVES

For anyone viewing librarians as managers of knowledge and information, and libraries as service organizations, there are four contexts or perspectives, each of which requires data collection and the relating of data to a planning process that addresses accountability, improved service performance, productivity, and informed decision making. These perspectives, in fact, apply not only to libraries but also to other programs and services within academe, and they provide evidence useful for assessment, accountability, and evaluation. "In general, when an educational institution or one of its components assesses its own performance, it's assessment; when others assess performance, it's accountability."[2] More specifically, "Assessment is a set of initiatives the institution takes to review the results of its actions, and make improvements; accountability is a set of initiatives others take to monitor the results of the institution's actions, and to penalize or reward the institution based on the outcomes"—results.[3] Evaluation, on the other hand, is narrower and, in the case of libraries, produces data to improve service and to ensure that the results relate to the stated mission, goals, and objectives.

The four perspectives discussed here view (1) the *institution and the communities served in the life of the library or the academic department/ program*; (2) the *library or academic department/program in the life of the institution*; (3) the *library, department/program, and institution in the life of the user/customer*; and (4) the *library, program/department, and institution in the life of stakeholders*. These perspectives are not mutually exclusive, and there may be different foci within a perspective (e.g., different expectations between government agencies and higher education accrediting organizations).

The first perspective (*library/academic-program centered*) focuses solely on the library or academic program, and data collection characterizes the library or program on its own terms: its perceived service/ educational priorities and its perceived success in meeting those priorities, as characterized by input, output, and performance measures. Input measures reflect the distribution of resources to accomplish program or service priorities, whereas output and performance measures are the direct products of program activities and are usually measured in terms of how much work the library, or other organizational unit, accomplishes. Output and performance measures focus on the result of having applied inputs. E-metrics tend to comprise output or performance measures. In essence, input, output, and performance measures enable a library or program to "speak" to the institutional administration and stakeholders in terms of what it believes is important, for instance, the number of students served in information literacy programs or the number of uses of a database.[4] Data collected for this perspective also enable libraries/departments/programs to benchmark their performance to other *comparable* libraries, departments, and programs, perhaps as a rationale for requesting additional resource allocation.

The second perspective (*institution centered*) is that of the institution or parent organization. Typically, an academic library/program competes within the institution for scarce resources. The library or academic program may use output and performance measures to demonstrate its contribution toward accomplishing the institution's mission and to define faculty productivity and an acceptable quality of student scholarship. Such measures, however, reflect neither how much students learned nor, in the case of libraries, their contribution to attracting new students and faculty and retaining them.

The third perspective (*user/customer centered*) is that of the students, faculty, staff, administration, and others served by the institution and its library. In part, an institution may treat its users as *customers*. A customer-focus applies more to the services of ancillary units (e.g., bookstores, student unions, and food services) than to educational programs. Nonetheless, this perspective looks directly at users and not at them through another perspective, such as that of the library. The intention is to compare user expectations with service performance—service quality—and to gather data that will document the gap between expectations and performance, and lead to improved service delivery. As Terry G. Vavra, president of Marketing Metrics and professor of marketing, explains, "Perceived performance may . . . reinforce, exceed, or fall short of expectations. If expectations are in any way not met, rendered satisfaction [or service quality] decreases from the baseline level established by expectations. If, on the other hand, expectations are met or exceeded, satisfaction [or service quality] increases and expectations in future . . . uses may be adjusted upward."[5] A critical question is "To what extent, do (should) customer expectations shape the services offered?"[6]

The fourth perspective (*stakeholder centered*) is that of stakeholders; to repeat, they have an interest in the extent to which the institution accomplishes its mission. That interest usually relates to funding or accreditation. They shape an institution's approach to documenting accountability for excellence. Thus, the type of data that libraries, academic programs, and institutions provide these stakeholders may reflect the first and second perspectives (library/program and institution centered). They may also interject new requirements for demonstrating institutional effectiveness and efficiency (e.g., fiscal accountability and educational quality). Those requirements may result in a focus on outcomes, or "what happened *because* of the outputs."[7] For example, in the United States, higher educational associations and regional accrediting organizations increasingly focus on student learning and questions such as:

- What should students learn?
- How well are they learning it?
- What measures and procedures does the institution use to determine the effectiveness of its educational programs?
- To what extent does the institution offer direct (and not so much

indirect) evidence that demonstrates its effectiveness to the public and the accrediting organization?

• What does the institution plan to do with this evidence to improve student learning?

Results-oriented questions such as these serve as a catalyst for the systematic application of outcomes assessment in higher education in the effort to measure, report, and improve institutional effectiveness. Institutions have reported outcomes for years. However, *student outcomes* and *student learning outcomes* differ. The former refer to aggregate statistics on groups of students (e.g., graduation, retention, and transfer rates). Such outcomes are really outputs as they reflect what the institution has accomplished; they do not reflect what (or how much) students have learned. Furthermore, these measures do not answer the five questions mentioned above.

Student learning outcomes document the change in knowledge, attitudes, skills, and behavior over the duration of a program of study, and they deal with question such as "What do students know that they did not know before?" and "What can they do that they could not do before?" For libraries, the key question is "What contribution did they make to the change in the student?" Outcomes assessment focuses on student learning outcomes and, as envisioned by higher education commissions and associations, goes beyond a single course and may look at the success of the partnership between classroom instructors and librarians from a program or institutional perspective. For instance, how does the library's information literacy program contribute to the academic expectations that students should achieve by the time of graduation? The answer to the question is intended to document a vital contribution of the library to the institution's educational programs, especially if the library can demonstrate its contribution to helping students master higher-ordered outcomes—those related to problem solving and critical thinking. However, the answer cannot be based solely on self-reports and anecdotal evidence.

As Kenneth R. Smith, the Eller Distinguished Service Professor of Economics and Faculty Associate to the Provost, University of Arizona, wrote:

[W]e . . . [need to move] from a model in which we package knowledge around the expertise of the faculty to a model based on the learning outcomes realized by students. These outcomes include not only what students know, but also the skills they develop, what they are able to do, and the attitudes of mind that characterize the way they will approach their work over a lifetime of change.[8]

He continues by noting that

This concept of learning requires a shift in focus from the teacher's knowledge to the student's understanding and capabilities. This shift in focus leads to a new perspective on the development of quality in the academic enterprise. More than anything, it requires the faculty to bring the strength of the research paradigm into the learning process.[9]

Peggy D. Rudd, state librarian of Texas, sees outcomes as having application beyond academe and as

benefits or changes for individuals or populations during or after participating in program activities, including new knowledge, increased skills, changed attitudes or values, modified behavior, improved condition, or altered status (e.g., number of children who learned a finger play during story time, . . . [and] number of children who maintained reading skills over the summer as a result of a summer reading program).

When she recommends a "number of people who report being better able to access and use networked information after attending information literacy classes,"[10] in effect, she advocates data collection that focuses on indirect methods (i.e., self-reports) as opposed to direct methods and the examination of their actual performance. Higher education outcomes assessment is beginning to look more at direct methods of gathering evidence and the tool chest of relevant methodologies. E-metrics are appropriate if they contribute to answering the five abovementioned questions.

Some academic librarians and the Association of Research Libraries (ARL) tend to treat customer satisfaction as an outcome. For example, the Association of College and Research Libraries (ACRL), Task Force on Academic Library Outcomes Assessment, maintains that "satisfaction on the part of the user is an outcome. So is dissatisfaction. The task force considers simple satisfaction as a facile outcome, however, too often unrelated to more substantial outcomes that hew more closely to the mission of libraries and the institutions they serve."[11] Educational associations and accrediting organizations in the United States do not all concur. This example illustrates a difference in perspectives and that, in this case, one measure does not apply to a different perspective— one looking at accreditation.

A cost-benefit or cost-effectiveness analysis might pertain to all four perspectives. For the fourth one (stakeholder centered), however, it would be more relevant to a government agency than to an accrediting organization. Clearly, libraries, programs, and institutions need to collect different types of data, ones that show their role and accomplishments from their own perspective, as well as to cast them as contributing to overall institutional effectiveness.

BALANCED SCORECARD

Many businesses and some libraries, mostly located outside the United States, have adopted the concept of the balanced scorecard as an evaluation method. The scorecard is a variety of measures that reflect the performance of the organization from the perspective of each of its stakeholders. The scorecard queries four key areas common to most organizations:

1. How do customers perceive us?
2. How do we look to decision-makers and the community? (financial perspective)
3. What must we excel at? (This question examines the internal working of the organization.)
4. Can we continue to improve and create value?[12]

The balanced scorecard is a tool for strategic management. Implementing the scorecard requires that the administration answer the above-mentioned questions in terms of the present situation and the organization's planning documents. The next step is to define the factors critical for success and then to identify measures that indicate success. All of the measures are combined to generate an overall score.

Roswitha Poll, chief librarian of the University and Regional Library Münster (Germany), discusses a balanced scorecard that includes four perspectives: those of "users," "finances," "processes," and "potentials."

The user perspective involves "reaching a large part of the population as possible and . . . satisfying their information needs with the services offered." Evidence for that perspective rests on outputs (e.g., the percentage of the population registered as actual users and percentage of the population using electronic library services) and simplified outcomes (e.g., user satisfaction rate and user satisfaction with opening times).[13] The next perspective, the financial one, examines the cost-effectiveness of the organization and collects inputs (e.g., total costs of the library per active user); and "processes" focuses on the organization of all processes and operations to support "investment into new developments and [the] improvement of service."[14] Evidence is gathered through the use of input measures (e.g., percentage of all staff costs spent on electronic services and average media processing time). Finally, the potentials perspective describes "the capability of the library to cope with future challenges and [it] addresses . . . [organizational] ability to change and improve."[15] Data collection focuses on inputs such as library budget as a percentage of the institution's budget and number of short-time illnesses per staff member.

Suffice to say, although the balanced scorecard, to some extent, may reflect the four perspectives discussed in this chapter, it infrequently places the customer/user at the center to the degree required in the third (customer-centered) perspective. The scorecard may not look at stakeholders that have a financial oversight role and sufficiently address outcomes assessment as stipulated by accrediting organizations. Undoubtedly, widespread use of the scorecard in the United States would require extensive restructuring and the reassignment of values in its point distribution if the goal is to accommodate outcomes assessment and the customer perspective, and to focus on indicators that have strategic relevance to the educational mission of institutions of higher education.

WHERE DO WE GO FROM HERE?

Coverage of the four perspectives is actually more complex than the previous section suggests, given that additional assessment and evaluation terminology may apply. For instance, outcomes assessment is important when the intent is to measure student learning and the effectiveness of the institution, programs, academic departments, and the library in producing educated graduates who are able to function as

Figure 11.1
Framework for Continuous Program Improvement

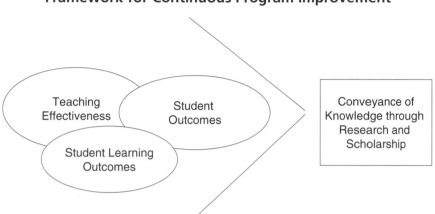

lifelong learners, as stipulated in educational mission and vision statements. However, not to be ignored are *research* outcomes, which view research as a *formal inquiry process* and address the extent to which students have mastered the components of that process. For instance, can they differentiate between a problem and purpose statement?[16] Other questions are "Do libraries have a role in setting and measuring research outcomes?" and "Can indicators of faculty productivity be viewed solely in terms of inputs and outputs?" Undoubtedly, classroom teaching contributes to achievement of student learning outcomes, but how does one determine the extent to which a faculty member has become a successful scholar and researcher? Most likely, the answer is through the use of outputs.

Figure 11.1 serves as a reminder that institutions tend not to look solely at learning. Traditionally, they also focus on teaching, scholarship, and the ability to generate funded research. The difficult issue is to examine the whole picture and accord proper recognition to improving the quality of learning.

For the customer-centered and stakeholder perspectives, a new body of measures, even input measures, might be developed. Figure 11.2 illustrates a set of input measures that address the customer perspective. The numbers are hypothetical but they illustrate a return on investment; tuition monies go for more than classroom instruction and institutional overhead. It is time for more data collection to go beyond merely self-reports. Database vendor usage statistics, for instance, "are

Figure 11.2
Tuition Dollars Contribute to Library Services

Service	Measure Applied	Factors	Total Savings
Studying, which requires the library to be open	Hours open during year = 3,810 $692,612 expended for all salaries, wages, and benefits 355 seats (excluding classroom in library) $692,612/3,810 = $181.79/hour to open $181.79/355 seats = $0.512/seat/hour	Use the library for 1 hour/week each semester That is 30 hours/year x $0.512/seat/hour = $15.36	$15.36
Borrow a reserve book	Average reserve book (undergraduate) = $37.32 Average reserve book (graduate) = $61.94 Average (both) = $42.13	Borrow one reserve book each semester (or two reserve books during the year)	$84.26
Ask a question of the reference staff *or* Use a subject guide created by the reference staff to answer a question	Answered 10,032 questions in FY 2002 Reference salaries = $187,778 plus benefits (18.7%) = $35,114 for a total = $222,892 Cost per question = $22.22	Ask one reference question *or* Use one reference-developed subject guide	$22.22
Use a reference book	Expended $63,431 on reference books (FY 2002) Purchased 336 volumes Average cost = $188.78/volume Assume value is half its cost = $94.39	Consult one reference book during the academic year	$94.39
Borrow a laptop computer	Rental rates seen from $20 to $50/hour Let's use $10/hour	Borrow a laptop once during the year	$10.00
Use a desktop computer to search for information	Rental rates (same as above) Let's use $10/hour	Use a desktop computer once during the year	$10.00
View a VHS videotape for a course	TV with VHS rental rates are $4–6/hour Let's use $4/hour	View a videotape in the library once during the year	$4.00
Access and download full-text articles for a paper from a subscription database *and* print them in the library	Vendor A charges $1–4/article; however, most of the information content is not scholarly Vendor B charges about $20.00/article, including the necessary copyright Let's use $10.00/scholarly article Then, use the library's printers to print the article pages (free at the library) Let's use 5 pages/article at $0.10/page (that's the per page cost to photocopy)	Let's say 2 scholarly articles per course (3 courses per semester; 2 semesters in academic year) Total of 12 articles for the entire year: $120.00 Print the article pages (12 articles at 5 pages/article = 60 pages) That is $6.00	$126.00

Figure 11.2 (continued)

Use the library's proxy server to access and download full-text articles while at home *or* at work	Do not have to come to the library to conduct research (therefore, do not need to pay to park or use subway) Normally take subway to school; $2.00 round trip	Save 1 trip to library each semester via subway That is a total of 2 round trips during the year	$4.00
Borrow a book from the general collection	The average academic book to purchase was $49.10 (2002) Let's use half that cost to reflect a "used book," therefore use = $24.55		$24.55

Total   **$394.78**

easy to obtain and process. However, the standardization of key usage statistics and [the] reporting format is critical."[17] Equally as important, these e-metrics focus on the library-centered, and somewhat on the institution-centered, perspective. They do not necessarily apply to the other two perspectives. However, if a library's information literacy program emphasized instruction in the use of Boolean search operators (e.g., use of AND), it might be hypothesized that as the school term progresses, the number of retrievals per search will be reduced from the number retrieved earlier in the term. Thus, if a vendor's statistics provide the "number of searches" and the "number of hits" per month, the staff could determine if the number of hits per search decreased over the term.[18] This example meets the expectations of accrediting organizations for outcomes assessment and comprises an e-metric, *Boolean search and retrieval (hits) rate*.

CONCLUSION

Institutional effectiveness examines the extent to which institutions meet their stated mission, goals, and objectives. From the vantage point of outcomes assessment, the planning and assessment process focuses on the effectiveness of student learning and the extent to which that learning and the institution's contributions to society center on educating individuals to become lifelong learners who can solve problems and engage in critical thinking. Libraries typically view themselves as playing an integral role in student learning; however, the measures they collect have generally failed to demonstrate that interconnection to the satisfaction of important segments of the stakeholder perspective, which views the educational mission of an academic institution in terms of accountability for excellence.[19] Clearly, mission statements should not be developed and then either discarded or ignored.

As the need to demonstrate accountability has moved beyond the reliance on self-reports and anecdotal evidence, the effort to demonstrate effectiveness increasingly focuses on *quality* measures, perhaps defined in terms of service quality; student satisfaction, graduates of the institution satisfaction, and donor satisfaction; and student learning. When academic institutions focus on knowledge generation and student learning, they might gather evidence of accountability through the use of direct methods more than through self-reports (indirect methods). Student learning outcomes serve as a basis for uniting campus administration and faculty in demonstrating the extent to which the educational mission is accomplished, and equally as important, such outcomes charge everyone with continuous improvement of student learning, or the development of, implementation of, and gathering of evidence (feedback loop) for judging and improving the assessment plan.

Finally, the library profession, and other groups, need to view the spectrum of measures from the four perspectives and to include relevant methodologies as part of their tool chest. Complicating matters, libraries and other institutional players may need guidance as they select from the various options. However, they should not be seduced into believing that measures applicable to the library-centered and institution-centered perspectives necessarily apply fully or adequately to the other two perspectives. The impact of outcomes assessment is only starting to unfold, and such assessment is intended to alter campus cultures over time. To be successful in an environment that increasingly focuses on accountability for excellence, academic libraries need to contribute broadly to student learning and to gain recognition for their successes. However, their contributions and successes will be linked to outcomes assessment and their ability to contribute to the development of educated individuals who become lifelong learners. Thus, any evidence gathered must demonstrate the development of students from the time of their entry into a program of study to their graduation: changes in behavior, knowledge, problem solving, critical thinking, and communication skills.

Such behavioral change, linked to a partnership role between classroom faculty and librarians, represents an expanded responsibility and a more active role in the learning process—a role that requires libraries to engage in outcomes assessment. Still, we must be mindful of the warning that Cecilia L. López, then associate director of the Higher Learning Commission, North Central Association of Colleges and Schools, issued when she wrote:

> In institutional self-studies and accreditation team reports, it is still unusual to find any reference to librarians' contributions to the development of learning objectives for information literacy skills or to the interpretation of the outcomes of assessing those skills. I would go one step further and suggest that it is an additional loss to the nationwide effort to assess and improve student learning that, although a number of librarians hold faculty status, they do not often appear in the membership of institutional or departments' assessment committees.[20]

The challenge for all of us engaged in assessment and evaluation is to be mindful of the four perspectives and the different uses of terminology. Each perspective is legitimate and performs an important function. Libraries exist in a larger environment, one shaped by their users and nonusers, the institution, and relevant stakeholders. In the future more measures, not all of which can be adequately captured as percentages, will emerge, and librarians and their institutional partners will need help in their application, especially when data collection depends on the use of (1) experimental designs involving pretesting and posttesting, and (2) longitudinal data collection (the use of repeated measures).

The jigsaw puzzle entitled "assessment and evaluation" continues to increase in size, scope, and the number of pieces. In fact, the picture that the puzzle represents is now clouded, but we all should enjoy assembling it, especially if funding organizations will support the assembly of a puzzle that depicts the four perspectives and the major players in each perspective.

NOTES

1. See J. Richard Hackman, *Leading Teams: Setting the Stage for Great Performances* (Boston: Harvard Business School Press, 2002); and J. Richard Hackman and Richard E. Walton, "Leading Groups in Organizations," in *Designing Effective Work Groups*, ed. Paul S. Goodman and Associates (San Francisco: Jossey-Bass, 1986), 72–120.

2. Richard Frye, *Assessment, Accountability, and Student Learning Outcomes* (Bellingham: Western Washington University, n.d.), 1, available at http://www.ac.wwu.edu/dialogue/issue2.html (accessed February 28, 2004).

3. Frye, *Assessment, Accountability.*

4. See Robert E. Dugan and Peter Hernon, "Outcomes Assessment: Not Synonymous with Inputs and Outputs," *The Journal of Academic Librarianship* 28 (November 2002): 376–380.

5. Terry G. Vavra, *Improving Your Measurement of Customer Satisfaction: A Guide to Creating, Conducting, Analyzing, and Reporting Customer Satisfaction Measurement Programs* (Milwaukee, Wisc.: ASQ Quality Press, 1997), 42.

6. Most of the techniques currently used to listen to library users (customers) involve self-reports. LibQUAL+, which enables libraries to compare themselves to peer institutions and to gather some general information about the expectations of the campus community, is now one of the more widely used survey instruments in academic libraries in the United States. However, instead of relying *solely* on an instrument that mostly generates a low response rate and does not produce results reflective of a multicultural environment, libraries need to settle on (and probe) those expectations related to use of a physical library building and a digital environment that they are willing to resource as service priorities. As a result, the user community realizes that its voice matters—leads to improved service.

7. K. Motylewski and C. Horn, "Frequently Asked OBE [Outcome-Based Evaluation] Questions" (Washington, D.C.: Institute of Museum and Library Services, n.d.), 2, available at http://www.imls.gov/grants/current/crnt_outcomes.htm (accessed February 28, 2004).

8. Kenneth R. Smith, "New Roles and Responsibilities for the University Library: Advancing Student Learning through Outcomes Assessment," *Journal of Library Administration* 35 (2001): 29.

9. Smith, "New Roles and Responsibilities."

10. Peggy D. Rudd, "Documenting the Difference: Demonstrating the Value of Libraries through Outcome Measurement," in *Perspectives on Outcome Based Evaluation for Libraries and Museums* (Washington, D.C.: Institute of Museum and Library Services, 1999), 20, available at http://www.imls.gov/pubs/pdf/pubobe.pdf (accessed February 28, 2004).

11. Peter Hernon and Robert E. Dugan, *An Action Plan for Outcomes Assessment in Your Library* (Chicago: American Library Association, 2002), 30. For a perspective on LibQUAL+ as providing evidence of outcomes, see Donald L. DeWitt, ed., "Evaluating the Twenty-first Century Library: The Association of Research Libraries New Measures Initiative, 1997–2001," *Journal of Library Administration* 35 (2001): 1–91.

12. Robert S. Kaplan and David P. Norton, "The Balanced Scorecard—Measures That Drive Performance," *Harvard Business Review* 70 (January-February 1992): 96.

13. Roswitha Poll, "Managing Service Quality with the Balanced Score-card," in *Advances in Library Administration and Organization*, vol. 20, ed. Edward D. Garten and Delmus W. Williams (Amsterdam: Elsevier Science, 2003), 216.

14. Poll, "Managing Service Quality," 222.

15. Poll, "Managing Service Quality," 223.

16. Hernon and Dugan, *An Action Plan for Outcomes Assessment in Your Library*, 67–68. An introductory research methods course therefore might have student learning outcomes, such as (1) develop one problem statement and its justification for basic research and another for applied research; (2) define research as an inquiry process and describe the steps involved—including the formulation of objectives and a hypothesis, and gathering data—maximizing reliability and internal validity; (3) distinguish between different types of research (e.g., descriptive, experimental, and qualitative); (4) identify the components of a research study and provide examples of each; (5) distinguish between independent, dependent, and control variables; (6) provide examples of research misconduct and assess their implications for the integrity of the peer review process; (7) explain how falsification can be intentional and unintentional; (8) distinguish between probability and nonprobability sampling (for a given problem, students might be asked to explain the type of sampling technique they would apply); (9) differentiate between type I and type II errors; and (10) distinguish between reliability and validity.

Given the number of outcomes that any researcher could generate, the list might be more manageable if someone grouped the outcomes selected by broad topic such as "introduction or overview of research," "statistical concepts," "ethical issues in research," "the problem statement," "measuring research variables," "experimental research," "descriptive research," and so on.

17. Wonsik Shim and Charles R. McClure, "Improving Database Vendors' Usage Statistics Reporting through Collaboration between Libraries and Vendors," *College & Research Libraries* 63 (November 2002): 499.

18. See Hernon and Dugan, *An Action Plan for Outcomes Assessment in Your Library*, 115.

19. In 2003, Congress deliberated about renewal of the Higher Education Act. Those deliberations stressed accountability and the cost of an education. Congress is looking "for ways to hold colleges more accountable for the performance of their students and to curb increases in the institutions' prices." For instance, see Stephen Burd, "Republican Leaders Stress Accountability and Cost Issues in Hearing on Higher Education Act," *The Chronicle of Higher Education* (May 14, 2003), 1, available at http://chronicle.com/daily/2003/05/2003051401n.htm (accessed May 20, 2003).

20. Cecilia L. López, "Assessment of Student Learning: Challenges and Strategies," *The Journal of Academic Librarianship* 28 (November 2002): 356.

CHAPTER 12

Institutional Perspectives

Robert E. Dugan

All stakeholders of, and groups within, higher education institutions have their own perspective about institutional effectiveness and accountability. In some cases, stakeholders and various groups share common characteristics among their different perspectives. Oftentimes, however, each stakeholder and group has a unique perspective that must be identified and understood when planning for and conducting the institutional assessment process. Complicating matters, accountability involves many stakeholders and constituent groups; for example,

- Institutional leadership (e.g., a chancellor or vice president for academic affairs, or a provost)
- Institutional academic administration (e.g., deans)
- Departmental and program chairs
- Faculty
- Students
- Parents
- Alumnae or alumni
- Regional and national accrediting organizations
- State executives (e.g., governors)
- State legislatures
- State education commissions
- Members of Congress

A shared perspective relates to institutional effectiveness. However, the purpose for undertaking an assessment effort varies by stakeholder and constituent group: Is institutional effectiveness conducted for evaluative purposes to satisfy an accountability requirement, or is it conducted to identify institutional functions and services that need improving? The underlying purpose for assessment—evaluation or improvement—oftentimes results in conflicting perspectives held by institutional stakeholders and constituent groups. Assessment efforts for evaluation are analogous to a reporting function. The institution conducts the assessment processes required to comply with accountability mandates from stakeholders (e.g., the federal government) and files a report such as one for a self-study.

Assessment efforts for self-improvement seek to (1) discover the degree of success in gaining institutional effectiveness and to improve continuously and (2) align better the measured learning outcomes with the institution's stated educational mission and expected learning achievements. The first perspective ascertains and focuses on educational quality, whereas the second one improves student learning. Both perspectives may be intertwined, and they are based on a systematic model of identifying objectives and measures of standards, implementing strategies to address the objectives, measuring progress toward meeting the identified standards, reviewing and evaluating the findings, and using the information from the evaluative step to identify and recommend changes. Any institutional perspective influences other institutional perspectives and, in turn, influences institutional culture.

INSTITUTIONAL PERSPECTIVE

A higher education institution is composed of both horizontal and vertical organizations. The vertical organization or structure includes the faculty, staff, and students of the various schools, disciplines, and departments, whereas the horizontal organization or structure represents the provision of institution-wide services and functions shared by two or more of the vertical structures, such as student activities, library, and financial aid. The institution's perspective is actually a hybrid and accumulation of the diverse perspectives held by the horizontal and vertical structures of the entire entity.

What influences the perspectives concerning accountability and institutional effectiveness? In addition to the individual and shared perspectives of the higher education institution's community (primarily student, faculty, and employees), other influences and contributors to the institutional perspective include the institution's governing authority (e.g., trustees) and extrainstitutional stakeholders and constituencies, such as the alumnae/alumni, prospective students and their parents, sources of funding, state educational governing bodies, accrediting organizations, and local, state, and federal government. Many of these stakeholders and constituencies eventually make judgments concerning the value and quality of the institution through individual and group actions and decisions evidenced in part, for instance, by recruitment, retention, and persistence; funding; and accreditation. Specifically, the perspective concerning institutional effectiveness influences, and is influenced by, the institution's culture as is reflected in planning and conducting assessment throughout the horizontal and vertical hierarchy, framed along a continuum of "we do it because we have to" to "we do it because it is a tool in helping the institution review, evaluate, and improve educational quality."

How does one discover the assessment culture and perspective of an institution? Institutional culture refers to the values, philosophies, and ideologies that characterize the institution—what people value and believe in. The institution's general education perspective—what it expects its students to learn and achieve—is most often found in its mission statement and in the educational objectives aligned with the core curriculum. Each horizontal and vertical unit comprising the institution has its own organizational culture; in reality, organizational and institutional perspectives and culture continually shape each other. Perspectives and culture may also be observed throughout the institutional assessment process; for example, documents from the strategic planning process including mission statements, values, goals, objectives (strategies and methodologies), and identified expectations (standards); extent of the visibility of the outcomes assessment effort and its reporting; and the availability and amount of resources (e.g., funding) directed toward the effort.

Additionally, "institutional effectiveness" may mean different things to different institutions and its community members. Do the institutional members have and share a common, locally developed language, or do they use a common language from the literature concerning assessment? The community should, at a minimum, agree on working definitions and their context for efficiency, effectiveness, evaluation, assessment, and outcomes. As an example, without agreement on the application of the definitions, institutional members may internally confuse outcomes with outputs, especially concerning aggregated student outcomes such as retention rate and graduation rate. Some institutions would consider these two measures to be outputs, and other institutions would label them as aggregate student outcomes.

A perspective is also discovered by identifying where campus leadership for assessment originates and/or is coordinated and facilitated. Does that leadership reside with the chancellor, the faculty, an assessment team appointed by the central administration, or an office of institutional research? Part of that discovery is to identify the holder of the most visible role in the institutional context concerning assessment. Is it personnel-driven, such as that of the president, board of trustees, department chairs, or individual faculty? Or, is the most visible role functional-based, such as the faculty assembly (senate), the senior administrative team, or the assembled department chairs?

Furthermore, the inclusiveness of the assessment process—the involvement of members of the institutional community—is also a perspective. A tightly held outcomes assessment process with little involvement will illustrate and influence the perspective of others as to the degree of institutional openness, and even to its trust of community members.

Commitment by community members to the assessment process is another example of institutional perspective. Institutional self-studies and external peer-review evaluation visits are a commonplace mechanism for accreditation, from which assessment may be characterized as "burdensome," "a chore," or "an add-on" to day-to-day responsibilities, arousing resistance to compliance and resulting, oftentimes, in a short-lived commitment.[1] There might be differences in the perspective depending on whether the commitment to assessing student learning were to come from within the institution—from administrators, faculty, and academic support departments.[2] Clearly, institutional administrators must be committed to the assessment process as an ongoing sustained process, and they must provide consistent support to the process as an institutional effort to improve learning.[3]

Continuous improvement will likely change institutional culture. For example, the commitment to continuous improvement via assessment cannot be delegated to faculty members while institutional administrators move on to other matters.[4] As evidence of effort, learning outcomes should be directly related to the institution's mission, and the assessment of those outcomes should be within the institution's financial and other resources.[5]

Besides the institutional inclusiveness and commitment to improvement, a perspective will also be evident in the means applied to conduct assessment, such as the types of assessment measurements applied. One perspective would be that the institution and faculty were satisfied with indirect measures such as student and alumni satisfaction surveys. Another institutional perspective would find such dependence on indirect measures inappropriate for the actual reporting of findings to institutional stakeholders. Reliance on commercial-produced standardized tools rather than developing institutional-based measures to capture local/institutional learning rather than "national-norms" may not be as well received as locally developed measurements for learned skills, values, content, and behaviors. Does the ability and willingness to differentiate between student outcomes and student learning outcomes, and the appropriate use and reporting of inputs, throughputs, and outputs as such—instead of reporting outputs as outcomes—exist?

Institutional support is a perspective. Does the institution train the faculty or expect them to learn assessment techniques and methodologies on their own? Does the institution support faculty attendance at assessment workshops and conferences? Is there a collection of assessment resources and support (how to construct a learning objective, for example) available and publicized to faculty? Institutional leaders need to frame a commitment to assessment as a professionally responsible endeavor, integral to teaching that contributes to higher education's learning about student learning.[6] A perspective would be evident in the emphasis on enhancement and improvement in the classroom as opposed to evaluating a faculty member.

Are there institutional communications concerning assessment and improvement? Is the evidence of learning and "best practices" shared and reported both internally and externally? Does an open, inclusive, and continuous evaluation process influence the planning and budgeting processes identifiable by all community members? By understanding institutional culture, a culture that both creates and reinforces values, one may engage institutional community members in ways that they will respond to and support.[7]

FACULTY PERSPECTIVE

Faculty may have differing perspectives from the institution. Faculty may see the "evaluation" process as a personnel issue and/or an administrative ploy to evaluate classroom teaching, and therefore they view it as a threat to their academic freedom rather than as an effort to improve learning. They may view the current grading system as adequate and appropriate assessment, and may be unwilling to spend time to design and implement a project that is filled with educational jargon, burdened by process, and expected to soon fade in both importance and urgency as did other, earlier educational experiments. Furthermore, promotion and tenure processes may not place any (or sufficient) value on advancing the learning process. Additionally, faculty may propose that outcomes assessment employ off-the-shelf standardized tests administered at the institutional or school level rather than at the departmental or course level.[8] Other faculty members may hold the perspective that assessment does not meet its stated objective of demonstrating whether or not learning occurs.[9]

Although regional accreditors hold institutions accountable for educational quality, student learning outcomes assessment is primarily a program- and course-based effort. As a result, institutions depend on faculty for identifying, designing, measuring, and reporting student learning outcomes. Considering the aforementioned perspectives held by some faculty concerning learning outcomes, how do institutions ally with the faculty to conduct and support the general assessment process?

Faculty must be included in the development of the general educational expectations of the institution as stated in the mission statement and delineated within the core curriculum. Additionally, it is important to determine what faculty members' value in their discipline, teaching, research, and service, and then to relate assessment to those values.[10] Based upon their perspectives, what are faculty willing to evaluate and be held accountable for?[11]

As stated previously, institutional perspectives and culture influence each other. Culture may be used to alter perspectives, and of course, institutional and organizational cultures influence one's perspective depending on where they are situated within the organizational structure. Therefore, institutional culture must proactively engage faculty members to become aware of, and to contemplate, their perspectives concerning outcomes assessment practices[12] by directly linking their contributions to the stated educational mission of the institution.

While it is the responsibility of institutional leadership to create an environment in which teaching, learning, and student achievement of expected learning outcomes are institutional priorities, faculty leadership must evolve and be involved in the institutional assessment process. Faculty members are responsible for student learning; their involvement enhances the quality of outcomes and the assessment process. The inclusion of faculty in the outcomes assessment process should be viewed as institutionally critical; to exclude faculty from the process will doom the assessment effort.[13]

The institution must directly confront the faculty perspective that the evidence of student learning compiled and reported from the outcomes assessment process will not be used as a teacher evaluation tool. Outcomes assessment is appropriately applied as measures over time in several courses and throughout a program or discipline, not as a singular occurrence.

The application of standardized tests may not be as effective as locally developed instruments. Faculty-developed tests can focus on the identified educational objectives of the institution and may, in fact, yield better projections of student performance throughout the curriculum for general education and the specific discipline.[14]

Additionally, changes and improvements need not be exhaustive and fully implemented simultaneously to be effective. Incremental changes can be applied and tested to ensure effectiveness is indeed improved rather than a larger, untested, and unproven series of changes that may do more harm than good.[15]

Providing incentives for participation would help convince faculty of the institution's commitment and support for the outcomes assessment effort. Does the institutional leadership publicly recognize faculty contributions? Are training and support funds made available to assist faculty to establish and maintain assessment practices?[16]

According to Raymond Rodrigues, "If assessment is to become part of the institution's culture, administrators need to recognize it as such and not perceive it as something to be assigned to faculty members while the administrators move on to other matters."[17] Does the institution review and respond to the findings reported by faculty to enhance and improve student learning, or are the reports merely filed for referral when it is time for reaccreditation?

AN ACADEMIC SUPPORT DEPARTMENT—THE LIBRARY

Perspectives of academic support departments, such as the library, may also vary from those of the institution and faculty. As with the faculty, the academic support unit must be familiar with the general education objectives of the institution as stated in its mission. What has the institution determined is important for students to learn or achieve? Additionally, the support department must also be aware of faculty-developed educational objectives at the department and/or course level in order to provide and sustain support for assessment efforts. Specifically, how does the academic library contribute to institutional-wide assessment? Furthermore, how is the contribution identified, measured, analyzed, and reported; to whom is it reported; and for what purposes?[18]

Libraries contribute to the overall education mission of the institution of which they are a part. They are changing from collecting and reporting informative measures concerning inputs and outputs to the actual assessment of various types of outcomes. Library input measures date back to the early twentieth century; output measures have been actively collected and analyzed since the 1980s. Inputs, and later outputs, were most often applied to managerial decision making such as collection development and staffing, and benchmarking—comparing the library's measured activities to its identified peers.[19] "Given a choice," wrote Sharon Markless and David Streatfield, "librarians would probably like to be judged on their ability to provide a wide range of freely available services to meet all likely needs and to measure their success in terms of quality of use."[20]

One of the most important educational contributions that academic libraries can provide to the institution is the linkage of information literacy to student learning outcomes. An information literacy program can be effective in increasing student information seeking, retrieval, and evaluation skills, and in developing the awareness of the value of life-long learning. Regrettably, one study found that few functional information literacy programs were underway and that even less assessment was conducted, even though there was institutional acceptance, however modest, for such an effort.[21]

Regional accrediting organizations have identified information literacy as a general education component and learning outcome. For example, the Commission on Higher Education of the Middle States Association of Colleges and Schools has determined information literacy to be a meta-outcome, "invoked any time a student attempts to learn anything, in any discipline, whether or not a library is involved in the information gathering process. In other words, information literacy is invoked during the acquisition of all other learning outcomes that an institution might incorporate in its curriculum."[22] Middle States expects information literacy to be addressed in the outcomes assessment plans of each member institution.[23]

Academic libraries have been instructing students concerning their information skills for more than a century. However, their effort has not been widely incorporated into the institutions' perspective of a desired, general education objective, as reflected in their mission statements. Information literacy, as an instructional service provided by the library to encourage and assist students when using its resources and services, has thus been culturalized as a perspective by the institution, the faculty, and the library as the librarian's "turf." As a result, the institution and the faculty may have lost a sense of responsibility for institutionalizing information literacy's skills and values.[24] Faculty may not allocate adequate class time to information literacy or see value in using class time for student instruction by librarians, and may expect that a computer literate student is also information literate.

The perspective of information literacy as the sole responsibility of the library is changing. For example, when considering information literacy in the institutions' self-studies for accreditation, Middle States expects that "all personnel involved in curriculum development, teaching, the assessment of learning, and individual and institutional improvement will confront the subject of information literacy."[25] Information literacy as a learning outcome is an institution-wide general education objective that is a direct support activity for the institution, but it cannot be viewed as the exclusive territory of librarians. Therefore, the library must guide the institution and faculty toward an understanding of the critical educational importance of information literacy as an educational, social, economic, and lifelong set of skills and values.

The library's perspective is changing as librarians reach out to faculty in a collaborative effort to derive a positive outcome for this educational objective. Librarians may create instruction modules that are offered in the library's instruction area, in a faculty member's classroom, and by other technology-based means such as the Web or video streaming. Librarians and faculty are "expected to work together to develop, implement, and assess a strategy for information literacy instruction that will lead to individual and institutional improvement."[26] Such collaboration encourages dialogue between librarians and faculty to find ways to improve academic programs and student learning.[27]

Librarians must leverage the information literacy efforts and work of the Association of College and Research Libraries (ACRL) to communicate the definition, characteristics, and standards of an "information-literate" person to the faculty and institution. Specifically, librarians can support and partner with faculty in the assessment process by identifying, measuring, analyzing, and reporting desired information literacy skills and competencies. Additionally, the library can support the institutional effort by applying the assessment process on other general education behaviors and values such as increasing student understanding and appreciation for intellectual property rights and information ethics (e.g., copyright and plagiarism). The findings are then applied by both faculty and librarians to improve pedagogy, educational content, and information services, and to review and revise as necessary educational objectives and identified performance indicators and their integrated, measurable standards.[28] As a result, the library can demonstrate its commitment and contributions to the institution's educational mission and its learning outcomes assessment efforts.

CONCLUSION

All constituencies and stakeholders of higher education institutions hold a perspective concerning institutional effectiveness. One prevalent perspective held is whether or not the institutional assessment process is used primarily as an evaluation process to document accountability, or for identifying needed improvements within the institution to increase its effectiveness. Perspectives held are often based upon place within the organizational structure. For example, faculty may hold a different perspective from that of an academic support unit or institutional leadership. The numerous and various stakeholders may each hold a different perspective from that of the other stakeholders.

Perspectives influence, and are influenced by, institutional and organizational culture. Existing institutional perspectives and culture may appear intractable and inflexible, but can be changed as the assessment process evolves, matures, and is itself *culturalized* by the constituencies and stakeholders. Factors influencing perspective and cultural change include each stakeholder's priority and commitment toward assessment, and the inclusiveness and openness of the process as undertaken. However, the expected outcome of the assessment process is the most critical underlying perspective, namely evaluation for accountability or the continuous improvement to increase effectiveness and to impact positively student learning.

NOTES

1. Peggy Maki, "Moving from Paperwork to Pedagogy," *AAHE Bulletin* (May 2002), available at http://aahebulletin.com/public/archive/paperwork. asp? (accessed June 8, 2003).

2. Maki, "Moving from Paperwork to Pedagogy."

3. Oswald M. T. Ratteray, "Information Literacy in Self-Study and Accreditation," *The Journal of Academic Librarianship* 28 (November 2002): 370.

4. Raymond Rodrigues, "Want Campus Buy-In for Your Assessment Efforts?" *AAHEBulletin.com* (September 2002), available at http://aahebulletin. com/member/articles/2002–10-feature02_pf.asp? (accessed June 8, 2003).

5. Ratteray, "Information Literacy in Self-Study and Accreditation," 370.

6. Maki, "Moving from Paperwork to Pedagogy."

7. Rodrigues, "Want Campus Buy-In for Your Assessment Efforts?"

8. Rodrigues, "Want Campus Buy-In for Your Assessment Efforts?"

9. Henk Vos, "How to Assess for Improvement of Learning," *European Journal of Engineering Education* 25 (2000): 228.

10. Rodrigues, "Want Campus Buy-In for Your Assessment Efforts?"

11. Cecilia L. López, "Assessment of Student Learning," *Liberal Education* 84 (Summer 1998): 36–44, EBSCOhost database (accessed June 6, 2003).

12. Rodrigues, "Want Campus Buy-In for Your Assessment Efforts?"

13. Charles D. Eisenman, "Faculty Participation in Assessment Programs," *North Central Association Quarterly* 66 (Fall 1991): 458–464.

14. López, "Assessment of Student Learning."

15. Vos, "How to Assess for Improvement of Learning," 229.

16. Rodrigues, "Want Campus Buy-In for Your Assessment Efforts?"

17. Rodrigues, "Want Campus Buy-In for Your Assessment Efforts?"

18. Martha Kyrillidou, "From Input and Output Measures to Quality and Outcome Measures, or, from the User in the Life of the Library to the Library in the Life of the User," *The Journal of Academic Librarianship* 28 (January-March 2002): 42.

19. Kyrillidou, "From Input and Output Measures," 43.

20. Sharon Markless and David Streatfield, "Developing Performance and Impact Indicators and Targets in Public and Education Libraries," *International Journal of Information Management* 21 (2001): 169.

21. Ratteray, "Information Literacy in Self-Study and Accreditation," 368.

22. Ratteray, "Information Literacy in Self-Study and Accreditation," 370.

23. Ratteray, "Information Literacy in Self-Study and Accreditation."

24. Ratteray, "Information Literacy in Self-Study and Accreditation," 369.

25. Ratteray, "Information Literacy in Self-Study and Accreditation," 370.

26. Ratteray, "Information Literacy in Self-Study and Accreditation."

27. Kathleen Dunn, "Assessing Information Literacy Skills in the California

State University: A Progress Report," *The Journal of Academic Librarianship* 28 (January/March 2002): 26.

28. Cecilia L. López, "Assessment of Student Learning: Challenges and Strategies," *The Journal of Academic Librarianship* 28 (November 2002): 356.

CHAPTER 13

An International Perspective

Peter Hernon

Stakeholders in the United States, especially government bodies (e.g., Congress, state legislatures, and federal and state departments of education) call for greater accountability in higher education with increased focus on excellence (in the learning environment and in the extent to which students actually learn what a program or institution expects) and affordability of an undergraduate education. Conversion of accountability for excellence into outcomes assessment has historically fallen on government departments and a decentralized system of accrediting organizations that largely monitor the quality of student learning through institutional and program compliance with a series of standards and policies directed at the learning environment. Today, both institutional and program accrediting organizations have revised how they understand, measure, and assess the ability of programs and institutions to provide relevant educational experiences to students. The accreditation process in the United States increasingly focuses on student learning outcomes, which depend on gathering evidence of acceptable levels of student performance and the use of that evidence for continued improvement in the quality of the educational experience. At the same time, state higher education boards and program accreditation bodies may require additional evidence—beyond the demonstration of what students learn—as part of their emphasis on accountability. That evidence might relate to faculty productivity and resource management at the program or institutional level.

The landscape of higher education views tuition and other forms of student revenues as playing an increasingly important role in financing postsecondary education. "As a result of the changed landscape, institutions have become more interested in the factors that drive student recruitment, satisfaction, and retention." Furthermore,

> Institutions have subsequently developed quality improvement, enrollment management, and evaluation processes that are intended to enhance strategic advantages in the competition for students. Institutions are challenged to integrate their quality improvement and enrollment management efforts with their mission, role, and strategic directions.[1]

Outcomes assessment is predominately a term used in the United States to provide evidence that demonstrates the extent to which the student-directed standards set by accrediting organizations are met. It represents an evolution in thinking and assessment from institutional efficiency to institutional effectiveness and the linkage of such effectiveness with accountability for excellence and planning—that is, planning for continuous improvement in learning.

Higher education in other countries may use the balanced scorecard (see Chapter 11) and other means to demonstrate accountability. In these countries, the focus is likely to be on *quality assurance*; however, that term may not be synonymous with *outcomes assessment*. Quality assurance is part of quality assessment, which is defined as systematic management and assessment procedures adopted by a higher education institution or system to monitor performance and ensure improved quality. The purpose of quality assurance is to provide stakeholders with validation that higher education manages and seeks to improve the quality of the educational experience.

Quality assurance is part of the broader quality movement, which is often associated with the use of effective business practices, the view of universities as big businesses, and pressure to provide a quality product—well-educated graduates able to enter the workforce and to read, write, conceptualize, engage in problem solving and critical thinking, and communicate effectively. Quality education may also depend on the application of good management practices, and it may be linked to efficiency and flexibility in the use of resources.

The increased emphasis on quality assurance seems to be a global phenomenon. The Organization for Economic Co-operation and Development (OECD), the International Academic Cooperation Association, and bodies within various countries all support this focus. The European Network for Quality Assurance (ENQA) does as well when it calls for the dissemination of "information, experiences, good practices and new developments in the field of quality assessment and quality assurance in higher education [in Europe] between interested parties: public authorities, higher education, institutions, and quality assurance agencies."[2] Such resources, in effect, promote benchmarking and the application of best practices (see Chapter 15).

Academic audits emerged in the United Kingdom (UK) around 1990 and have spread to Sweden, Australia, New Zealand, and Hong Kong. Such audits "evaluate what are coming to be called 'education-quality processes'—the key faculty activities required to produce, assure, and regularly improve the quality of teaching and learning." As William F. Massy, professor emeritus of education and business administration at Stanford University, explains, "An audit asks how professors organize their work and the kinds of data they use to make decisions, as well as how faculty members can use resources available to them and work collegially to do better."[3]

The purpose of this chapter is to provide a general overview of some international developments, especially those within the UK, Australia, New Zealand, and Canada. As a guide to these and other countries, *Managing Quality in Higher Education*, which John Brennan and Tarla Shah edited, provides case studies on a number of countries.[4] Different chapters in their book illustrate the impact of different national systems of quality assessment on management, planning, and decision making in the individual institutions that implemented those case studies. Quality assessment is clearly a complex phenomenon that is multifaceted and in a state of considerable flux. Furthermore, there are nuances in the definition and application of quality assessment.

UNITED KINGDOM

Since the late 1980s, government policy in the UK has tried to align higher education with the contemporary needs of society and to make education more accountable for the public investment. For example, the report of the National Committee of Inquiry into Higher Education (NCIHE), often cited as the Garrick report in Scotland and the Dearing report elsewhere, "provides a blueprint for a strategic change in the national focus of [accountability] regulation, from one concerned primarily with the quality of the educational process and the students' learning experience, to one concerned primarily with the quality of the outcomes of the educational process. The term standards-based quality assurance . . . [describes] the overall approach,"[5] and it focuses on the linkage of an institution's performance related to student learning to the standards set by a national, statutory body.

Established in 1997, the Quality Assurance Agency for Higher Education (QAAHE), which is an independent body funded by subscriptions from higher education institutions and contracts with funding bodies, develops policies based on NCIHE's proposals. The agency reviews, promotes, and supports efforts to enhance the "quality of provision and standards of awards" in higher education institutions in the UK.[6] QAAHE defines quality assurance as covering accountability or "all aspects of the ways in which organizations try to make sure that their activities are fully fit for their intended purposes."[7] Continuous improvement, or "enhancement, . . . is an integral part of quality assurance. . . . In a mature and reflective [academic] institution, the self-knowledge that internal and external review and evaluation provide will lead, inexorably, to the conscious recognition of strengths and weaknesses and the identification of areas for improvement and development."[8]

Peter Williams of the QAAHE notes that

> institutions are responsible for their enhancement activities and it is not our job [i.e., that of the agency] to try to improve or develop teaching and learning directly. Our task is to help institutions improve the management of their academic quality and standards, by providing them with opportunities to know and understand themselves better, making available information about how other institutions set about the task, and acting as a catalyst for the development of new approaches to this area of their responsibility. Indirectly this should lead to more effective learning and better teaching, and of course we hope it does.[9]

Obviously, QAAHE plays more of an indirect role than do the accrediting organizations in the United States in shaping the institutional approach to, and evidence necessary to support claims of, institutional effectiveness. To meet its enhancement responsibilities, QAAHE has gathered information about "good and not so good institutional practice in the assurance of quality and standards," and it shares the results through reports, seminars, and discussion groups.[10]

The Higher Education Funding Council for England, Universities UK, and the Standing Conference of Principals created the Teaching Quality Enhancement Committee (TQEC) to focus on enhancing the quality of teaching and learning and to shift attention from quality assurance to quality enhancement. "The spotlight has now turned away from questions of accountability towards enhancement," with the latter focusing on continuous improvement.[11] In comparison, within the United States, accrediting organizations would consider enhancement as accountability, that is, accountability within the context of student learning outcomes and continuous quality improvement—improvement of the delivery and mastery of teaching and learning. Accountability is not the same as the regulation of academic practice: "Regulation is a difficult and emotive concept for academic communities which value, above all other values, personal and institutional autonomy (the right of individuals and institutions to decide how to perform their core activities) and academic freedom (the absence of outside interference, censure or obstacle to academic practice)."[12]

Outcomes assessment preserves institutional autonomy and academic freedom, but it expects programs of study to demonstrate how a collection of core and elective courses leads to the result declared in formal mission and goal statements. Similar to the TQEC, the purpose of outcomes assessment is quality enhancement. However, the U.S. approach exceeds the UK goal of "enthusing students and capturing and retaining their commitment to learning" and produces more explicit measures of learning outcomes—ones useful for continuous improvement in the educational process.[13]

In a report issued in 2003, TQEC proposed the creation of a single, central body—the Higher Education Academy—to support the enhancement of learning and teaching in higher education.[14] The enhancement of teaching requires the exploration of different techniques to maximize learning when increasingly students engage in independent study outside the classroom; to forge links between theory and practice; to develop students' communication skills; and to encourage students to become critical, creative thinkers who engage in lifelong learning.

In summary, both quality assurance and quality enhancement are conducted on behalf of funding councils by an agency with substantial university representation. Apparently, this arrangement is effective but it is also complex and costly. It seems that, in the UK, when the term *learning outcomes* is used, it tends to refer to what students will be able to do upon completion of a course or of a course module. The impetus for such assessment appears to come from external assessors and prospective employers. The national government also views learning outcomes as an integral part of standards adopted by "vocationally-oriented tertiary education."[15] In 2002, the QAAHE renewed its commitment to academic audits, which are intended to improve educational quality without adding to the costs for academic institutions.

The years 2002 and 2003 also saw universities such as the one at Northumbria begin to explore *impact assessment*. This type of assessment is still at the conceptual level but could emerge as the equivalent to outcomes assessment in the United States.

AUSTRALIA

Because education is one of the nation's primary export industries and education functions in a highly competitive international market, there is increased emphasis on quality assurance. In fact, competition among Australian universities, combined with the delivery of distance education outside the country, makes the nation "well aware that it needs to have a leading-edge approach to quality assurance."[16] The government wants to ensure that the universities have quality assurance mechanisms in place in part to maintain market position for the education industry.

As a result, the universities have quality assurance and improvement plans that identify their goals, the strategies adopted, and the indicators they use to assess their success in achieving those goals. The plans also reflect on data gathered from two national surveys that assess the employment success of recent graduates as well as the perception of those graduates in the teaching that they experienced. Most universities also have a system of formal, cyclical review. Despite these developments,

> the rigor with which an institution approaches its quality assurance across all aspects of provision is entirely at its discretion. Another weakness is that, with some exceptions related to State Government audit requirements, there is no external review or audit of its claims. Further, there is no way of knowing whether a given degree in a given institution is of acceptable standard or how it compares with similar degrees elsewhere at other institutions. Additionally, our claims in the international marketing arena lack a degree of credibility as a result of our current hands-off approach.[17]

Clearly, the focus of the quality movement is on benchmarking performance and claims made within and across institutions. With increased government expectations for accountability in higher education and "heavy reliance of Australian institutions on the fees paid by overseas students," forecasts based on benchmarking will improve as will the demand for an independent method of validating the "sound quality for Australian degrees and graduates."[18]

To advance the measurement of quality enhancement, Australia has already identified the knowledge and skills that employers expect of university graduates, and many universities have identified the attributes they want their graduates to possess.[19] The resultant knowledge, skills, and attributes could conceivably be converted into outcomes that rely on the gathering of direct and indirect methods of evidence and that might demonstrate the improvement in the quality of student learning over time. Anyway, in March 2000, the Ministerial Council on Education, Employment Training and Youth Affairs recommended the establishment of a national agency, the Australian Universities Quality Agency (AUQA), to provide an independent verification of the quality assurance of Australian higher education through its efforts to monitor, audit, and report on quality assurance. The agency was then established, and in 2001, it began to conduct academic audits.

"Government accountability strategies," according to Felicity McGregor of the University of Wollongong in New South Wales, "are shaping a higher education environment increasingly focused on market share generation and commercial opportunities." She notes that "student expectations of all university services have sharpened in the context of tuition fees and tough employment markets."[20] As a result,

> Performance indicators . . . need to reflect the strategic priorities of the parent body and to provide data to key stakeholders on broad organizational performance such as return on investment and success in creating value. Indicators are also needed to predict competitive position and future sustainability—usually considered to be applicable only to business organizations.
>
> Measuring performance against a recognized business excellence or quality framework can deliver a range of benefits for libraries. These include recognition both within and outside the university and library sectors and the reinforcement of a culture of assessment.
>
> Business excellence frameworks challenge libraries to think about, and develop performance indicators for previously unfamiliar concepts such as future sustainability, marketing strategy, risk management and image capital.[21]

In this instance, library performance is linked to best practice and overall organizational performance. Apparently, there is no movement toward adopting measures that demonstrate the extent of student progress in becoming educated lifelong learners and in ensuring that the educational mission of a university has been accomplished. Rather, the AUQA has adopted the ADRI (*a*pproach, *d*eployment, *r*esults, and *i*mprovement) system that the Australian Business Excellence Framework advocates. The ADRI will be used to audit all Australian universities and accrediting organizations.

CANADA AND NEW ZEALAND

Canada has also embraced quality assurance, with the universities themselves producing most of the relevant literature. Part of the focus within those universities has been on international education and

- Adapting business English and business etiquette to the needs of international clients
- Acquiring basis skills in an additional language or languages
- Developing Canadian and global perspectives
- Developing intercultural competence
- Demonstrating coping and resiliency skills[22]

An examination of the types of measures that universities gather and report in their planning documents emphasizes student outcomes, especially graduation, employment, student default, and satisfaction— that of students and employers—rates. These rates are characterized as *performance indicators*.[23]

Since the late 1980s, New Zealand has embraced quality assurance and improved the audit process for the nation's eight universities.[24] However, there is no evidence that quality audits in either country look at student learning in the same way that outcomes assessment in the United States now does.

CONCLUSION

Although institutions of higher education and educational bodies in different countries increasingly focus on accountability for excellence, the scholarly literatures for library and information science, higher education, and assessment and evaluation tend to ignore cross-national boundaries and, instead, look at the specific activities of the higher education community and its stakeholders within a given country. These literatures tend to document how the community tries to improve educational quality. Although there are some different emphases, the international lexicon of terminology related to assessment shares some common threads: it provides evidence to demonstrate accountability but enables individual institutions and their academic programs some flexibility within the context of their written assessment plans or self-study reports. Accountability indicates that learning has occurred, but the type of evidence provided to demonstrate the effectiveness of that learning in those plans or reports may vary from country to country and from institution to institution.

The broad academic community and its stakeholders would benefit from a common understanding of what occurs on a global basis. With the advent of the Internet, we are constantly reminded of an intertwining global village, the existence of shared interests, and the emergence of a learning society. Yet, for outcomes assessment, that global village has not yet formed, and the international assessment community uses different (1) terminology to describe accountability for excellence and (2) kinds of evidence as provided through quality or academic audits.

Higher education anywhere, especially from the vantage point of a country's stakeholders, should be (and often is) interested in "the quality of the student experience and the standards set for, and achieved by, students."[25] Finally, it would seem that the United States is moving toward implementation of one of the most rigorous interpretations of quality assurance and quality enhancement. Academic institutions in the United States are starting to provide evidence of student learning and the extent to which they attain student outcomes, and they do so through the use of direct and indirect methods linked to a planning process of continuous quality improvement.

Outcomes assessment for higher education in the future might be reserved more for student learning outcomes than for aggregate student outcomes, which, in effect, comprise outputs. Still, inputs (the distribution of financial resources), outputs (the volume of activity reported), and outcomes together provide evidence of diverse activities and priorities within a broad characterization of course, program, and institutional effectiveness. As is evident, accountability for excellence and evidence documenting student learning, especially in the United States, are moving beyond individual courses to embrace academic programs and the entire institution. Elsewhere, the emphasis might remain on the course or course module level. However, even in those countries, there are variations among institutions.

Still, countries such as the UK have a rich heritage of accountability for public organizations and for providing evidence that demonstrates the quality of services and processes, which underpin their delivery to local populations. One example is the impact of performance measurement as reflected in the best value report, *Building Better Libraries*, of the Audit Commission, which was established in 1983. This insightful and blunt report identifies steps that UK public libraries need to implement in order to improve their performance.[26]

NOTES

1. John F. Welsh and Sukhen Day, "Quality Management and Quality Assurance in Higher Education," *Quality Assurance in Education* 10 (2002): 18.

2. See *European Network for Quality Assurance in Higher Education* (Helsinki: European Network for Quality Assurance in Higher Education, 2004), available at http://www.enqa.net/index.lasso (accessed March 2, 2004).

3. William F. Massy, "Auditing Higher Education to Improve Quality," *The Chronicle of Higher Education* (June 20, 2003): B16.

4. John Brennan and Tarla Shah, ed., *Managing Quality in Higher Education: An International Perspective on Institutional Assessment and Change* (Buckingham, U.K.: OECD, SRHE, and Open University Press, 2000); for coverage of quality assurance in Europe, see C. Campbell, S. Kanaan, B. Kehm, B. Mockiene, D. F. Westerheijden, and R. Williams, *The European University: A Handbook on Institutional Approaches to Strategic Management, Quality Management, European Policy and Academic Recognition* (Torino, Italy: European Training Foundation, 2000); and J. P. Scheele, P.A.M. Massen, and D. F. Westerheijden, eds., *To Be Continued: Follow-up of Quality Assurance in Higher Education* (Maarssen, Netherlands: Elsevier/De Tijdstroom, 1998).

5. Norman Jackson, "Understanding Standards-Based Quality Assurance: Part I—Rationale and Conceptual Basis," *Quality Assurance in Education* 6, no. 3 (1998): 132; for the report, see National Committee of Inquiry into Higher Education, *Higher Education in the Learning Environment* (London: Her Majesty's Stationery Office, 1997).

6. Quality Assurance Agency for Higher Education, "About QAA" (Gloucester, U.K.: Quality Assurance Agency for Higher Education, 2004), available at http://www.qaa.ac.uk/aboutqaa/aboutQAA.htm (accessed March 2, 2004).

7. Peter Williams, "Higher Quality 11: November 2002" (Gloucester, U.K.: Quality Assurance Agency for Higher Education, 2002), 1, available at http://www.qaa.ac.uk/public/hq/hq11/hq11.htm (accessed October 13, 2003); for information about the agency, see http://www.qaa.ac.uk/aboutqaa/aboutQAA.htm.

8. Williams, "Higher Quality 11," 2.

9. Williams, "Higher Quality 11."

10. Williams, "Higher Quality 11."

11. Williams, "Higher Quality 11," 1.

12. Jackson, "Understanding Standards-Based Quality Assurance," 133.

13. Teaching Quality Enhancement Committee, *Final Report* (TQEC, January 2003), available at http://www.hefce.ac.uk/learning/ (accessed October 15, 2003).

14. The Higher Education Academy, "History" (York, U.K.: The Higher Education Academy, n.d.), available at http://www.heacademy.ac.uk/history.asp (accessed March 2, 2004).

15. Centre for the Enhancement of Learning and Teaching, Educational and Staff Development Section, "The 'Aims and Learning Outcomes' Approach" (Aberdeen, U.K.: Robert Gorden University, n.d.), available at http://www2.rgu.ac.uk/subj/eds/pgcert/specifying/speci3.htm (accessed March 2, 2004).

16. Don Anderson, Richard Johnson, and Bruce Milligan, *Quality Assurance and Accreditation in Australian Higher Education: An Assessment of Australian and International Practice* (Canberra, Australia: Department of Education, Higher Education Division, Training and Youth Affairs, May 2000), 2, available at http://www.detya.au/highered/eippubs/eip00_1/fullcopy00_1.pdf (accessed October 15, 2003).

17. Anderson, Johnson, and Milligan, *Quality Assurance and Accreditation*, 16.

18. Anderson, Johnson, and Milligan, *Quality Assurance and Accreditation*, 17.

19. Anderson, Johnson, and Milligan, *Quality Assurance and Accreditation*, 27–29.

20. Felicity McGregor, "Benchmarking with the Best," in *Library Measures to Fill the Void: Assessing the Outcomes*, unpublished conference notebook, Fifth Northumbria International Conference on Performance Measurement in Libraries and Information Services (Durham, U.K.: 2003), 72.

21. McGregor, "Benchmarking with the Best."

22. Conestoga College, "Documents—Strategic Plan: Trends in International Education" (Kitchener, Ont.: Conestoga College, n.d.), available at http://www.conestogac.on.ca/jsp/documents/stplan/trends/internationaledtrends.jsp (accessed March 2, 2004).

23. See, for instance, Government of Ontario, Ministry of Education, Ministry of Training, Colleges and Universities, "Information on Program Out-

comes" (Toronto, Ont.: Ministry of Education, 2003), available at http://www.edu.gov.on.ca.eng/general/postsec/ps_overview.html (accessed October 15, 2003).

24. Anderson, Johnson, and Milligan, *Quality Assurance and Accreditation*; pages 35–41 provide an overview of New Zealand's approach to quality assurance.

25. Mantz Yorke, "Assuring Quality and Standards in Globalised Higher Education," *Quality Assurance in Education* 7 (1999): 9, available at the Emerald database.

26. See the Audit Commission (London: Commission, 2003), available at http://www.audit-commission.gov.uk (accessed October 15, 2003).

CHAPTER 14

Assessment: A Case Study in Synergy

Sandra Bloomberg and Melaine McDonald

Critics who question the efficacy of higher education frequently cite external forces as the primary catalysts for improvement.[1] They consider factors such as for-profit, corporate, and virtual universities, state and federal governments, stakeholder groups, regional accrediting organizations, and professional accrediting bodies to be essential for change to occur. University administrators and faculty alike live with the consequences of government opinion and action. They hear calls for accountability from an outspoken public, they are acutely aware of the expectations of accrediting organizations, and they are positioned in a global education environment that is becoming increasingly competitive. However, are these the forces that motivate change? Admittedly, from an administrative perspective these critical challenges are confronted on a daily basis. They are challenges that require time and resources and are likely to precipitate administrative action if the need for change is acknowledged.

The question remains: "Are these the forces that motivate faculty to act?" Faculty are cognizant of the issues. They threaten the foundation upon which the academy is built and challenge many of its most cherished tenets. However, these issues are peripheral to the lives of most educators. These matters are relegated to the "administrative side." Many faculty select their professions because they believe they can make a difference. They find satisfaction in helping others to learn and to grow. Those who are so oriented define their success in terms of the success of their students.[2] For them, regional accreditation, state government, and media demands for increased accountability are not necessarily calls to action. Such events do not lack relevance; they simply lack the immediacy and personal power of success and failure in the classroom.

Given the growing complexity of facilitating learning in today's classroom and the fact that university faculty are prepared as disciplinary experts rather than educators, it is not surprising that faculty, both new and experienced, are sometimes perplexed by the challenges they face. It is these challenges and the frustration that result (when faculty input and quality of outcomes lack congruency) that give rise to calls to action.[3]

Such was the case with a majority of faculty in the College of Professional Studies, one of three colleges within a moderately sized urban university (one with approximately 10,000 students) and a unit that graduates approximately 41 percent of the university's undergraduates each year. Major areas of study are business administration, criminal justice/security, fire science, health sciences, and nursing, with more than a dozen specialties represented.

FACULTY INTEREST (SPRING 1999)

Two events seemed to give life to an interest in teaching and learning. The first was a fall term memorandum conceived as much in hope as in expectation, seeking faculty interested in participating in research related to pedagogy. Two-thirds of faculty responded affirmatively. The second was the response to a 1998 survey in which a majority of faculty reported a strong desire for teaching and learning development activities. Subsequent to both events, the dean convened a meeting intended to elicit specific suggestions. Ideas proposed focused primarily on teaching, learning, and assessment. The tone of the conversation was tentative, and reflected concern for the potential difficulty encountered when collaborating across disciplines. Frequent meetings were encouraged and supported every few weeks to provide a venue for continued discussion. Some faculty shared ideas and opinions while others contributed articles. The discussions that spring, while extremely productive, progressive, and enthusiastic, placed many more questions than answers on the table.

Every process has an early, foundational phase, and it is worth noting that the elemental, grassroots conversations about teaching and learning initiated that spring were the stimulus for the assessment activity that has now started to engage faculty campuswide. Thus, the initial stimulus was accepted and endorsed. A successful effort to institutionalize assessment must be rooted in faculty support.

AN INFRASTRUCTURE (SUMMER 1999)

In June 1999, I attended the American Association for Higher Education's (AAHE) assessment conference and learned more about a national effort, the Carnegie Academy for the Scholarship of Teaching and Learning (CASTL), sponsored by the Carnegie Foundation for the Advancement of Teaching and coordinated by AAHE. One component of the project (Carnegie Teaching Academy Campus Program) was designed to engage faculty in carefully crafted discussion about the Scholarship of Teaching and Learning (SoTL). The similarities between our campus conversations and the national dialogue were quickly apparent and at once both reassuring and energizing. The aggregation of so many thoughtful and enthusiastic educators made the entire enterprise vivid and the road ahead far less daunting.

Upon my return to campus, I shared the information with faculty and sought—and found—consensus for applying to the Campus Program as a participating school. The college now had an infrastructure (albeit an external one) that would provide direction, intellectual resources, and, perhaps most important, a national network of commonly committed institutions.

THE CARNEGIE ACADEMY CAMPUS FACULTY—
AN IDENTITY (FALL 1999)

That fall the college announced its intent to participate in the Carnegie Academy Campus Program and invited all faculty to an information session to discuss the program's rationale and the benefits of participation. Nearly two-thirds of the faculty attended, some desiring to become involved, others curious. Approximately 50 percent continued participation, committing to the prescribed activities: defining the scholarship of teaching, identifying obstacles to the scholarship of teaching, and supporting factors in the campus environment. During this time the group began to read and reflect on Ernest Boyer's seminal report, *Scholarship Reconsidered: Priorities of the Professoriate*,[4] and *Scholarship Assessed*.[5]

At the same time an interest and desire was growing on the part of many in the college to shift our learning paradigm from one that tended to be more traditionally oriented (i.e., faculty centered) to a more student-centered model. Efforts were also underway to review disciplinary and cross-curricular student learning outcomes.

A MISSION (SPRING 2000)

We continued our SoTL work, but faculty remained interested in focusing on the foundations of teaching, learning, and assessment, as well as on theories, principles, research, and applications. Following two months of reading and discussion, fifteen core faculty who were regularly participating were now reviewing Thomas Angelo and Patricia Cross's *Classroom Assessment Techniques*.[6] There was intense interest in so many aspects of teaching and learning that it was suggested we survey the faculty using the Delphi method to narrow the scope of ideas, set priorities, and help establish a plan of action. Responses yielded two areas of highly concentrated interest, importance, and performance. The results of the survey indicated that the categories or topics found to be "perceived at the highest level of importance" were:

1. Learning more about teaching and learning
2. How to create high quality courses that are student centered and online
3. Developing and using outcomes

In contrast, the two categories "perceived as low performance" were areas related to:

1. Change
2. Assessment

Group members requested that experts in the areas identified be retained to work with them to accelerate the pace of learning. They then established three requirements: (1) all presentations made by consultants must be as interactive as possible, (2) the efforts must be viewed as long term, and (3) it must be developmental, with one expert building upon the work of another. The president and the vice president for academic affairs supported the effort with additional development funds for the 2000–2001 academic year.

A PLAN (FALL 2000)

The four questions that emerged from the spring survey were:

1. How do we best support faculty in the transition from teacher-centered learning to a student-centered learning paradigm?
2. How do we assist faculty in their efforts to become more knowledgeable about how people learn?
3. How do we develop and evaluate assessment rubrics?
4. How do we best adapt to change?

The next step was to find presenters with whom we could effectively work.

The group continued to read and present articles focused on topics such as culturally responsive teaching, deep learning, and collaborative learning. I had just read Sharon Silverman and Martha Casazza's *Learning and Development: Making Connections to Enhance Teaching*[7] and asked if anyone would like to read or review it (everyone did). This book, in particular, helped the group to organize its thinking and set priorities.

I facilitated conversations and events entirely within my college until the fall term; however, it soon appeared that the process had evolved sufficiently to benefit from the expertise of colleagues in the College of Education. Two senior, well-respected education faculty were invited to participate and lead discussion for the academic year. Their expertise and knowledge of adult education (in which we were the participants), and the attendant affirmation, were especially helpful in encouraging confidence and resolve.

The SoTL project progressed and student learning outcomes (disciplinary and cross-curricular competencies) continued to be discussed within the departments. Word of our activities, their apparent promise, and the continuing strengthening influence on faculty thought and conversation began to generate both interest and excitement.

ENGAGEMENT (SPRING 2001)

We sent representatives to the AAHE's invitational CASTL conference that spring and attended to the prescribed SoTL activities. However, conversation continued around questions such as:

- How can we better communicate to colleagues what *student-centered* means?
- How can we effectively apply the principles of student-centered learning?
- How do different learning styles and teaching preferences affect teaching and learning?
- What motivates students to learn?
- How does goal setting occur?

To help us reflect on these questions, we invited several presenters. Most presentations or workshops were scheduled for a single day and included a half day of active faculty involvement. Presenters were requested to forward materials in advance of the event to help participants prepare. The topics included "Self-Regulation and Goal Setting," "Multicultural Education and Campus Climate Issues," "Developing Team Skills: The Key to Leading Change in the Next Decade," and "Assessment of Student Competencies." Each presentation was assessed by participants, and suggestions for change and improvement were requested. The assessment feedback was instrumental in identifying areas of strength, weakness, and opportunity. In response to the interest our work was stimulating, faculty—university-wide—were invited to three of the four presentations sponsored through the college.

The vice president for academic affairs made additional travel funds available so that Carnegie faculty, regardless of discipline, could attend national and regional higher education conferences and workshops where they could share their work without being compelled to present. These trips were significant as they permitted faculty to experience the broader context in which similar activities were occurring, provided new ideas and insights, and helped develop professional networks, sometimes among disciplines. Faculty returned, impressed with what they experienced, affirmed concerning the work on campus, and committed to pressing on. Some faculty, heartened by the positive manifestations observed on campus and at these meetings, began presenting their work pertaining to pedagogy at education and technology conferences.

Plans to proceed with activities were agreed upon and decisions were made concerning the nature and extent of expert assistance required for academic year (AY) 2001–2002. Faculty requested more interaction, more hands-on participation, information specific to content areas, and a better understanding of how to effectively assess. A planning subcommittee was established to relieve the committee because members felt too much time was being devoted to planning and too little to discussion and performance. In addition to the workshop readings, faculty were provided a copy of *The Seven Principles in Action: Improving Undergraduate Education*[8] along with occasional related articles from various journals.

PROGRESS CONTINUES (SUMMER 2001)

The Carnegie Academy Campus Faculty mapped its SoTL progress and maintained membership in AAHE's CASTL program.

GROWTH (FALL 2001)

The Carnegie faculty, continuing to focus on teaching/learning, assessment, and change, retained experts in the areas of "developing a learning style/teaching style assessment model for diverse populations," "personalities and perspectives," "program assessment," and "learning styles and preferences." Presentations were becoming more hands-on, presenters were asked to return to provide greater continuity, and they were requested to include follow-up activities as part of their presentation.

At this point, faculty university-wide were invited to all but a few specialized presentations. Eighty percent of College of Professional Studies faculty participated in one or more of the presentations. The reading (parable) for the Carnegie faculty was *Who Moved My Cheese?*[9] a work that has earned significant recognition as a useful tool for encouraging dialogue.

EXPANDING THE NETWORK (SPRING 2002)

Most observers agreed that the college was making progress. Faculty in general were satisfied. Spontaneous, informed conversations concerning teaching and learning were occurring more frequently in departments and in meetings. As syllabi and new course and program proposals were generated, they more clearly addressed outcomes, assessment, and criteria for assessment, and they were more oriented toward a student-centered learning paradigm. Comparison of documents created then with similar documents from spring 1999 clearly reflected the significant progress that all participants believed was occurring.

Several additional days of development were sponsored during the spring term. A three-day "teaching institute" was held during winter break and a two-day outcomes assessment workshop was added later. Both were open to all faculty. Chairpersons were included as a distinct group for a half-day portion of the assessment workshop. In our college, a consultant was retained for two days to work with one large department that was making significant progress and would benefit from assistance in completing their student outcomes plan.

One of the more significant outcomes that resulted from the development activities was the requests of a number of faculty (several of whom were not Carnegie participants) who asked if it would be possible to work one-on-one with two of our consultants. Before their arrival we asked the consultants (who worked collaboratively) to identify goals in conjunction with these faculty. This was accomplished via e-mail and telephone conversations. The goals determined were to:

- Engage in a personal conversation about one's teaching practice in order to validate specific aspects.
- Reflect on ways to enhance it and develop a plan for continuous development toward a learner-centered classroom.
- Begin to partner with a colleague and students to jointly develop teaching and learning goals that lead to realistic change and further dissemination of effective practice.

Twelve faculty participated in the original group, and each semester the number has grown. The consultants typically visit once per semester for two days. They hold a general meeting with the group for two hours and meet with faculty one-on-one in their classrooms (during class) or offices. The consultants work confidentially with faculty and communicate with individuals between visits when questions arise. This group is named Partners for Innovation in Teaching and Learning.

With the guidance of the retained consultants and ongoing administrative support, departments were working persistently on cross-curricular student learning outcomes, determining how to integrate them systematically into the curriculum and how to appropriately assess. However, during students' junior and senior years, the faculty uniformly believed their work would be more easily accomplished if there were broader (university-wide) participation, particularly in the area of general education. Until AY 2002–2003, university policy prohibited students from declaring majors until they had completed the 66 general studies credit requirements. Fifty percent of the students in the College of Professional Studies are transfer and the other half originate as first-time, full-time freshmen.

COLLABORATION (SUMMER 2002)

In response to the faculty request for "broader participation," a proposal was submitted, on behalf of the university (not simply the College of Professional Studies), indicating interest in participating at AAHE's Summer Academy with project groups from other colleges and universities. The goals of the summer project as described in the proposal were to:

- Identify six cross-curricular competencies [learning outcomes] considered essential in the general studies curriculum and in the major curricula.
- Develop rubrics for the assessment of these competencies.
- Outline a strategic three-year plan designed to actively engage departments in using the rubrics for the purpose of course, program, and university-wide assessment.
- Foster institutional support for implementation of a university-wide assessment plan.

Nine faculty and five staff (the director of the library, the director of cooperative education, the assistant to the dean of professional studies, and the deans of arts and sciences and of professional studies) were designated through a variety of means (e.g., Carnegie faculty participants, recommendations from chairpersons, deans, and the vice president for academic affairs). They met several times prior to the July workshop and identified five, often-cited, cross-curricular learning outcomes: (1) writing, (2) oral presentation, (3) information literacy, (4) technology, and (5) critical thinking.

At the conclusion of the summer workshop, rubrics were completed for four of the learning outcomes, while critical thinking required further development. A loosely framed strategic plan that included suggestions for involving the entire campus was completed.

On their return to campus, the group began fine-tuning the proposed plan for presentation to the vice president for academic affairs and the president. They became identified as the Carnegie Taskforce on Teaching and Learning and met at least once each month to plan, organize, and assess.

Their first recommendation was that a pilot study be conducted during the fall term that would include at least ten faculty, each using one of the outcomes and their rubrics for assessment in a class. The same exercise, but on a larger scale, would be conducted during the spring term. The primary purpose of the pilot studies was to gather information from faculty and students on the four completed outcomes/rubrics from faculty and students; that information included their ease of use and appropriateness. The initial drafts of the rubrics were long and, in some instances, cumbersome.

In the strategic plan the taskforce advised that continued development was essential if the adoption, integration, and assessment of rubrics were to occur successfully. They recommended an active schedule for the faculty at large, the chairpersons, and themselves.

As a result of this intense summer project,

- A greater sense of cohesiveness developed across disciplinary and college boundaries among participants.
- A better (and shared) understanding of the "language" of pedagogy emerged.
- Exposure to best practices of other colleges and universities was informative.

- Gaining a sense of the broader vision of education and its issues, compatible with the vision of the project participants and the university, was affirming.

COMMON PURPOSE (FALL 2002)

The vice president for academic affairs approved the first-year plan. The taskforce met one to two times each month to plan, organize, and assess. The first university-wide activity sponsored by the taskforce in conjunction with the office of the vice president for academic affairs was a two-day workshop on the fundamentals of assessment conducted by Peggy Maki, then AAHE's senior scholar for assessment. Chairpersons were included in separate sessions focused on change, implementation, support, and other issues specific to the position of a unit leader. The vice president for academic affairs and the taskforce also met with the consultant independently.

The topic of the subsequent workshop was developing a teaching portfolio. As planned, this five-hour workshop dovetailed nicely with the previous workshop because the focus was on teaching/learning, student learning outcomes, and their assessment.

The four rubrics (writing, oral presentation, information literacy, and technology) were being piloted by ten faculty, and work began anew on the critical thinking rubric. An expert who is nationally known for his scholarship in the area of critical thinking was invited to work with our faculty on this complex area. At the conclusion of the fall semester, it was nearly ready to be piloted. Guidelines for using the rubrics were also developed.

As feedback came to the taskforce from the classrooms, it was apparent that the forms needed to be refined immediately and that the use of paper forms was cumbersome and wasteful. The summer project members and faculty using the rubrics began meeting to refine and shorten them. Contact was made with the Information Technology Systems Department (ITS) to request assistance in determining how the rubric forms could be made available and used on the World Wide Web rather than used with paper. *A Taxonomy for Learning, Teaching, and Assessing*[10] was distributed during the Critical Thinking Workshop and made available for taskforce members and others.

AFFIRMATION (SPRING 2003)

Relieved of the planning function by a subcommittee, the Carnegie faculty chose to become a reading group effective fall 2003. The first book selected was Parker Palmer's *The Courage to Teach*.[11] All faculty and staff were invited to participate, thus opening the group to university-wide participation. Books were distributed to eighteen faculty members during the summer. The group met twice during October 2003 to discuss the book. The second reading for the semester was Mary Huba and Jann Fried's *Learner-Centered Assessment on College Campuses*.

Faculty and staff development continued with the focus on "change" and "building a culture of assessment." Three well-attended workshops were offered during the spring term.

Requests for proposals were posted for an "assessment symposium" to be held in May, sponsored and coordinated by the Carnegie Academy Campus Faculty to be held in May. The purpose of the symposium was to provide a forum for faculty to share their progress, observations, successes, and frustrations working with the rubrics during the spring semester. Seven faculty presented for thirty to forty-five minutes each and seven individuals or departments contributed poster presentations.

The item of greatest importance on the spring term agenda was the nature of the instrument utilized by faculty and students for monitoring (student outcomes) progress. A consultant from ITS was assigned to work with the taskforce to investigate the potential for development of a system to record and track student outcomes during their stay at the university. The project, of course, was deemed feasible and work continued throughout the summer refining the instrument and the process. One of the many positive outcomes of this exercise was the commitment to attempting to use the information available through the new tracking system to develop a means of creating student portfolios.

The critical thinking rubric was piloted and the chairperson of the mathematics department offered to convene interested faculty to begin development of a quantitative reasoning rubric. The university joined with seven other universities in a national (AAHE) project, the goal of which is to support, promote, and share results from the scholarship of teaching and learning efforts, aimed at understanding and improving student learning and development during the first critical year of college. The purpose of the first phase of the project is to identify five to seven common, core learning outcomes for the first-year curriculum and co-curriculum. Work on this project will continue for three years.

Two notable accomplishments for the year were the use of the business administration student outcomes grid, which was used in an assessment publication, and the printing of the information literacy learning outcomes and rubrics, which were printed in a handbook used by our regional accrediting organization. It has also been translated into four languages.

COMING FULL CIRCLE (FALL 2003)

Development of the "Student Competency [Outcome] Software System" was complete. It provided easy data maintenance through the use of electronic bubble forms, relatively straightforward reporting of student competency (outcome) scores, and comprehensive student reporting through the integration of the data (i.e., student and course) with other student data in our PeopleSoft Reporting System.

The software system was unveiled at the fall university assembly by the vice president for academic affairs. The ITS consultant demonstrated the features of the system and how to use it. Two senior, well-respected faculty (also taskforce members) discussed the guidelines for using the system and entertained questions.

Following the demonstration, five rooms were set aside in which the respective student learning outcomes/rubrics were to be discussed. One taskforce member was assigned to each room as a facilitator. From these meetings, it was determined which faculty were interested in using which outcomes/rubrics. Prior to the assembly, three dates were established during the fall semester when each group would meet to discuss its experiences using the rubrics and share practical applications. The dates did not overlap so that, if they wished, faculty could participate with more than one rubric group.

Twelve members remain on the taskforce; four withdrew and were replaced by four new members. Participation on the taskforce is open to faculty who are interested and who have the time to regularly participate at meetings. Neither released time nor any additional compensation is offered to members.

A second assessment symposium was scheduled for the conclusion of the fall term. The keynote topic, "The Scholarship of Teaching and Learning," was presented by Barbara Cambridge, director for AAHE Teaching Initiatives. Following the address, faculty were invited to offer thirty-minute presentations about their experiences using the rubrics, with emphasis on application. Poster presentations were also requested. Based on these exchanges of ideas, faculty in the college now feel that they are better prepared to engage in the "scholarship of teaching and learning," and they are. With this symposium, the college has come full circle.

CONCLUSION

The primary lesson to be drawn from our experience and the experiences of our colleagues is that the permutations of assessment models are infinite. The perceptions and realities of success are limitless, as are the circumstances and characteristics of the more than 3,000 institutions of higher education in the United States. In short, there are no perfect models.

Our success has been achieved at a public, urban university located in the Northeast, established in 1927 first as a teacher's college. Our students are diverse; many are new immigrants and the first generation of their families to attend college. Some are educationally disadvantaged. Most work, many full time. Our faculty is predominately tenured. We have a tradition of strong shared governance and our campus is unionized. Our environment is competitive. These are our realities.

In the fabric of reality are woven opportunities. The urban landscape is rich with choices. Our students create a fascinating tapestry. They have a strong work ethic. They are motivated to "get ahead" and get out. Some are educationally disadvantaged. They bring work experience to the classroom. Our faculty are experienced. Many consider themselves educators—first. There is a tradition of working and planning from the bottom up. There is a history of collaboration among administration, faculty, students, and the union. Our environment is competitive. These are our opportunities.

Our progress at times has seemed glacial, our path circuitous, and our outcomes occasionally serendipitous—and that is simply how it is. We have planned, we have sought opportunities, and we have created and used synergy. This is our success.

The following competencies and rubrics were developed by the university's task force on teaching and learning and renewed, revised, and graciously edited by numerous faculty and staff. Rubrics remain works in progress.

COMPETENCY
CRITICAL THINKING

Student Name: _____ **Date:** _____

Course Title: _____ **Reference #:** _____

NJCU students must be able to think critically by performing specific cognitive tasks.

COMPETENCY	ASSESSMENT CRITERIA	N/A*	N/E**	Novice	Proficient	Accomplished
1. REMEMBER						
A. Recalls content and details		☐	☐	☐ Recalls some content and details but not always accurately	☐ Recalls most content and details accurately	☐ Recalls all significant content and details accurately
B. Identifies classifications, principles, methodologies and theories		☐	☐	☐ Identifies some classifications, principles, methodologies and theories	☐ Identifies most classifications, principles, methodologies and theories accurately	☐ Identifies significant classifications, principles, methodologies and theories accurately
C. Restates main ideas, concepts and principles		☐	☐	☐ Restates main ideas, concepts and principles with difficulty	☐ Restates main ideas, concepts and principles with minimal assistance	☐ Restates main ideas, concepts and principles clearly and accurately
2. UNDERSTAND						
A. Explains ideas, concepts and principles		☐	☐	☐ Explains ideas, concepts and principles with limited accuracy and irrelevant examples	☐ Explains ideas, concepts and principles with some accuracy and relevant examples	☐ Explains ideas, concepts and principles accurately and relevant examples
B. Contextualizes ideas, concepts and principles		☐	☐	☐ Contextualizes ideas, concepts, and principles with difficulty	☐ Contextualizes ideas, concepts and principles with minimal difficulty	☐ Contextualizes complex ideas, concepts and principles easily
C. Demonstrates awareness		☐	☐	☐ Demonstrates minimal awareness of the depth and breadth of one's knowledge	☐ Demonstrates some awareness of the depth and breadth of one's knowledge	☐ Demonstrates a clear awareness of the depth and breadth of one's knowledge

* Not Applicable
** No Evidence

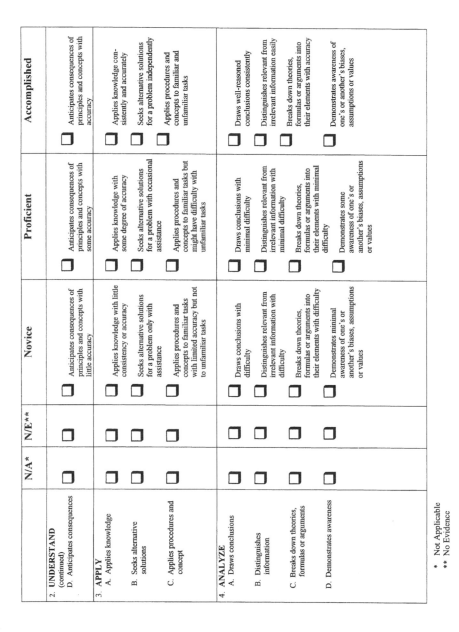

	N/A*	N/E**	Novice	Proficient	Accomplished
2. UNDERSTAND (continued)					
D. Anticipates consequences	☐	☐	☐ Anticipates consequences of principles and concepts with little accuracy	☐ Anticipates consequences of principles and concepts with some accuracy	☐ Anticipates consequences of principles and concepts with accuracy
3. APPLY					
A. Applies knowledge	☐	☐	☐ Applies knowledge with little consistency or accuracy	☐ Applies knowledge with some degree of accuracy	☐ Applies knowledge consistently and accurately
B. Seeks alternative solutions	☐	☐	☐ Seeks alternative solutions for a problem only with assistance	☐ Seeks alternative solutions for a problem with occasional assistance	☐ Seeks alternative solutions for a problem independently
C. Applies procedures and concept	☐	☐	☐ Applies procedures and concepts to familiar tasks with limited accuracy but not to unfamiliar tasks	☐ Applies procedures and concepts to familiar tasks but might have difficulty with unfamiliar tasks	☐ Applies procedures and concepts to familiar and unfamiliar tasks
4. ANALYZE					
A. Draws conclusions	☐	☐	☐ Draws conclusions with difficulty	☐ Draws conclusions with minimal difficulty	☐ Draws well-reasoned conclusions consistently
B. Distinguishes information	☐	☐	☐ Distinguishes relevant from irrelevant information with difficulty	☐ Distinguishes relevant from irrelevant information with minimal difficulty	☐ Distinguishes relevant from irrelevant information easily
C. Breaks down theories, formulas or arguments	☐	☐	☐ Breaks down theories, formulas or arguments into their elements with difficulty	☐ Breaks down theories, formulas or arguments into their elements with minimal difficulty	☐ Breaks down theories, formulas or arguments into their elements with accuracy
D. Demonstrates awareness	☐	☐	☐ Demonstrates minimal awareness of one's or another's biases, assumptions or values	☐ Demonstrates some awareness of one's or another's biases, assumptions or values	☐ Demonstrates awareness of one's or another's biases, assumptions or values

* Not Applicable
** No Evidence

275

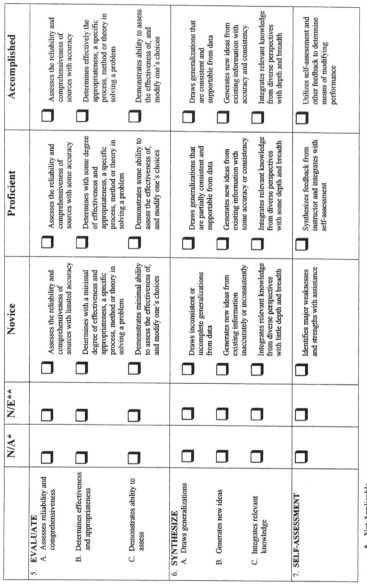

	N/A*	N/E**	Novice	Proficient	Accomplished
5. EVALUATE A. Assesses reliability and comprehensiveness	☐	☐	☐ Assesses the reliability and comprehensiveness of sources with limited accuracy	☐ Assesses the reliability and comprehensiveness of sources with some degree of accuracy	☐ Assesses the reliability and comprehensiveness of sources with accuracy
B. Determines effectiveness and appropriateness	☐	☐	☐ Determines with a minimal degree of effectiveness and appropriateness, a specific process, method or theory in solving a problem	☐ Determines with some degree of effectiveness and appropriateness, a specific process, method or theory in solving a problem	☐ Determines effectively the appropriateness, a specific process, method or theory in solving a problem
C. Demonstrates ability to assess	☐	☐	☐ Demonstrates minimal ability to assess the effectiveness of, and modify one's choices	☐ Demonstrates some ability to assess the effectiveness of, and modify one's choices	☐ Demonstrates ability to assess the effectiveness of, and modify one's choices
6. SYNTHESIZE A. Draws generalizations	☐	☐	☐ Draws inconsistent or incomplete generalizations from data	☐ Draws generalizations that are partially consistent and supportable from data	☐ Draws generalizations that are consistent and supportable from data
B. Generates new ideas	☐	☐	☐ Generates new ideas from existing information inaccurately or inconsistently	☐ Generates new ideas from existing information with some accuracy or consistency	☐ Generates new ideas from existing information with accuracy and consistency
C. Integrates relevant knowledge	☐	☐	☐ Integrates relevant knowledge from diverse perspectives with little depth and breadth	☐ Integrates relevant knowledge from diverse perspectives with some depth and breadth	☐ Integrates relevant knowledge from diverse perspectives with depth and breadth
7. SELF-ASSESSMENT	☐	☐	☐ Identifies major weaknesses and strengths with assistance	☐ Synthesizes feedback from instructor and integrates with self-assessment	☐ Utilizes self-assessment and other feedback to determine means of modifying performance

* Not Applicable
** No Evidence

COMPETENCY
INFORMATION LITERACY

Student Name: _____   **Date:** _____

Course Title: _____   **Reference #:** _____

Information Literacy involves the ability to define, retrieve, evaluate and use information found, ethically and legally, and to become independent lifelong learners in a society that is deluged with the volume and variety of information sources. Information literacy is crucial in developing an informed citizenry, an up-to-date professional, and a self-aware social human being.

COMPETENCY	ASSESSMENT CRITERIA				
	N/A*	N/E**	Novice	Proficient	Accomplished
1. Formulates and defines an information need clearly					
A. Topic / keyword identification	☐	☐	☐ No idea of topic / keyword and how to phrase question	☐ Some idea of topic / keyword and how to phrase question	☐ Knows exactly what topic / keyword and phrase to use
B. Extent and depth of information needed	☐	☐	☐ No idea of extent and depth of information needed	☐ Some idea of both extent and depth	☐ Clear idea of extent and depth
2. Knows information sources					
A. Types[1]	☐	☐	☐ No idea of types	☐ Some idea of types	☐ Knows all the types
B. Formats[2]	☐	☐	☐ No idea of formats	☐ Some idea of formats	☐ Knows all the formats

* Not Applicable
** No Evidence
[1] Primary vs. secondary, general vs. discipline-specific, popular vs. scholarly, current vs. historical, local vs. external sources, interlibrary loan, etc.
[2] Print: book (encyclopedias, handbooks, dictionaries, indexes, etc.), periodicals, AV, microform: <u>Electronic</u>: database, website, on-line catalogs, etc.

Competencies	N/A*	N/E**	Novice	Proficient	Accomplished
3. Constructs/implements effective search strategies					
A. Knowledge of information organization and how to look for materials	☐	☐	☐ No knowledge	☐ Knows about library classification system, etc., and how materials are organized	☐ Uses knowledge to focus on searching topic
B. Knowledge of searching tools[3]	☐	☐	☐ No knowledge	☐ Some knowledge	☐ Knows searching tools and how to use them
C. Knowledge of search strategies[4] or how to refine search	☐	☐	☐ Does not know how to refine search	☐ Knows some strategies	☐ Applies all strategies as relevant
4. Applies criteria for evaluating information					
A. Relevance	☐	☐	☐ Cannot judge relevance	☐ Can judge relevance	☐ Can distinguish gradations of relevancy
B. Reliability / authority	☐	☐	☐ Accepts all information found	☐ Some idea which information is reliable	☐ Questions authority all the time
C. Timeliness	☐	☐	☐ Does not check for timeliness	☐ Checks dates of information found	☐ Selects the most up-to-date information depending on the topic

*   Not Applicable
** No Evidence
[3] Searching Tools: (Reference books above), on-line catalog, library databases, Internet search engines and directories, etc.
[4] Strategies: Boolean, proximity, nesting, truncation, etc.

Competencies	N/A*	N/E**	Novice	Proficient	Accomplished
5. Follows institutional guidelines which relate to access, information and copyright	☐	☐	☐ Has rudimentary understanding of plagiarism	☐ Understands plagiarism, and does not plagiarize; cites sources in proper format	☐ Obtains copyright permission, stores and disseminates text, data, images, and sounds within legal and institutional guidelines
6. Self-Assessment	☐	☐	☐ Identifies major weaknesses, and strengths with assistance	☐ Synthesizes feedback from instructor and integrates with self-assessment	☐ Utilizes self-assessment and feedback to determine means of modifying performance

COMPETENCY
COMMUNICATION: ORAL PRESENTATION

Student Name: _____ Date: _____

Course Title: _____ Reference #: _____

Students will be able to speak and to present to an audience with precision and clarity in standard American English.

COMPETENCY ASSESSMENT CRITERIA	N/A*	N/E**	Novice	Proficient	Accomplished
1. Clarity of Purpose (thesis)	☐	☐	☐ Purpose (thesis) is evident	☐ Purpose (thesis) is clear	☐ Purpose (thesis) is clear and well-developed
2. Timing	☐	☐	☐ Inappropriate use of time	☐ Close to allotted time	☐ Completed in allotted time
3. Structure A. Opening / Closing	☐	☐	☐ May lack clear opening or closing ☐ Organization is uneven or confusing	☐ Organization is clear with an identifiable opening and closing ☐ Some unevenness exists	☐ Clear and effective opening and closing ☐ Sequence and relationships of ideas are easy to follow, clear and effective
B. Development	☐	☐			

* Not Applicable
** No Evidence

	N/A*	N/E**	Novice	Proficient	Accomplished
4. Verbal A. Grammar & Syntax B. Vocal Variety[1]	☐ ☐	☐ ☐	☐ Errors interfere with understanding ☐ Limited vocal variety	☐ Clear, reflects few errors ☐ Vocal variety[1] supports the expression of ideas and information	☐ Effective, compelling presentation ☐ Vocal variety[1] enhances quality of presentation
5. Non-verbal A. Body language B. Eye contact	☐ ☐	☐ ☐	☐ Body language somewhat supports message ☐ Minimal eye contact	☐ Body language complements message ☐ Frequent eye contact	☐ Body language strongly supports and strengthens message ☐ Consistently uses eye contact to strengthen presentation
6. Communication aids	☐	☐	☐ Poorly prepared or inappropriately used	☐ Contribute to the quality of the presentation	☐ Professionally prepared to complement and enhance the presentation
7. Use of disciplinary knowledge and language	☐	☐	☐ Able to apply concepts / theories and use examples	☐ Able to organize ideas, concepts, and theories and differentiate	☐ Shows evidence of ability to evaluate and generate ideas and hypotheses
8. Assessment of Audience A. Awareness / Sensitivity B. Response	☐ ☐	☐ ☐	☐ Has limited awareness of audience biases and peculiarities toward topic and speaker ☐ Attempts to incorporate responses of audience	☐ Recognizes audience biases and peculiarities ☐ Incorporates responses of audience	☐ Demonstrates sensitivity to audience biases and peculiarities ☐ Uses responses to support presentation
9. Self-Assessment	☐	☐	☐ Independently identifies strengths and weaknesses	☐ Needs assistance regarding how to address strengths and weaknesses	☐ Utilizes self-assessment and other feedback to determine means of modifying performance

[1]Vocal variety: pitch, rate, volume, energy.
* Not Applicable
** No Evidence

COMPETENCY
COMMUNICATION: WRITTEN

Student Name: _____   **Date:** _____

Course Title: _____   **Reference #:** _____

Students will develop the ability to communicate clearly and effectively through written form.

COMPETENCY / ASSESSMENT CRITERIA	N/A*	N/E**	Novice	Proficient	Accomplished
1. Thesis (or purpose) A. Supportability B. Clarity C. Complexity	☐ ☐ ☐	☐ ☐ ☐	Thesis demonstrates <u>rudimentary</u>: ☐ supportability ☐ clarity ☐ complexity	Thesis demonstrates <u>adequate</u>: ☐ supportability ☐ clarity ☐ complexity	Thesis demonstrates <u>advanced</u>: ☐ supportability ☐ clarity ☐ complexity
2. Organization of ideas to support thesis or purpose A. Clarity of purpose B. Logical development C. Supporting evidence	☐ ☐ ☐	☐ ☐ ☐	Organization demonstrates <u>rudimentary</u>: ☐ clarity of purpose ☐ logical development ☐ supporting evidence	Organization demonstrates <u>adequate</u>: ☐ clarity of purpose ☐ logical development ☐ supporting evidence	Organization demonstrates <u>advanced</u>: ☐ clarity of purpose ☐ logical development ☐ supporting evidence

* Not Applicable
** No Evidence

282

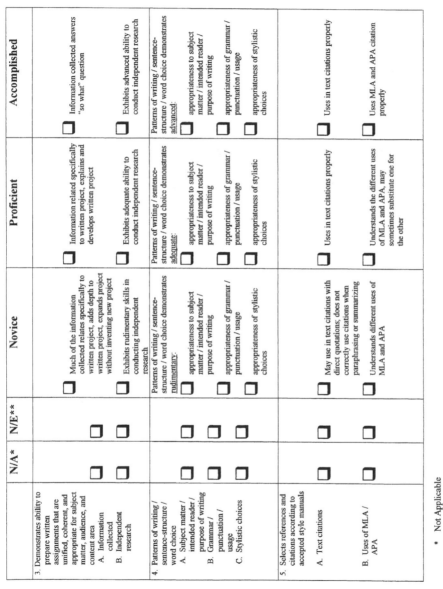

	N/A*	N/E**	Novice	Proficient	Accomplished
3. Demonstrates ability to prepare written assignments that are unified, coherent, and appropriate for subject matter, audience, and content area					
A. Information collected	☐	☐	Much of the information collected relates specifically to written project, adds depth to written project, expands project without inventing new project	Information related specifically to written project, explains and develops written project	Information collected answers "so what" question
B. Independent research	☐	☐	Exhibits rudimentary skills in conducting independent research	Exhibits adequate ability to conduct independent research	Exhibits advanced ability to conduct independent research
4. Patterns of writing / sentence-structure / word choice			Patterns of writing / sentence-structure / word choice demonstrates rudimentary:	Patterns of writing / sentence-structure / word choice demonstrates adequate:	Patterns of writing / sentence-structure / word choice demonstrates advanced:
A. Subject matter / intended reader / purpose of writing	☐	☐	appropriateness to subject matter / intended reader / purpose of writing	appropriateness to subject matter / intended reader / purpose of writing	appropriateness to subject matter / intended reader / purpose of writing
B. Grammar / punctuation / usage	☐	☐	appropriateness of grammar / punctuation / usage	appropriateness of grammar / punctuation / usage	appropriateness of grammar / punctuation / usage
C. Stylistic choices	☐	☐	appropriateness of stylistic choices	appropriateness of stylistic choices	appropriateness of stylistic choices
5. Selects references and citations according to accepted style manuals					
A. Text citations	☐	☐	May use in text citations with direct quotations; does not correctly use citations when paraphrasing or summarizing	Uses in text citations properly	Uses in text citations properly
B. Uses of MLA / APA	☐	☐	Understands different uses of MLA and APA	Understands the different uses of MLA and APA, may sometimes substitute one for the other	Uses MLA and APA citation properly

* Not Applicable
** No Evidence

	N/A*	N/E**	Novice	Proficient	Accomplished
6. Differentiates between scholarly and popular sources	☐	☐	☐ Sometimes is unable to distinguish between scholarly and popular sources	☐ Distinguishes between scholarly and popular sources	☐ Uses higher level scholarly sources
7. A. Demonstrates ability to analyze, synthesize, and integrate ideas	☐	☐	☐ Exhibits rudimentary ability to integrate written assignments with assigned readings	☐ Exhibits adequate ability to integrate written assignments with assigned readings	☐ Possesses advanced ability to integrate written assignments with assigned readings
B. Demonstrates ability to analyze, synthesize, and integrate ideas	☐	☐	☐ Rarely or never questions current knowledge on the subject matter	☐ Begins to question current knowledge on the subject matter	☐ Questions current knowledge on subject matter and is able to show significance of new knowledge
8. A. Examines validity of author's position	☐	☐	☐ Exhibits beginning understanding of need to move beyond personal experience in examining author's position	☐ Exhibits more developed understanding of moving beyond personal experience / values in examining author's position	☐ Exhibits ability to move beyond personal experience / values in examining author's position
B. Examines values of author's position	☐	☐	☐ Recognizes values reader brings to the page and how those values may differ from author	☐ Exhibits beginning ability to reconcile values discrepancy between self / author	☐ Takes worldview in reconciling values discrepancy between self / author
9. Self-Assessment	☐	☐	☐ Synthesizes feedback from instructor and students with assistance	☐ Synthesizes feedback and integrates with self-analysis	☐ Utilizes self-assessment and feedback to determine means of modifying performance

* Not Applicable
** No Evidence

284

COMPETENCY
QUANTITATIVE REASONING

Student Name: _____   **Date:** _____

Course Title: _____   **Reference #:** _____

Students must be able to use the knowledge, skills, and attitudes of mathematics and the sciences for effective quantitative reasoning.

COMPETENCY	ASSESSMENT CRITERIA				
	N/A*	N/E**	Novice	Proficient	Accomplished
1. Results and conclusions					
A. Reasonableness of results	☐	☐	☐ Results often unreasonable	☐ Results usually reasonable	☐ Results almost always reasonable
B. Checks results for correctness	☐	☐	☐ Very seldom checks	☐ Usually checks	☐ Almost always checks
C. Justifies conclusions	☐	☐	☐ Very little justification	☐ Some justification but incomplete	☐ Extensive justification
2. Uses the language and methods of mathematics in other contexts					
A. Correctly	☐	☐	☐ Many errors	☐ Some errors	☐ Very few errors
B. Independently	☐	☐	☐ Requires much help	☐ Requires some help	☐ Very seldom needs help
3. Uses the language and methods of the sciences in other contexts					
A. Correctly	☐	☐	☐ Many errors	☐ Some errors	☐ Very few errors
B. Independently	☐	☐	☐ Requires much help	☐ Requires some help	☐ Very seldom needs help
4. Uses scientific methods of analysis and experimentation					
A. Appropriately	☐	☐	☐ Applications often inappropriate	☐ Applications seldom inappropriate	☐ Applications never inappropriate
B. Accurately	☐	☐	☐ Many errors	☐ Some errors	☐ Very few errors
C. With insight and knowledge	☐	☐	☐ Exhibits little knowledge or insight	☐ Exhibits considerable knowledge and insight	☐ Exhibits full knowledge and insight
D. With complete documentation	☐	☐	☐ Very little documentation	☐ Some documentation but incomplete	☐ Complete documentation

*   Not Applicable
** No Evidence

285

	N/A*	N/E**	Novice	Proficient	Accomplished
5. Use examples, counter-examples and mathematical proof					
A. With understanding and insight	☐	☐	☐ Exhibits almost no understanding or insight	☐ Exhibits considerable understanding and insight	☐ Exhibits complete understanding and insight
B. Correctly	☐	☐	☐ Makes many errors	☐ Makes some errors	☐ Makes very few errors
6. Uses conjecture and testing, mathematical modeling, computer simulation, and statistical techniques for realistic and relevant real world applications	☐	☐	☐ Requires considerable guidance and explanation	☐ Requires some guidance and explanation	☐ Requires very little guidance and explanation
7. Uses various measurements, data gathering techniques, sampling, probability, and descriptive and inferential statistics to support or reject claims of size, relationship, or relative accuracy					
A. With understanding and insight	☐	☐	☐ Exhibits almost no understanding or insight	☐ Exhibits considerable understanding and insight	☐ Exhibits complete understanding and insight
B. Correctly	☐	☐	☐ Makes many errors	☐ Makes some errors	☐ Makes very few errors
8. Uses a variety of graphical, tabular, numerical, algebraic, verbal, schematic, and experimental techniques to represent, interpret, and draw inferences from data or function values					
A. Correctly	☐	☐	☐ Many errors	☐ Some errors	☐ Very few errors
B. Independently	☐	☐	☐ Requires much help	☐ Requires some help	☐ Very seldom needs help
C. With understanding	☐	☐	☐ Can represent but cannot interpret or draw inferences	☐ Can represent and interpret but not draw inferences	☐ Can represent, interpret, and draw inferences with much understanding
9. Create generalizations from observed patterns and develop specific examples from general statements	☐	☐	☐ Requires much assistance	☐ Requires some assistance	☐ Requires very little assistance
10. Self-Assessment	☐	☐	☐ Synthesizes feedback with assistance	☐ Synthesizes feedback and integrates with self-analysis	☐ Utilizes self-assessment and feedback to modify performance

* Not Applicable
** No Evidence

COMPETENCY
TECHNOLOGY

Student Name: _____

Course Title: _____

Date: _____

Reference #: _____

Students will be expected to use technology proficiently and ethically to access information, use productivity tools to solve problems and produce products and presentations. They will be expected to locate and analyze various sources of information for problem solving and conducting research.

COMPETENCY	ASSESSMENT CRITERIA				
	N/A*	N/E**	Novice	Proficient	Accomplished
1. Demonstrates an ability to operate technology					
A. Operations/Tasks	☐	☐	☐ Does basic operations with help	☐ Performs routine tasks with minimal assistance	☐ Performs complex tasks independently
B. Troubleshoot	☐	☐	☐ Unable to troubleshoot	☐ Troubleshoots common operational difficulties	☐ Troubleshoots some advanced operational difficulties
2. Uses technology tools collaboratively, safety, responsibly and ethically					
A. Collaboration	☐	☐	☐ Seldom works cooperatively and/or collaboratively using technology	☐ Usually works cooperatively and/or collaboratively using technology	☐ Takes a leadership role in collaborative work using technology
B. Ethics	☐	☐	☐ Demonstrates little evidence of ethical use of technology	☐ Demonstrates ethical use of technology	☐ Models a high level of respect and ethical behavior in the use of technology
C. Responsibly/Safety	☐	☐	☐ Demonstrates little evidence or concern for personal or physical safety	☐ Uses technology with appropriate concern for personal and physical safety	☐ Models technology with appropriate concern for personal and physical safety

* Not Applicable
** No Evidence

287

	N/A*	N/E**	Novice	Proficient	Accomplished
3. Uses technology as a problem-solving tool	☐	☐	☐ Demonstrates little evidence of formulating problems or choosing appropriate strategies for using technology	☐ Formulates problems and chooses appropriate strategies with some guidance using technology	☐ Formulates problems and chooses appropriate strategy using technology
4. Use of technological resources	☐	☐	☐ Uses few or inefficient technology resources to gather information	☐ Uses a variety of technology resources to gather information	☐ Consistently uses the most appropriate technology resources to gather information
5. Use of assessment resources	☐	☐	☐ Seldom evaluates accuracy, relevance, appropriateness, comprehensiveness and bias of electronic information sources	☐ Usually evaluates accuracy, relevance, appropriateness, comprehensiveness and bias of electronic information sources	☐ Almost always researches and evaluates the accuracy, relevance, appropriateness, comprehensiveness, and bias of electronic information sources
6. Uses technology to produce class assignments and projects					
A. Designs and develops	☐	☐	☐ Needs much assistance to produce a product using technology	☐ Uses technology to design, develop, publish and present a product with minimal assistance	☐ Designs and develops advanced products with little or no assistance
B. Communication	☐	☐	☐ Communicates and/or illustrates ideas with difficulty using technology	☐ Communicates and/or illustrates ideas using technology with minimal assistance	☐ Fluently communicates and/or illustrates ideas with technology
7. Uses technology to locate, evaluate and collect information from a variety of sources	☐	☐	☐ Discovers the use of technology to locate, evaluate and collect information from a variety of sources using search engines for the purpose of gathering electronic data	☐ Analyzes which search engines are more effective in locating a variety of electronic information to conduct research and/or solve a problem	☐ Assesses and evaluates the credibility of electronic information to ascertain the authenticity, reliability and bias of the data gathered before using it
8. Self-Assessment	☐	☐	☐ Identifies major weaknesses and strengths with assistance	☐ Synthesizes feedback from instructor and integrates with self-assessment to continue growth in the use of technology	☐ Utilizes self-assessment and other feedback to determine means of modifying performance

Adapted from www.jls.palo-alto.ca.us/eslr/eslrTechnology.pdf

* Not Applicable

** No Evidence

NOTES

1. See A. W. Astin, *Assessment for Excellence: The Philosophy and Practice of Assessment and Evaluation in Higher Education* (Phoenix, Ariz.: Oryx Press, 1991); T. W. Banta & Associates, *Building a Scholarship of Assessment* (San Francisco: Jossey-Bass, 2002); P. Eckel, M. Green, and B. Hill, *On Change V— Riding the Waves of Change: Insights from Transforming Institutions* (Washington, D.C.: American Council on Education, 2002); and A. F. Lucas & Associates, *Leading Academic Change: Essential Roles for Department Chairs* (San Francisco: Jossey-Bass, 2000).

2. See J. R. Davis, *Better Teaching, More Learning: Strategies for Success in Postsecondary Settings* (Phoenix, Ariz.: Oryx Press, 1993); G. Highet, *The Art of Teaching* (New York: Vintage Books, 1959); and Parker J. Palmer, *The Courage to Teach: Exploring the Inner Landscape of a Teacher's Life* (San Francisco: Jossey-Bass, 1998).

3. Davis, *Better Teaching, More Learning*.

4. Ernest L. Boyer, *Scholarship Reconsidered: Priorities of the Professoriate* (San Francisco: Jossey-Bass, 1990; Princeton, N.J.: The Carnegie Foundation for the Advancement of Teaching, 1990).

5. Charles Glassick, Mary T. Huber, and Gene I. Maeroff, *Scholarship Assessed: Evaluation of the Professorate* (San Francisco: Jossey-Bass, 1997).

6. Thomas A. Angelo and K. Patricia Cross, *Classroom Assessment Techniques: A Handbook for College Teachers*, 2nd ed. (San Francisco: Jossey-Bass, 1993).

7. Sharon L. Silverman and Martha E. Casazza, *Learning and Development: Making Connections to Enhance Teaching* (San Francisco: Jossey-Bass, 2000).

8. Susan R. Hatfield, ed., *The Seven Principles in Action: Improving Undergraduate Education* (Boston: Anker Pub. Co., 1995).

9. Spencer Johnson, *Who Moved My Cheese?* (New York: Putnam, 1998).

10. Lorin W. Anderson, David R. Krathwohl, P. W. Airasian, K. A. Cruikshank, R. E. Mayer, P. R. Intrich, J. Raths, and M. C. Wittrock, *A Taxonomy for Learning, Teaching, and Assessing* (New York: David McKay Co., 2001).

11. Palmer, *The Courage to Teach*.

CHAPTER 15

Preparing for the Future: A View of Institutional Effectiveness

Peter Hernon

Michael F. Middaugh, assistant vice president for institutional research and planning at the University of Delaware in Newark, points out that "American higher education is a complex enterprise in which various types of institutions deliver teaching, research, and service; the relative emphasis on each of these components relates to institutional mission and the diversity of the population they serve." He continues:

> Historically, colleges and universities have taken a generic approach to explaining what faculty and the institutions themselves do. In years past, this sufficed. But since 1990, higher education has clearly been a prime target for accountability in terms of how faculty spend their time, what the products of higher education are, and what costs are associated with those products.[1]

Accountability for excellence focuses on institutional effectiveness, a concept that aligns institutional activities and programs with the institution's mission. Outcomes assessment, which is definitely not a passing fad, becomes a means for ensuring such effectiveness and for engaging in continuous improvement in student learning. Outcomes assessment applies to student learning, both at the undergraduate and graduate levels, and, over time, "will become a critical component of faculty productivity."[2] Traditionally, faculty productivity has been measured from activities such as the number of professional papers published in peer-reviewed journals, the number of professional conference paper presentations given, the number of active memberships in professional associations, the number and amount of grants received, and the nature and scope of faculty- or curriculum-development activities. Program productivity, the collective course offerings in a department or across departments that culminates in the awarding of academic degrees, has been viewed in terms of measures such as undergraduate persistence and graduation rates, the proportion of graduating students who found program-related employment within twelve months after graduation, the extent of student satisfaction with their interaction with faculty, and the proportion of graduating seniors who pursue graduate or professional education.

Faculty productivity regarding teaching and learning will increasingly not be viewed merely in terms of faculty output and classroom teaching (what is presented and how—and how well—it is learned). Accountability for excellence now focuses on program results: how the combination of courses that students take in their subject major produces the intended learning results.

Recognizing a changing environment, one more focused on institutional effectiveness, this chapter looks at institutional culture and identifies some obstacles to overcome for outcomes assessment to thrive. It also suggests that program, regional, and national accreditation agencies are likely to increase their expectations of higher education institutions once the faculty and administrators at these institutions become more familiar with outcomes assessment, provide direct evidence of student learning, and seek to improve the learning environment over time.

INSTITUTIONAL CULTURE

"Institutional culture refers to the values, philosophies and ideologies that characterize the institution—that is, what people value, believe in, and consider admirable in the institution." Because an institution consists of various subunits, each of which has its own culture,[3] institutional culture encompasses those subcultures or organizational cultures. Organizational cultures, for instance, might be characterized as clan, hierarchical, or market; these categories are not mutually exclusive. A market culture focuses on the projection of an institutional image, and the changes in that image may be more cosmetic than substantive. "Organizations that are dominated by the hierarchical and clan cultures are typically focused on maintaining the status quo, keeping control of their processes and outcomes, and providing an enjoyable working environment for employees. These organizations are typically less concerned with fostering new ideas, implementing change, and transforming the organization into something new."[4] Yet, institutions with hierarchical cultures generally have "a strong sense of mission," "are less innovative than other institutions," and rate "significantly lower than other institutions on organizational effectiveness."[5]

Institutional culture has a significant impact on students' disposition to learning. British educators P. Hodkinson and M. Bloomer found that, over the period of time spent at the institution, common sets of dispositions became established in students' learning. Their interactions with faculty, staff, and other students shaped their dispositions, while simultaneously shaping—and being shaped by the—the institutional culture. Furthermore, institutional culture transforms individual beliefs and intentions.[6]

George D. Kuh, professor of higher education at Indiana University, Bloomington, describes institutional culture as a combination of influences that encompass the entire college experience, including how people behave and what is (and is not) important to administrators, faculty, staff, and students. This broad characterization addresses curriculum accreditation, denominational affiliation, mission and vision statements, the type of student attracted to the institution, and so on.[7]

In their analysis of quality in higher education, Jann E. Freed, associate professor of business management and chair of the Behavioral Science Division at Central College (Pella, Iowa), and Marie R. Klugman, associate professor of statistics in the College of Business and Public Administration at Drake University (Des Moines, Iowa), note that "the implementation of continuous improvement is a change in the culture of an institution." Conversely, "if the culture does not change, the institution is not truly dedicated to continuous improvement." They maintain that college and university administration, at the upper levels, must be committed to continuous quality improvement and that with turnover of those individuals it is imperative that change occur.[8] The commitment to change must go beyond certain individuals if continued improvement of the learning environment is to become an end, one that has gained broad institutional support.

One purpose of outcomes assessment is to encourage the development of a structure and climate supportive of cultural change and to move clan, hierarchical, and market cultures to accept a quality structure. Clearly, the approach taken to the adoption of outcomes assessment represents managed evolution or the linkage of outcomes assessment to an evolutionary planning process. A discussion of how to accomplish or manage change is beyond the scope of this chapter and book.[9] However, faculty and those evaluating them for promotion and tenure need to understand and value their contributions to accomplishing the educational mission of the institution. They need to look beyond the teaching of specific courses and the number of students enrolled in a class, and show how individual courses contribute to the accomplishment of program outcomes—significant behavioral and performance change by the time of graduation.

The proponents of outcomes assessment in accreditation bodies tend to favor a gradual approach to its implementation: get started and develop the assessment structure over time. This does not mean that institutions can ignore outcomes assessment; they must set the foundation and, over time, build on their solid beginning.

GETTING STARTED

An accrediting organization might define institutional effectiveness as the systematic application of clearly defined assessment and planning procedures, determination of the extent to which an institution fulfills its mission and achieves its goals, periodic publication of the results to its constituencies, the use of the evidence gathered to improve student learning, and the alignment of that evidence with the formal assessment plan. As a result, the first step is to develop a written assessment plan to guide the development and implementation of outcomes assessment and ensure continuous improvement in student learning. The Middle States Commission on Higher Education, for instance, identifies the components of that plan as providing

- A foundation in the institution's mission, goals, and objectives
- Periodic assessment of institutional effectiveness that addresses the total range of educational offerings, services, and processes, including planning, resource allocation, and institutional renewal processes; institutional resources; leadership and governance; administration; institutional integrity; and student learning outcomes
- Support and collaboration of faculty and administration

- Systematic and thorough use of multiple qualitative and/or quantitative measures, which maximize the use of existing data and information
- Evaluative approaches that yield results that are useful in institutional planning, resource allocation, and renewal
- Realistic goals and a timetable, supported by appropriate investment of institutional resources
- Periodic evaluation of the effectiveness and comprehensiveness of the institution's assessment plan

Linked to that plan should be an identification of how the data collected from those "evaluative approaches" will provide evidence of how the institution's mission, goals, and objectives are met, as well as how the learning experience is improved. Furthermore, the plan should discuss how the assessment results will be used to "improve and gain efficiencies in administrative services and processes, including activities specific to the institution's mission (e.g., services, outreach, and research)."[10]

The plan should indicate the audience from whom evidence will be gathered (e.g., each level of undergraduate class, masters' students, or doctoral students) and the method of gathering evidence (whether it is a national examination, relies on direct or indirect methods of gathering evidence, and involves qualitative or quantitative data collection).

Learning outcomes can be subdivided into "higher order" and "lower order" competencies based on Bloom's *A Taxonomy of Educational Objectives*.[11] Lower-order competencies refer to the attainment of skills, information gathering, and the types of resources that the information seeker uses, whereas higher-order competencies relate to problem solving and critical thinking. Higher-order competencies encompass knowledge of theories, structures, principles, conventions, trends, and so on; comprehension; application; analysis; synthesis; and evaluation. For example, an outcome might be

> Students will think logically and critically in solving problems; be able to evaluate, critique, and apply the thinking of others; and reach an appropriate conclusion.

Analysis and synthesis might involve the understanding of complex issues, the ability to explore the connections among ideas, and the for-

Figure 15.1
Planning Student Learning Outcomes

Desired Outcome	Strategy	Method(s) of Assessment	Level of Assessment	Recommendations	Changes in Learning
What knowledge or skills should students exhibit?	How will students be given the opportunity to gain that knowledge/ skill?	Is it direct or indirect? Which method? Why?	Is assessment at the course, program, or institutional level?	Based on the evidence gathered, what are the suggestions for improving student learning?	What resulted from implementation of the recommendations?

mulation of a defensible (valid) independent conclusion. Two key questions are "How will evidence be gathered?" and "How will it be judged?" An assessment plan should recognize the methods appropriate to achieve a particular learning outcome, distinguish between higher- and lower-order competencies, and answer the types of questions depicted in Figure 15.1.

A desired outcome might be "competence in oral and written communication will be characterized by clarity, logic, coherence, persuasion, and precision." Competence refers to the ability to:

- Assimilate, analyze, and present a body of information clearly and succinctly.
- Communicate in various modes and media, including through the use of appropriate technology.
- Be able to sustain a consistent point of view.
- Compose effective written materials for various audiences.

The five assessment criteria for judging each of the four abilities center on a definition of: (1) clarity, (2) logic, (3) coherence, (4) persuasion, and (5) precision. By the way, the home pages of the South Seattle Community College (http://www.southseattle.edu/campus/slo. htm) and Saint Louis University's Office of Institutional Study (http:// www.slu.edu/servicices/ois/SLU_Assesment/slu_student_outcomes.html) provide other examples of student learning outcomes.

Figure 15.2
Introductory Source Material

Angelo, Thomas A., and K. Patricia Cross. *Classroom Assessment Techniques: A Handbook for College Teachers*. San Francisco: Jossey-Bass, 1993.

Association of College and Research Libraries. *Information Literacy Competency Standards for Higher Education*. Chicago: Association of College and Research Libraries, 2000. Available at http://www.ala.org/Content/NavigationMenu/ACRL/Standards_and_Guidelines/Informat ion_Literacy_Competency_Standards_for_Higher_Education.htm, accessed September 28, 2003.

Astin, Alexander W., Trudy W. Banta, K. Patricia Cross, Elaine El-Khawas, Peter T. Ewell, Pat Hutchings, Theodore J. Marchese, Kay M. McClenney, Marcia Mentkowski, Margaret A. Miller, E. Thomas Moran, and Barbara D. Wright. *9 Principles of Good Practice for Assessing Student Learning*. Washington, D.C.: American Association for Higher Education, AAHE Assessment Forum, n.d. Available at http://www.aahe.org/assessment/principl.htm, accessed September 28, 2003. (The principles also appear as Figure 8.3 in this book.)

California Polytechnic State University, San Luis Obispo. *General Education Assessment Library*. San Luis Obispo: California Polytechnic State University, n.d. Available at http://www.calpoly.edu/~acadprog/gened/library.htm, accessed March 2, 2004.

Council for Higher Education Accreditation. *Assessment and Accreditation in Higher Education: Bibliography*. Washington, D.C.: Council for Higher Education Accreditation, 2003. Available at http://www.chea.org/Commentary/biblio.cfm, accessed September 28, 2003.

Hernon, Peter, and Robert E. Dugan. *An Action Plan for Outcomes Assessment in Your Library*. Chicago: American Library Association, 2002.

Middle States Commission on Higher Education:
- Assessment Web site, http://www.msache.org/ (exercises, practices, and guidelines), accessed March 2, 2004.
- *Developing Research & Communication Skills: Guidelines for Information Literacy in the Curriculum* (Philadelphia, 2003)
- *Student Learning Assessment: Options and Resources* (Philadelphia, 2003)

North Carolina State University. "Internet Resources for Higher Education Outcomes Assessment." Raleigh: North Carolina State University, 2003. Available at http://www2.acs.ncsu.edu/UPA/assmt/resource.htm, accessed March 2, 2004.

"Outcomes Assessment in Higher Education." *The Journal of Academic Librarianship*.
- Volume 28, nos. 1–2 (January/March 2002):
  - Ronald L. Baker, "Evaluating Quality and Effectiveness: Regional Accreditation Principles and Practices"
  - Elizabeth W. Carter, "'Doing the Best You Can with What You Have': Lessons Learned from Outcomes Assessment
  - Robert E. Dugan, "Managing Technology in an Assessment Environment"
  - Bonnie Gratch-Lindauer, "Comparing the Regional Accreditation Standards: Outcomes Assessment and Other Trends"

As the institution develops its plan, the faculty and administration might review the previous chapters in this book, the standards for accreditation of the relevant program and regional accrediting organizations, the general readings listed in Figure 15.2, and this book's bibliography. Chapter 8 of *An Action Plan for Outcomes Assessment in*

Figure 15.2 (continued)

- o Martha Kyrillidou, "From Input and Output Measures to Quality and Outcome Measures, or, from the User in the Life of the Library to the Library in the Life of the User"
- o Peggy L. Maki, "Developing an Assessment Plan to Learn about Student Learning"
- Vol. 28, no. 6 (November 2002)
  - o Robert E. Dugan and Peter Hernon, "Outcomes Assessment: Not Synonymous with Inputs and Outputs"
  - o Cecilia L. López, "Assessment of Student Learning: Challenges and Strategies"
  - o Oswald M. T. Ratteray, "Information Literacy in Self-Study and Accreditation"

Pullman, George. "Electronic Portfolios Revisited: The Efolios Project." *Computers and Composition* 19 (2002): 151–169.

"Report on Educational Effectiveness Assessment" [an assessment plan template]. Fairbanks: University of Alaska, 1998. Available at http://www.uaf.edu/provost/outcomes/downloads.html, accessed March 2, 2004.

Sustein, Bonnie S., and Jonathan H. Lovell, eds. *The Portfolio Standard: How Students Can Show Us What They Know and Are Able to Do.* Portsmouth, N.H.: Heinemann, 2000.

University of Wisconsin–Madison, Office of Provost. "Outcomes Assessment: Using Assessment for Academic Program Improvement." In section IV.A, *Assessment Manual*. Madison: University of Wisconsin, Office of Provost, n.d.

Your Library, for example, discusses "evidence demonstrating the achievement of outcomes," and the López article builds on that discussion by identifying academic institutions that have been successful in their application of the different methods for measuring learning.

Some methods provide direct evidence that outcomes have been achieved and that the desired change has occurred. Other methods offer indirect evidence and any association about change must be inferred.

Direct Methods of Student Learning

As identified in previous chapters, some options for direct methods include:

• *Capstone course evaluation.* "Capstone courses integrate knowledge, concepts, and skills associated with an entire sequence of study in a program. For academic units where a single capstone course is not feasible or desirable, a department may designate a small group of courses where competencies of completing majors will be measured."[12] Another option is a capstone *experience* in which students might take a problem or issue and make a presentation in which they demonstrate knowledge of the issue and communication skills. Naturally, the experience covered must be addressed through stated outcomes. Whatever approach is taken, such courses or experience provide a culminating common experience for students in the program.

• *Course-embedded assessment.* "The embedded methods most commonly used involve the development and gathering of student data based on questions placed in course assignments. These questions, intended to assess student outcomes, are incorporated or embedded into final exams, research reports, and term papers [in their final year of the program]. . . . The student responses are then evaluated by two or more faculty to determine whether or not the students are achieving the prescribed educational goals and objectives of the department. This assessment is a separate process from that used by the course instructor to grade the exam, report, or term paper."[13]

• *Tests (locally designed or commercially produced standardized tests).* Tests enable academic units to determine if students have acquired the requisite knowledge. "A well-constructed and carefully administered test that is graded by two or more judges for the specific purpose of determining program strengths and weaknesses remains one of the most popular instruments for assessing most majors. . . . In most cases, standardized testing is useful in demonstrating external validity."[14]

In some instances, academic units might administer tests "at the beginning and at the end of courses or academic programs. These test results enable faculty to monitor student progression and learning throughout prescribed periods of time."[15] Such assessment might even involve performance evaluation as viewed from either videotapes or audiotapes.

• *Portfolio evaluation.* These portfolios, whether print or electronic, represent "collections of student work that exhibit to the faculty and the student the student's progress and achievement in given areas. Included in the portfolio may be research papers and other process reports, multiple-choice or essay examinations, self-evaluations, personal essays, journals, computational exercises and problems, case studies, [and so on.]. . . . Information about the students' skills, knowledge, development, quality of writing, and critical thinking can be acquired through a comprehensive collection of work samples."[16]

• *Paper/thesis/dissertation/paper evaluation.* Departments might use theses, dissertations, a research project, or a performance paper "to demonstrate a mastery of an array of skills and knowledge."[17] This method might even use content analysis to identify examples of critical thinking.

In conjunction with some of the above-mentioned methods, those individuals conducting the assessment might use think-aloud protocol, a type of verbal protocol analysis that seeks information about a participant's cognitive thoughts using verbal reports. These reports occur during data collection and should be compared with verbal reports given after the completion of the task. The subsequent reports, known as "think afters," are important because some participants might not be able to articulate their thoughts or actions well as they carry out a task that involves complex cognitive processing. Think afters can produce pertinent insights in such a situation, but they might be influenced by forgetting and fabrication.[18]

Indirect Methods of Student Learning

The choices for indirect methods include:

• *Surveying (student and exit interviewing, alumni and employer surveying).* Such surveys provide evidence of "the educational needs [and expectations] of students." During such surveying, students "reflect on what they have learned as majors in order to generate information for program improvement."[19] "Surveying of alumni is a useful tool for generating data about student preparation for professional work, program satisfaction, and curriculum relevancy." Employer surveys, on the other hand, "can provide information about the curriculum, programs, and students that other forms of assessment cannot produce."[20] Surveying might even include the use of focus group interviews so that students or others could be brought together and given the opportunity to interact with their peers.

• *Curriculum and syllabus evaluation.* "As one technique to keep a focus on the agreed-upon objectives, curriculum analysis provides a means to chart just which courses will cover which objectives. The chart then provides assurance to the department that, assuming certain sequences are taken by the student candidates for that major, they will in fact have the opportunity to learn those objectives. Syllabus analysis is an especially useful technique when multiple sections of a department course are offered by a variety of instructors. It provides assurance that each section will cover essential points without prescribing the specific teaching methods to be used in helping the students learn those objectives."[21]

• *External reviewer evaluation.* Peer reviewers determine the extent to which student achievement matches departmental goals and objectives. They can also identify program strengths and weaknesses as they review a sample of student work from a progression of courses.

• *Other*. This miscellaneous category includes persistence, retention, transfer, and graduation rates; the length of time to complete a degree; enrollment trends; transcript analysis; and job placement data.

The tool chest of methods for gathering evidence might also include observation and self-assessment. Observation involves watching, listening, asking questions, and collecting examples of student work so that the evaluators can "describe what goes on, who or what is involved, when and where things happen, [and] how they occur."[22] Observation balances observing and participating, but also relies on judicious interviewing. As for self-assessment, students might be asked to assess what they have learned and the extent to which they have mastered certain outcomes. Where they find themselves deficient, they might be asked if (and how) they would offset those deficiencies. Naturally, self-assessment might result in bias and a distorted picture. However, when combined with other data collection, it might result in a meaningful dialogue with students.

COMPLETING THE FOUNDATION—SUSTAINABLE OUTCOMES

As programs and institutions build on the foundation discussed in the previous section, faculty and administrators should verify that the assessment results are useful for improving (and are actually used to improve) student learning (e.g., pedagogy, classroom instruction, the curriculum, and the quality and availability of learning resources) and student services on an ongoing basis. Faculty and administrators should also ask, "Do the assessment results inform decision making at all levels?" and "How well are needed resources linked to planning and budgeting processes?" Such questions relate to the assessment plan that the program and institution have developed.

When getting started, faculty and administrators should restrict the number of outcomes they develop. Once they become more familiar with outcomes assessment and the use of the evidence gathered, they can expand the number of outcomes they employ. The mix of higher-order and lower-order competencies merits review. The purpose is to ensure the progression toward the use of higher-order competencies and the reliance on direct evidence of learning that, for instance, demonstrates that students can distill previously learned knowledge and skills to produce something new (*synthesis*) or that they can apply previously learned information in new and concrete situations to solve problems (*application*). At the same time, faculty and administrators can reach into that methodological tool chest and select more methods that collectively provide a richer and more complete picture of the current state of student learning. Sustainable outcomes therefore become those outcomes that will continue over time and guide the collection of evidence.

OBSTACLES

To change institutional culture, faculty must understand that the evidence gathered to assess the accomplishment of outcomes is not a reflection on them as educators and will not be used in a negative manner (e.g., for annual financial compensation, promotion, or tenure). At the same time, administrators must resist a desire to consider the evidence as a reflection on a faculty member's classroom teaching. Course-embedded assessment (see below) is not the same as teacher/course evaluation that students typically complete at the end of the school term. The teaching faculty tend to view learning within the context of the courses they teach and the grades they assign. Outcomes assessment for a program or institution, on the other hand, looks at the entire learning experience—an undergraduate's major or graduate student's entire program of study.

The evidence gathered may contain weaknesses in the extent of its generalizability to an institution as a whole, reliability, and internal validity. During the getting-started phase, the faculty can identify the most critical weaknesses for the application of program and institutional outcomes and develop mechanisms to overcome them. Thus, sustainable outcomes are revised and improved over time, and a rigorous gathering and interpretation of evidence guides the assessment of student performance as reflected in whatever outcomes are used. It may take time for the obstacles to disappear, and it may require regional and program accrediting organizations to adopt a firm stance as they pressure institutions to provide evidence of accountability for excellence and to use that evidence to improve the learning experience.

BEST PRACTICE

Some accrediting organizations and professional associations, as well as individual institutions, maintain Web sites that convey *best practice*. Best practice refers to the processes, practices, and systems that performed exceptionally well and are widely recognized as improving an organization's performance and effectiveness. Any institutions highlighted exemplify excellence in developing and using institution-wide plans for student learning outcome assessment and in applying direct and indirect methods of gathering and reporting the evidence gathered. Successfully identifying and applying best practice can improve organizational efficiency and effectiveness, and provide guidance in creating assessment plans and developing strategies that document how institutions have used the information gathered to improve student learning.

As the U.S. General Accounting Office notes in one of its many reports on best practice:

> In identifying best practices among organizations, the "benchmarking" technique is frequently used. In benchmarking with others, an organization (1) determines how leading organizations perform a specific process(es), (2) compares their methods to its own, and (3) uses the information to improve upon or completely change its process(es). Benchmarking is typically an internal process, performed by personnel within an organization who already have a thorough knowledge of the process under review.[23]

Thus, consideration of best practice enables other institutions to study what worked well elsewhere and to adapt those plans and processes, systems, and practices to meet local needs. However, a problem in relying on Web sites for identifying best practice is that the examples and content are not always updated on a regular, ongoing basis, and the criteria for inclusion are not always specified.

EXAMPLES

Peter Hernon and Robert E. Dugan have identified a set of verbs applicable to outcomes assessment. Using such verbs, faculty "develop concrete statements that reflect what precisely they expect learners to know and be able to do to achieve an outcome. Furthermore, these action-oriented verbs are interactive and decision-focused—they are not ambiguous. Each expresses something that is measurable and clearly understood."[24]

Student Learning Outcome

North Carolina State University's College of Engineering has developed an Annotated Template for Program Outcomes, which is adaptable beyond engineering. The template takes eleven different outcomes and explains how to interpret and measure them. In fact, faculty might review this document at the "getting started stage."[25] Although the template does not actually enable one to "construct and implement effectively a search strategy to locate information resources for a problem-oriented course assignment," the examples illustrate how to approach and refine such a learning outcome. Using *Student Learning Assessment* and other resources,[26] faculty could identify the components of a search strategy that they consider most important. It is necessary to standardize those components to guide others in their review of student work. Assessment then centers on the course-embedded, program, or institutional approach, and it produces evidence likely gathered through the application of direct methods. That evidence must relate to the written assessment plan.

Research Outcome

A research outcome for students in an academic program might be to "apply 'relevant' research to problem-centered course assignments," or it might focus on the following six competencies:

1. Analyze a problem in its full complexity.
2. Identify and relate relevant literature to the problem under investigation.
3. Select or develop a theoretical framework appropriate to solving that problem.
4. Select an appropriate procedure (research design and methodologies) that addresses study objectives, research questions, and hypotheses.
5. Adopt appropriate indicators of reliability and validity.

6. Demonstrate effective written, oral, and presentation skills to convey study findings and how those findings match the stated problem statement.

A research outcome assumes the presence of a foundation course on research methods and elective courses that include assignments that advance the realization of that outcome.

Most likely, faculty would refine that outcome so that anyone evaluating student work could see an evolution in students' problem-solving ability. A component of one outcome might be to "differentiate between a problem and purpose statement," with the latter comprising a subset of a problem statement.[27] Another component would be to demonstrate, over time, an improvement in the language used to state a problem so that the justification for the proposed study is more forcefully and fully stated. In other words, instead of just being able to express the components of a problem statement, students improve their effective communication of such a statement.[28]

Clearly, any of the direct methods already highlighted would be applicable. In the beginning, the faculty might select one method (e.g., capstone evaluation, portfolio evaluation, or course-embedded assessment) and apply and refine it, as they develop objective means to interpret the results. Over time, they can expand on those means of interpretation and explore other direct methods, as they take a multimethods approach to assessment—the purpose of which is to develop a richer picture of student learning, identify areas requiring improvement, and implement strategies to improve that learning.

CONCLUSION

As Ronald L. Baker, associate executive director of the Commission on Colleges and Universities, Northwest Association of Schools and of Colleges and Universities, notes, "Shifts in societal attitudes and expectations are forcing higher education to move toward specific meaningful assessment and reporting of the quality of its infrastructures, processes, and outcomes." These shifts are occurring at a time when "higher education's role as sole arbitrator of institutional effectiveness has eroded, due, in part, to a decrease in public confidence regarding the ability of colleges and universities to authenticate the achievement of results." Undoubtedly, the high cost of higher education, combined with the expectation of a direct and immediate economic return on the investment in that education, contributes to this erosion of public confidence. He further points out that higher education has been slow to adapt to the changing environment, "believing that society's interests are best served by advancing the academy's interests and therefore, the public should simply trust in higher education's ability to regulate itself."[29] Within this context, outcomes assessment and the assessment plan preserve "long-held educational values of quality improvement and self-regulation while simultaneously addressing society's needs for accountability and quality assurance."[30] Furthermore, "Because improving student learning *really* does matter to the personal growth of individuals and to the economic health of our nation and the world, it should be the reason for every accredited institution's continued existence."[31]

NOTES

1. Michael F. Middaugh, *Understanding Faculty Productivity: Standards and Benchmarks for Colleges and Universities* (San Francisco: Jossey-Bass, 2001), 163.

2. Middaugh, *Understanding Faculty Productivity*, 151.

3. "Assessment—Institutional Effectiveness" (Sacramento: California State University, 2000), available at http://www.csus.edu/portfolio/institutional_portfolio/assess_doc_institution.htm (accessed March 2, 2004).

4. "Assessment—Institutional Effectiveness."

5. "Assessment—Institutional Effectiveness."

6. P. Hodkinson and M. Bloomer, "Stokingham Sixth Form College: Institutional Culture and Dispositions towards Learning," *British Journal of Sociology of Education* 21 (2000): 187–203.

7. George D. Kuh, "Shaping Student Character," *Liberal Education* 84, no. 3 (1998): 18–25.

8. Jann E. Freed and Marie R. Klugman, *Quality Principles and Practices in Higher Education: Different Questions for Different Times* (Phoenix, Ariz.: Oryx Press, 1997), 205, 206.

9. Freed and Klugman, *Quality Principles and Practices*, 42–44, 46–53, 127–128, 131–137.

10. Middle States Commission on Higher Education, *Characteristics of Excellence in Higher Education: Eligibility Requirements and Standards for Accreditation* (Philadelphia: Middle States Commission on Higher Education, 2002), available at http://www.msache.org/ (accessed March 2, 2004); see also

Peggy L. Maki, "Developing an Assessment Plan to Learn about Student Learning," *The Journal of Academic Librarianship* 28 (2002): 8–13.

11. Benjamin S. Bloom and David R. Krathwohl, *Taxonomy of Educational Objectives: The Classification of Educational Goals. Handbook I: Cognitive Domain* (New York: Longmans, Green, 1956).

12. University of Wisconsin–Madison, Office of the Provost, "Outcomes Assessment: Using Assessment for Academic Program Improvement" (Madison: Office of the Provost, University of Wisconsin, April 2000), 1, available at http://www.wisc.edu/provost.assess/manual.html (accessed March 10, 2003).

13. University of Wisconsin–Madison, "Outcomes Assessment," 2.

14. University of Wisconsin–Madison, "Outcomes Assessment," 3.

15. University of Wisconsin–Madison, "Outcomes Assessment," 5

16. University of Wisconsin–Madison, "Outcomes Assessment."

17. University of Wisconsin–Madison, "Outcomes Assessment," 6.

18. See Jennifer L. Branch, "Investigating the Information-Seeking Processes of Adolescents: The Value of Using Think Alouds and Think Afters," *Library & Information Science Research* 22 (2000): 371–392; John S. Carol and Eric J. Johnson, *Decision Research: A Field Guide* (Newbury Park, Calif.: Sage, 1990).

19. University of Wisconsin–Madison, "Outcomes Assessment," 6.

20. University of Wisconsin–Madison, "Outcomes Assessment," 7, 8.

21. University of Wisconsin–Madison, "Outcomes Assessment," 8.

22. Margaret LeCompte, Judith Preissle, and Tesch Renata, *Ethnography and Qualitative Design in Educational Research*, 2nd ed. (New York: Academic Press, 1993), 196.

23. U.S. General Accounting Office, National Security and International Affairs Division, *Best Practices Methodology: A New Approach for Improving Government Operations*, GAO/NSIAD-95–154 (Washington, D.C.: General Accounting Office, May 1995), 11.

24. Peter Hernon and Robert E. Dugan, *An Action Plan for Outcomes Assessment in Your Library* (Chicago: American Library Association, 2002), 72.

25. North Carolina State University, College of Engineering, "Annotated Template for Program Outcomes," prepared by Michael Carter (Raleigh: North Carolina State University, 2000), available at http://www.engr.ncsu.edu/abet/criterion-3/template-3.html (accessed March 2, 2004).

26. Middle States Commission on Higher Education, *Student Learning Assessment: Options and Resources* (Philadelphia: Middle States Commission on Higher Education, 2003).

27. Hernon and Dugan, *An Action Plan for Outcomes Assessment*, 67.

28. An introductory research methods course therefore might have student learning outcomes, such as (1) develop one problem statement and its justification for basic research and another for applied research; (2) define research as an inquiry process and describe the steps involved—including the formula-

tion of objectives and a hypothesis, and gathering data—maximizing reliability and internal validity; (3) distinguish between different types of research (e.g., descriptive, experimental, and qualitative); (4) identify the components of a research study and provide examples of each; (5) distinguish between independent, dependent, and control variables; (6) provide examples of research misconduct and assess their implications for the integrity of the peer review process; (7) explain how falsification can be intentional and unintentional; (8) distinguish between probability and nonprobability sampling (for a given problem students might be asked to explain the type of sampling technique they would apply); (9) differentiate between type I and type II errors; and (10) distinguish between reliability and validity.

Given the number of outcomes that any researcher could generate, the list might be more manageable if someone grouped the outcomes selected by broad topic such as "introduction or overview of research," "statistical concepts," "ethical issues in research," "the problem statement," "measuring research variables," "experimental research," "descriptive research," and so on.

29. Ronald L. Baker, "Evaluating Quality and Effectiveness: Regional Accreditation Principles and Practices," *The Journal of Academic Librarianship* 28 (November 2002): 3.

30. Baker, "Evaluating Quality and Effectiveness."

31. Cecilia L. López, "Assessment of Student Learning: Challenges and Strategies," *The Journal of Academic Librarianship* 28 (November 2002): 367.

CHAPTER 16

Continued Development of Assorted Measures

Peter Hernon and Robert E. Dugan

Outcomes assessment draws on qualitative and quantitative research methods, assorted research designs (e.g., based on probability and nonprobability sampling, and experimental and nonexperimental designs), various types of input and other measures, and the four perspectives presented in Chapter 11. Based on that chapter, it is clear that no general model depicting input, output, and outcome measures has emerged that addresses all of the perspectives, encourages the use of measures that go beyond mere organizational or institutional reporting, and provides evidence directly useful for program and service improvement. This chapter addresses that deficiency and offers a research agenda, one that, it is hoped, will appeal to faculty in different disciplines, peer-reviewed journals in those disciplines, funding organizations, and various stakeholders. The goal is to create and maintain a cross-disciplinary and international dialogue.

CONCEPTUALIZATION OF DIFFERENT TYPES OF MEASURES

Figure 16.1 depicts institutional effectiveness in the context of continuous quality improvement. It shows that such effectiveness does not represent a linear progression from inputs and activities to outputs and from those outputs to service quality, satisfaction, and outcomes. Nor does the figure show a loop back from service quality, satisfaction, and

Figure 16.1
Institutional Effectiveness and Improvement

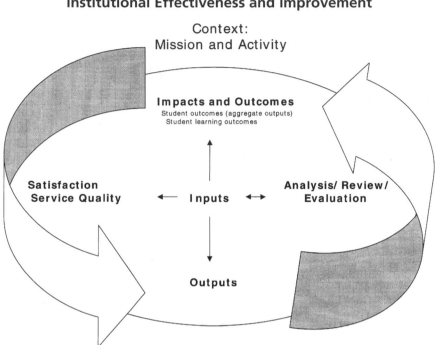

Context:
Mission and Activity

Impacts and Outcomes
Student outcomes (aggregate outputs)
Student learning outcomes

**Satisfaction
Service Quality** ← **Inputs** ↔ **Analysis/ Review/
Evaluation**

Outputs

outcomes to inputs. The development and use of outcomes assessment, as reflected in this book, are not consistent with such a characterization of institutional effectiveness. The reason is that there need not be a progression from outputs to outcomes; rather, inputs can lead directly to student learning outcomes without passing through a middle concept—outputs. As a result, the figure illustrates that, within the context of an educational mission and activity (e.g., one focused on effectiveness or efficiency), an institution, program, or service can proceed from inputs to outcomes, outputs, or a customer-focused orientation. The inclusion of "analysis/review/evaluation" in the figure serves as a reminder that organizations or institutions must constantly question and rely on the practical value of the data collected. Are they merely for report provision or do they have value for self-improvement?

While some outcomes, in fact, comprise outputs, learning outcomes are not necessarily outputs. Outputs are directly based upon inputs, the resources made available for services and resources. Outputs are workload measures of the efficiency and effectiveness of applying or expending the identified inputs. Learning outcomes, however, are the measured or perceived impact or influence of a conducted process on an individual. An output is institutionally or organizationally based; a learning outcome's basis is measured upon an individual person.

A brief example may help explain this concept. An oft-identified institutional educational objective is to instill its community members with the value of "lifelong learning." An academic library may decide to contribute toward meeting this institutional educational objective by providing instruction, emphasizing the vocational and personal values of lifelong learning to instruction session participants (students). Applying this objective to the general system model of planning (inputs, throughputs/process, outputs, and feedback mechanism), for example, may identify the activities of the inputs, process, and outputs:

• Inputs (the available resources for an identified formal library objective, one relating to lifelong learning, and suggested processes—instruction services—included in the library's long range or strategic plan). Examples include the number and titles of library staff and other personnel resources available to conduct library instruction, costs for these personnel resources, space (square feet) available to conduct instruction, the number of computer workstations available to conduct the instruction, and the number of planned instruction modules available for use.

• Throughputs/process (the use of the available resources). Examples include informing faculty and students of availability of instruction services, conducting instruction, and gathering information about the sessions conducted.

• Outputs. Examples are a count of the number of sessions conducted, count of the number of attendees, reported demographics of attendees and courses supported (e.g., 100 freshman students received library instruction in four sections of English), ratios of session demographics reported compared to identified institutional demographics (e.g., percentage of student FTE session participants to total student FTE), average cost per instruction session, average cost per instruction attendee, and library's contribution to the identified education objectives via a report. Creating and making available a report concerning the outputs is simply another output.

Learning outcomes are measures of the impact accrued as a result of the instruction process on the individual student attending; these outputs do not measure any impact on the individual attendee.

A library may not compile, measure, and report learning outcomes.

However, most libraries compile output measures for reporting purposes. The outputs, as listed above, are measurable indicators and are useful when applied against an identified standard from the planning process, as organizational, institutional, and peer efficiency and effectiveness benchmarks concerning the inputs applied.

How would these outputs measure the outcome (impact) of "lifelong learning"? When is "lifetime" measured as an output? It is the instruction process that influences the presence or occurrence of an outcome, not the mere presence of an output. If it is a "lifelong" objective, will an immediate measurement as an output result in an identified and measured outcome? The answer is no, because it would be impossible to relate directly an immediate measurable output (e.g., count of number of instruction sessions) to the outcome of lifelong learning. Furthermore, other processes may influence a learning outcome as time passes; for example, individual and group experiences occurring after the instruction or forgotten influences such as a friend showing someone a shortcut (e.g., the difference between a keyword and subject search) when searching for information. Are these library outputs? No, they are outcomes. Outputs are measurable and must be compiled, gathered, or counted to be an output; impacts are not so readily and easily measured.

Consequently, a library can have both outputs and outcomes; outcomes are not dependent upon outputs, but are dependent upon the processes used to convert inputs into outputs or into outcomes. Thus, Figure 16.1 does not depict outcomes as a direct result of outputs; clearly, outcomes, student learning outcomes, need not pass through a stage of outputs.

STUDENT OUTCOMES AND STUDENT LEARNING OUTCOMES

There is nothing wrong with using different types of data collection, some for report provision, some for use in self-improvement, and others for benchmarking performance with peer institutions. In fact, most likely, institutions use assorted measures. Unfortunately, no standard terminology exists globally or across disciplines and stakeholders. Stakeholders, a broad term that encompasses many groups, might use terminology differently; they might even disagree about what comprises an *outcome*. Nonetheless, as this book illustrates, one key stakeholder group considers outcomes to be *student outcomes* (aggregate statistics on groups of students) and *student learning outcomes* (which reflect what students actually learned). Student outcomes are really outputs as they reflect what the institution has accomplished; they neither reflect what (or how much) students actually learned nor measure changes in students as a result of their college or university experience.

In contrast to aggregate statistics on an institution- or programwide basis, student learning outcomes are concerned with attributes and abilities, both cognitive and affective, which reflect how students' experiences at the institution supported their development as individuals. Because students are asked to demonstrate the acquisition of specific knowledge and skills, critical questions become:

- What do they know that they did not know before?
- What can they do that they could not do before?

In a coordinated effort to answer these results-oriented questions, higher education governing and monitoring bodies have revised the standards that institutions use to demonstrate their effectiveness, efficiency, and compliance with the expectations of those bodies. It is through these standards that accountability is set and student learning outcomes are imposed.

In the past, prescriptive standards that regional accrediting organizations established to accredit individual higher education institutions have been input and output based, focused on measuring and reporting the processes and structures concerning the delivery and use of institutional programs and services. To increase accountability practices, regional accrediting organizations are placing more pressure on institutions to measure what students learn by applying assessment processes, replacing traditional standards with less prescriptive ones that require the gathering of outcome measures—institutional outcomes and student learning outcomes.[1] Regional accreditors might also require member institutions to prepare assessment plans that set and measure outcomes, especially student learning outcomes, within the institution, and that provide a framework for continuous quality improvement over time.

OUTCOMES AND IMPACTS

Learning outcomes, a type of impact measure, apply to students at both the undergraduate or graduate level. Research outcomes are most appropriate for graduate students, but some programs at the undergraduate level have required research methods and statistics courses as well as elective courses to hone student ability to conduct and interpret research. As a result, there is a need for measures at both the undergraduate and graduate levels that reflect student ability to grasp and apply various components of the research process.

A neglected question is "Can outcomes assessment apply to faculty members?" Peter Hernon and Robert E. Dugan show that, in a way, it can. Academic libraries, they point out, might develop "faculty support outcomes assessment plans" that identify how an institution's library supports faculty research and contributes to their teaching efforts. For clarity, they note:

> For example, what library resources do faculty need to conduct research and to teach? Is the library providing those resources? Has faculty research improved/benefited from the growth of library resources, such as office and off-campus access to electronic resources? Have library resources aided in teaching? Do faculty members collaborate with library staff concerning classroom support and/or professional responsibilities? How may the library improve our efforts to support the faculty?
>
> Faculty support performance indicators (outcomes) focus on the ability and willingness of the faculty to use the library as a resource supporting their course requirements, such as reserves, collections, reference staff, facility; to instruct students on general and specific basic, intermediate, and advanced information literacy skills; to instruct students on course-specific, topic-based research processes; as a resource to support the information needs as a result of faculty research, publication, and other professional responsibilities and endeavors; [and] to update and maintain faculty information seeking, retrieval, and evaluation skills so that they can transfer these skills to students, as well as applying them to their professional responsibilities effectively and efficiently.[2]

They proceed to identify objectives to guide outcomes assessment, and they offer direct and indirect measures relevant to outcomes assessment. They even provide a five-page faculty library services survey as an indirect measure.[3]

Looking at faculty from a department, college, and institutional perspective, rather than a library perspective, raises the question "Is outcomes assessment part of faculty productivity?" Outcomes assessment does not reflect the totality of faculty activities. For example, some teaching assessments might include inputs, such as the number of students taught, and course evaluations (instructor focused). However, such indicators do not reflect the learning process at either the course or program level, nor do the grades given (e.g., the number of As versus the number of Cs) reflect the extent of learning that has occurred over time. Faculty productivity, most often, is viewed within the context of research, scholarship, and grant seeking; such productivity might be presented as input and output measures. Outcomes assessment is not intended to replace such indicators of productivity, but it goes beyond individual faculty members and their performance as renowned scholars and researchers. Outcomes assessment examines how a set of courses fit together to achieve the program and institutional mission.

Michael F. Middaugh believes that "the current climate in higher education . . . demands accountability with respect to both [faculty] productivity and program quality." He foresees "that activities related to the assessment of academic programs and outcomes will become a critical component of faculty productivity over the next several years."[4]

As the example of faculty productivity illustrates, assessment and evaluation occur at different times: (1) annually for salary increases; (2) for promotion, tenure, and contract renewal; and (3) to demonstrate how faculty teaching contributes to an effective and dynamic program and to the continued development of a prestigious institution, one known for its learning and intellectual environment. In such settings, there is a need to collect various measures, some of which relate directly to institutional effectiveness. Accrediting organizations and other stakeholders expect institutional effectiveness to reflect program review. Accountability is more than a mere collection of inputs, outputs, and traditional measures of faculty productivity—or measures that focus on an individual rather than on how a set of courses fit together to achieve the educational mission and to enhance the student's learning experience. Clearly, faculty productivity is an evolving concept, one likely to become more complex and to consider faculty contributions to institutional accountability or effectiveness. The issue is less how much faculty do (inputs and outputs) and more what is the quality of what they do (e.g., outcomes and impacts).

A MODEST RESEARCH AGENDA

Outcomes assessment encompasses student outcomes, student learning outcomes, and student research outcomes. Furthermore, student satisfaction and the fulfillment of student expectations through *service quality*[5] may have an indirect relationship to student receptivity to, and mastery of, what is taught within a course or over the duration of a program or lifelong learning. As stressed in other chapters, outcomes assessment deals with accountability and provides various stakeholders, institutions, and programs with the evidence necessary to judge whether or not educational missions are met. Outcomes assessment also addresses impact assessment and value for money. Given this situation, any research agenda, such as the following one, encourages faculty and administrators at institutions of higher education to consider outcomes assessment as a legitimate area of scholarship. In fact, more faculty should be encouraged to develop the research and conceptual foundation of outcomes assessment. A research agenda might include the following:

- Flesh out the four perspectives discussed in Chapter 11 and the different types of measures and any interrelations. Examine the use of terminology (e.g., inputs, outputs, outcomes, impacts, effectiveness, and efficiency measures) in different disciplines and fields of study, and across stakeholder groups.

- Review Figure 16.1 from different perspectives and make refinements as necessary.

- Develop more state-of-the-art analyses of outcomes assessment that are international in scope so that the use of terminology worldwide is better understood.

- Apply experimental designs to measure the extent to which learning occurs and lifelong learning is achieved. Such assessment should be both formative and summative.

- Develop easy-to-apply strategies for data collection, including data collection instruments and instructions about how to implement them.

- Examine effectiveness within a team context as faculty and librarians work together to achieve program and institutional goals and expectations. That context might pertain to student learning outcomes. With teams now so common in the workplace, there is a need to examine the perspective of social and organizational psychologist J. Richard Hackman about teams and to see how applicable his concept is to different disciplines and work environments.[6]

- Examine any relationship among outcomes assessment, service quality, and satisfaction.

- Investigate outcomes that apply to the local community and have a cultural impact (e.g., result in greater appreciation of art and music). Cultural and community measures exist inside and outside higher education; pertain to a city, town, or a virtual community; and affect the overall quality of life for, and lifelong learning of, members of that community.[7]

- Identify the totality of impact measures and how outcomes assessment fits within that context.

CONCLUSION

It seems that those engaged in writing and research on performance, input, output, customer-based, and outcomes measures do not necessarily use terminology in a similar manner. They may even fail to appreciate subtle or significant differences in their use of the terminology. For example, as this chapter has shown, there are different perspectives on outcomes. This book focuses on only one perspective—a significant perspective that addresses impact, benefits, differences, or changes in individuals, but still only one perspective. Anyone dealing with stakeholders (e.g., accrediting organizations) and institutional effectiveness, however, must understand and apply that perspective.

As Figure 16.1 illustrates, research in different areas and from different perspectives enriches the field of assessment and evaluation, as we start to move above the trees and to create an image of the entire forest. That forest is populated with different varieties, shapes, and sizes of trees. Each tree contributes to the overall health of the forest and impacts the overall environment. Now is the time for all of us to examine the forest and to go beyond working from tree to tree.

NOTES

1. Beth McMurtrie, "Accreditors Revamp Policies to Stress Student Learning," *The Chronicle of Higher Education* (July 7, 2000): A29.

2. Peter Hernon and Robert E. Dugan, *An Action Plan for Outcomes Assessment in Your Library* (Chicago: American Library Association, 2002), 147.

3. Hernon and Dugan, *An Action Plan for Outcomes Assessment*, 147–148, 164–169.

4. Michael F. Middaugh, *Understanding Faculty Productivity: Standards and Benchmarking for Colleges and Universities* (San Francisco: Jossey-Bass, 2001), 151, 156.

5. See Peter Hernon and Ellen Altman, *Assessing Service Quality: Satisfying the Expectations of Library Customers* (Chicago: American Library Association, 1998).

6. J. Richard Hackman, *Leading Teams: Setting the Stage for Great Performance* (Boston: Harvard Business School Press, 2002); and J. Richard Hackman and Richard E. Walton, "Leading Groups in Organizations," in *Designing Effective Work Groups*, ed. P. S. Goodman (San Francisco: Jossey-Bass, 1986), 72–119.

7. Hernon and Dugan, *An Action Plan for Outcomes Assessment in Your Library*, 56–63.

Bibliography

Articles

Angelo, Thomas A. "Reassessing (and Defining) Assessment," *AAHE Bulletin* 48 (November 1995): 7.

Baker, Ronald L. "Evaluating Quality and Effectiveness: Regional Accreditation Principles and Practices," *The Journal of Academic Librarianship* 28 (2002): 3–7.

Barclay, Donald. "Evaluating Library Instruction: Doing the Best You Can with What You Have," *RQ* 33 (Winter 1993): 195–202.

Barrowman, Carole E. "Improving Teaching and Learning Effectiveness by Defining Expectations," *New Directions for Higher Education* 24 (Winter 1996): 103–114.

Bartlett, Thomas. "Take My Chair (Please)," *The Chronicle of Higher Education* (March 7, 2003): A36–A38.

Bogue, E. Grady. "Quality Assurance in Higher Education: The Evolution of Systems and Design Ideals," *New Directions for Institutional Research* 25, no. 3 (1998): 7–18.

Branch, Jennifer L. "Investigating the Information-Seeking Processes of Adolescents: The Value of Using Think Alouds and Think Afters," *Library & Information Science Research* 22 (2000): 371–392.

Burd, Stephen. "Accountability or Meddling?" *The Chronicle of Higher Education* (September 20, 2002): A23.

———. "Bush's Next Target?" *The Chronicle of Higher Education* (July 11, 2003): A18–A20.

———. "Will Congress Require Colleges to Grade Themselves?" *The Chronicle of Higher Education* (April 4, 2003): A27.

Daugherty, Timothy K., and Elizabeth W. Carter. "Assessment of Outcome-Focused Library Instruction in Psychology," *Journal of Instructional Psychology* 24 (1997): 29–33.

DeWitt, Donald L., ed. "Evaluating the Twenty-first Century Library: The Association of Research Libraries New Measures Initiative, 1997–2001," *Journal of Library Administration* 35 (2001): 1–91.

Dugan, Robert E., and Peter Hernon. "Outcomes Assessment: Not Synonymous with Inputs and Outputs," *The Journal of Academic Librarianship* 28 (November 2002): 376–380.

Dunn, Kathleen. "Assessing Information Literacy Skills in the California State University: A Progress Report," *The Journal of Academic Librarianship* 28 (2002): 26–35.

Eaton, Judith S. "Regional Accreditation Reform," *Change* 33, no. 2 (March/ April, 2001): 38–45.

Eisenman, Charles D. "Faculty Participation in Assessment Programs," *North Central Association Quarterly* 66 (Fall 1991): 458–464.

Ewell, Peter T. "A Matter of Integrity: Accountability and the Future of Self-Regulation," *Change* 26, no. 6 (1994): 24–29.

Fraser, Bruce T., Charles R. McClure, and Emily H. Leahy. "Toward a Framework for Assessing Library and Institutional Outcomes," *Portal: Libraries and the Academy* 2 (2002): 505–528.

Gratch-Lindauer, Bonnie. "Comparing the Regional Accreditation Standards: Outcomes Assessment and Other Trends," *The Journal of Academic Librarianship* 28 (January 2002): 14–25.

———. "Defining and Measuring the Library's Impact on Campuswide Outcomes," *College & Research Libraries* 59 (November 1998): 546–570.

Gray, Peter J. "Viewing Assessment as an Innovation: Leadership and the Change Process," *New Directions for Higher Education* 100 (1997): 5–16.

Hodkinson, P., and M. Bloomer. "Stokingham Sixth Form College: Institutional Culture and Dispositions towards Learning," *British Journal of Sociology of Education* 21 (2000): 187–203.

Hudgins, James L. "Institutional Effectiveness: A Strategy for Renewal," *Community College Journal* 63, no. 5 (1993): 41–44.

Jackson, Norman. "Understanding Standards-Based Quality Assurance: Part I— Rationale and Conceptual Basis," *Quality Assurance in Education* 6 (1998): 132–140.

Kaplan, Robert S., and David P. Norton. "The Balanced Scorecard—Measures That Drive Performance," *Harvard Business Review* 70 (January/February 1992): 71–79.

Kuh, George D. "Shaping Student Character," *Liberal Education* 84, no. 3 (1998): 18–25.

Kyle, D. W., and R. A. Hovda. "Action Research: Comments on Current Trends and Future Possibilities," *Peabody Journal of Education* 64 (1989): 170–175.

Kyrillidou, Martha. "From Input and Output Measures to Quality and Outcome Measures, or, from the User in the Life of the Library to the Library in the Life of the User," *The Journal of Academic Librarianship* 28 (January-March 2002): 42–46.

López, Cecilia L. "Assessment of Student Learning: Challenges and Strategies," *The Journal of Academic Librarianship* 28 (2002): 356–367.

——. "Classroom Research and Regional Accreditation: Common Ground. Special Insert," *Briefing* 14, no. 3 (1996): 1–4.

Major, C. H. "Connecting What We Know and What We Do through Problem-Based Learning," *AAHE Bulletin* 51, no. 7 (March 1999): 7–9.

Maki, Peggy L. "Developing an Assessment Plan to Learn about Student Learning," *The Journal of Academic Librarianship* 28 (January–March 2002): 8–13.

——. "From Standardized Tests to Alternative Methods," *Change* 33, no. 2 (March/April 2001): 28–31.

Markless, Sharon, and David Streatfield. "Developing Performance and Impact Indicators and Targets in Public and Education Libraries," *International Journal of Information Management* 21 (2001): 167–179.

Massy, William F. "Auditing Higher Education to Improve Quality," *The Chronicle of Higher Education* (June 20, 2003): B6–B7.

McKeon, Howard P. "Point of View: Controlling the Price of College," *The Chronicle of Higher Education* (July 11, 2003): B20.

McMurtrie, B. "Accreditors Revamp Policies to Stress Student Learning," *The Chronicle of Higher Education* (July 7, 2000): A29.

Messick, S. "The Matter of Style: Manifestations of Personality in Cognition, Learning and Teaching," *Educational Psychologist* 29 (1994): 121–136.

Moore, Kay McCullough. "Assessment of Institutional Effectiveness," *New Directions for Community Colleges* 14, no. 4 (1986): 49–60.

Paulson, L. F., P. R. Paulson, and C. Meyer. "What Makes a Portfolio a Portfolio," *Educational Leadership* 48, no. 5 (1991): 60–63.

Peters, Roger. "Some Snarks Are Boojums: Accountability and the End(s) of Higher Education," *Change* 26, no. 6 (1994): 16–23.

Ratteray, Oswald M. T. "Information Literacy in Self-Study and Accreditation," *The Journal of Academic Librarianship* 28 (November 2002): 368–375.

Shim, Wonsik, and Charles R. McClure. "Improving Database Vendors' Usage Statistics Reporting through Collaboration between Libraries and Vendors," *College & Research Libraries* 63 (November 2002): 499–514.

Smith, Kenneth R. "New Roles and Responsibilities for the University Library: Advancing Student Learning through Outcomes Assessment," *Journal of Library Administration* 35, no. 4 (2001): 29–37, available at http://www.arl.org/stats/newmeas/HEOSmith.html (accessed March 2, 2004).

Vos, Henk. "How to Assess for Improvement of Learning," *European Journal of Engineering Education* 25 (2000): 227–233.

Welsh, John F., and Sukhen Dey. "Quality Measurement and Quality Assurance in Higher Education," *Quality Assurance in Education* 10 (2002): 17–25.

Wolff, Ralph A. "Restoring the Credibility of Accreditation," *Trusteeship* 1, no. 6 (1993): 20–21, 23–24.

Yorke, Mantz. "Assuring Quality and Standards in Globalised Higher Education," *Quality Assurance in Education* 9 (1999): 14–24.

Books

Anderson, Lorin W., David R. Krathwohl, P. W. Airasian, K. A. Cruikshank, R. E. Mayer, P. R. Intrich, J. Raths, and M. C. Wittrock. *A Taxonomy for Learning, Teaching and Assessing*. New York: David McKay Co., 2001.

Angelo, Thomas A., and K. Patricia Cross. *Classroom Assessment Techniques: A Handbook for College Teachers*, 2nd ed. San Francisco: Jossey-Bass, 1993.

Astin, A. W. *Assessment for Excellence: The Philosophy and Practice of Assessment and Evaluation in Higher Education*. Westport, Conn.: Oryx Press, 1991.

Banta, Trudy W., and Associates. *Building a Scholarship of Assessment*. San Francisco: Jossey-Bass, 2002.

Bloom, Benjamin S., and David R. Krathwohl. *Taxonomy of Educational Objectives: The Classification of Educational Goals. Handbook I: Cognitive Domain*. New York: Longmans, Green, 1956.

Boyer, Ernest L. *Scholarship Reconsidered: Priorities of the Professorate*. San Francisco: Jossey-Bass, 1990; Princeton, N.J.: The Carnegie Foundation for the Advancement of Teaching, 1990.

Brennan, John, and Tarla Shah, ed. *Managing Quality in Higher Education: An International Perspective on Institutional Assessment and Change*. Buckingham, UK: OECD, SRHE, and Open University Press, 2000.

Campbell, C., S. Kanaan, B. Kehm, B. Mockiene, D. F. Westerheijden, and R. Williams. *The European University: A Handbook on Institutional Approaches to Strategic Management, Quality Management, European Policy and Academic Recognition*. Torino, Italy: European Training Foundation, 2000.

Carol, John C., and Eric J. Johnson. *Decision Research: A Field Guide*. Newbury Park, Calif.: Sage, 1990.

Commission on Colleges and Universities, Northwest Association of Schools and of Colleges. *Accreditation Handbook*. Bellevue, Wash.: Commission on Colleges and Universities, 1999.

Commission on Higher Education, Middle States Association of Colleges and Schools. *Characteristics of Excellence in Higher Education: Standards for Accreditation*. Philadelphia: The Commission, 1994.

Davis, J. R. *Better Teaching, More Learning: Strategies for Success in Postsecondary Settings*. Phoenix, Ariz.: Oryx Press, 1993.

Eaton, Judith S. *An Overview of U.S. Accreditation*. Washington, D.C.: Council for Higher Education Accreditation, 2002.

Eckel, P., M. Green, and B. Hill. *On Change V—Riding the Waves of Change: Insights from Transforming Institutions*. Washington, D.C.: American Council on Education, 2001.

Ewell, Peter, and Dennis P. Jones. *Indicators of Good Practice in Undergraduate Education: A Handbook for Development and Implementation*. Boulder, Colo.: National Center for Higher Education Management Systems, 1996.

Freed, Jann E., and Marie R. Klugman. *Quality Principles and Practices in Higher Education: Different Questions for Different Times*. Phoenix, Ariz.: Oryx Press, 1997.

Gardner, Howard. *Frames of Mind: The Theory of Multiple Intelligences*. New York: Basic Books, 1993.

Glassick, Charles, Mary T. Huber, and Gene I. Maeroff. *Scholarship Assessed: Evaluation of the Professorate*. San Francisco: Jossey-Bass, 1997.

Hackman, J. Richard. *Leading Teams: Setting the Stage for Great Performances*. Boston: Harvard Business School Press, 2002.

Hatfield, Susan R., ed. *The Seven Principles in Action: Improving Undergraduate Education*. Boston: Anker Pub. Co., 1995.

Hernon, Peter, and Ellen Altman. *Assessing Service Quality: Satisfying the Expectations of Library Customers*. Chicago: American Library Association, 1998.

Hernon, Peter, and Robert E. Dugan. *An Action Plan for Outcomes Assessment in Your Library*. Chicago: American Library Association, 2002.

Highet, G. *The Art of Teaching*. New York: Vintage Books, 1959.

Huba, Mary E., and Jann E. Freed. *Learner-Centered Assessment on College Campuses: Shifting the Focus from Teaching to Learning*. Boston: Allyn and Bacon, 2000.

Jenkins, R. R., and K. T. Romer. *Who Teaches? Who Learns? Authentic Student/Faculty Partners*. Providence, R.I.: IVY Publishers, n.d.

Johnson, Spencer. *Who Moved My Cheese?* New York: Putnam, 1998.

Kolb, D. A. *Individual Learning Styles and the Learning Process*. Cambridge, Mass: MIT Press, 1971.

LeCompte, Margaret, Judith Preissle, and Tesch Renata. *Ethnography and Qualitative Design in Educational Research*, 2nd ed. New York: Academic Press, 1993.

Leef, George C., and Roxana D. Burris. *Can College Accreditation Live Up to Its Promise?* Washington, D.C.: American Council of Trustees and Alumni, 2002.

Lucas, A. F., and Associates. *Leading Academic Change: Essential Roles for Department Chairs*. San Francisco: Jossey-Bass, 2000.

Middaugh, Michael F. *Understanding Faculty Productivity: Standards and*

Benchmarks for Colleges and Universities. San Francisco: Jossey-Bass Publishers, 2001.

Middle States Commission on Higher Education. *Characteristics of Excellence in Higher Education: Eligibility Requirements and Standards for Accreditation.* Philadelphia: The Commission, 2002.

———. *Developing Research & Communication Skills: Guidelines for Information Literacy in the Curriculum.* Philadelphia: The Commission, 2003.

———. *Student Learning Assessment: Options and Resources.* Philadelphia: Middle States Commission on Higher Education, 2003.

Northwest Commission on Colleges and Universities. *Accreditation Handbook.* Redmond, Wash.: Northwest Commission on Colleges and Universities, 2003.

Palomba, Catherine A., and Trudy W. Banta. *Assessment Essentials: Planning, Implementing, and Improving Assessment in Higher Education.* San Francisco: Jossey-Bass, 1999.

Parker, Palmer. *The Courage to Teach: Exploring the Inner Landscape of a Teacher's Life.* San Francisco: Jossey-Bass, 1998.

Scheele, J. P., P.A.M. Maassen, and D. F. Westerheijden. *To Be Continued: Follow-up of Quality Assurance in Higher Education.* Maarssen, Netherlands: Elsevier/De Tijdstroom, 1998.

Silverman, Sharon L., and Martha E. Casazza. *Learning and Development: Making Connections to Enhance Teaching.* San Francisco: Jossey-Bass, 2000.

Vavra, Terry G. *Improving Your Measurement of Customer Satisfaction: A Guide to Creating, Conducting, Analyzing, and Reporting Customer Satisfaction Measurement Programs.* Milwaukee, Wisc.: ASQ Quality Press, 1997.

Wiggins, G., and J. McTighe. *Understanding by Design.* Alexandria, Va.: Association for Supervision and Curriculum Development, 1998.

Book Chapters

Banta, Trudy W. "Characteristics of Effective Outcomes Assessment: Foundations & Examples," in *Building a Scholarship of Assessment*, edited by Trudy W. Banta and Associates, 260–283. San Francisco: Jossey-Bass, 2002.

Duffy, T. M., and D. J. Cunningham. "Constructivism: Implications for the Design and Delivery of Instruction," in *Handbook of Research for Educational Communications and Technology*, edited by David H. Jonassen, 170–198. New York: Macmillan, 1996.

Hackman, J. Richard, and Richard E. Walton. "Leading Groups in Organizations," in *Designing Effective Work Groups*, edited by Paul S. Goodman and Associates, 72–119. San Francisco: Jossey-Bass, 1986.

Poll, Roswitha. "Managing Service Quality with the Balanced Scorecard," in *Advances in Library Administration and Organization*, vol. 20, edited by Edward D. Garten and Delmus E. Williams, 213–227. Amsterdam: Elsevier, 2003.

Government Documents

National Committee of Inquiry into Higher Education. Higher Education in the Learning Environment. *Report*. London: Her Majesty's Stationery Office, 1997.

U.S. Department of Education, National Center for Education Statistics, *Defining and Assessing Learning: Exploring Competency-Based Initiatives*, NCES 2002–159, prepared by Elizabeth A. Jones and Richard A. Voorhees, with Karen Paulson. Washington, D.C.: Council of the National Postsecondary Education Cooperative Working Group on Competency-Based Initiatives, 2002.

U.S. General Accounting Office, National Security and International Affairs Division. *Best Practices Methodology: A New Approach for Improving Government Operations*, GAO/NSIAD-95–154. Washington, D.C.: General Accounting Office, May 1995.

Web Resources

ACT. "ACT Assessment." Iowa City, Iowa: ACT. Available at http://www.act.org/aap/, accessed March 2, 2004.

Alabama State University, College of Business Administration. "Student Writing and Quantitative Skills." Montgomery, Ala., n.d. Available at http://www.cobanetwork.com/soap.htm, accessed August 15, 2003.

Allan, Joanna. "Learning Outcomes in Higher Education," *Studies in Higher Education* 21 (March 1996): 93–109. Available at EBSCOhost, Academic Search Premier database, accessed June 6, 2003.

Alverno College. "About Alverno." Milwaukee, Wisc.: Alverno College, n.d. Available at http://www.alverno.edu/about_alverno/ability_curriculum.html, accessed September 4, 2003.

———. "About Alverno: Ability-Based Curriculum." Milwaukee, Wisc.: Alverno College, n.d. Available at http://www.alverno.edu/about_alverno/ability_curriculum.html, accessed September 4, 2003.

———. "About Alverno: Alverno's Eight Abilities." Milwaukee, Wisc.: Alverno

College, n.d. Available at http://www.alverno.edu/about_alverno/ability.
html accessed September 4, 2003.

———. "AC*CEL: The Diagnostic Digital Portfolio." Milwaukee, Wisc.: Alverno College, 2002. Available at http://ddp.alverno.edu/, accessed August 15, 2003.

———. "Quick Facts about Alverno." Milwaukee, Wisc.: Alverno College, n.d. Available at http://www.alverno.edu/about_alverno/quick_facts.html, accessed September 4, 2003.

American Association for Higher Education. "Principles of Good Practice for Assessing Student Learning." Washington, D.C.: American Association for Higher Education. Available at http://www.aahe.org/assessment/principl.htm, accessed June 8, 2003.

American College Personnel Association. [clearinghouse of assessment instruments]. Washington, D.C.: American College Personnel Association. Available at http://www.acpa.nche.edu/comms/comm09/dragon/dragon-index.html, accessed March 2, 2004.

American Library Association. *American Library Association Presidential Committee on Information Literacy: Final Report*. Chicago: American Library Association, 1989. Available at http://www.ala.org/Content/Navigation Menu/ACRL/Publications/White_Papers_and_Reports/Presidential_Committee_on_Information_Literacy.htm, accessed September 28, 2003.

American Library Association, Association of College and Research Libraries. *Information Literacy Competency Standards for Higher Education*. Chicago: Association of College and Research Libraries, 2000. Available at http://www.ala.org/ala/acrl/acrlstandards/informationliteracycompetency.htm, accessed March 2, 2004.

———. *Objectives for Information Literacy Instruction: A Model Statement for Academic Librarians*. Chicago: Association of College and Research Libraries, 2001. Available at http://www.ala.org/ala/acrl/acrlstandards/objectivesinformation.htm, accessed March 2, 2004.

Anderson, Don, Richard Johnson, and Bruce Milligan. *Quality Assurance and Accreditation in Australian Higher Education: An Assessment of Australian and International Practice*. Canberra, Australia: Department of Education, Higher Education Division, Training and Youth Affairs, May 2000. Available at http://www.detya.au/highered/eippubs/eip00_1/fullcopy00_1.pdf, accessed August 15, 2003.

Angelo, Thomas A. "Doing Assessment as If Learning Matters Most." *AAHE Bulletin* (May 1999). Available at http://aahebulletin.com/public/archive/angelomay99.asp, accessed August 12, 2003.

"Assessment—Institutional Effectiveness." Sacramento: California State University, Sacramento, 2000. Available at http://www.csus.edu/portfolio/

institutional_portfolio/assess_doc_institution.htm, accessed August 15, 2003.

Audit Commission. [Home page]. London: Audit Commission. Available at http://www.audit-commission.gov.uk, accessed March 2, 2004.

Brenau University. "Assessment at Brenau: An Overview—Assessment and Planning." Gainesville, Ga.: Brenau University, n.d. Available at http://intranet.brenau.edu/assessment/Guide/guideframe.htm, accessed September 4, 2003.

———. "Assessment at Brenau: An Overview—Assessment Roles, Responsibilities, and Time Frames: Educational Programs." Gainesville, Ga.: Brenau University, n.d. Available at http://intranet.brenau.edu/assessment/Guide/guideframe.htm, accessed September 4, 2003.

———. "Assessment at Brenau: An Overview—Cross Curricular Goals: Criteria Statements and Support Documents," *A Guide to Assessment.* Gainesville, Ga.: Brenau University, n.d. Available at http://intranet.brenau.edu/assessment/ccgoals.doc, accessed September 4, 2003.

———. "Assessment at Brenau: An Overview—Guidelines for Developing Assessment Plans in Educational Programs." Gainesville, Ga.: Brenau University, n.d. Available at http://intranet.brenau.edu/assessment/Guide/guideframe.htm, accessed September 4, 2003.

———. "Assessment at Brenau: An Overview—Outcomes Assessment Reporting Cycle at Brenau University." Gainesville, Ga.: Brenau University, n.d. Available at http://intranet.brenau.edu/assessment/Guide/guideframe.htm, accessed September 4, 2003.

———. "Assessment at Brenau: An Overview—Purpose and Planning." Gainesville, Ga.: Brenau University, n.d. Available at http://intranet.brenau.edu/assessment/Guide/guideframe.htm, accessed September 4, 2003.

———. "Purpose Statement." Gainesville, Ga.: Brenau University, n.d. Available at http://intranet.brenau.edu/assessment/purpose.htm, accessed September 4, 2003.

Burd, Stephen. "Republican Leaders Stress Accountability and Cost Issues in Hearing on Higher Education Act," *The Chronicle of Higher Education* (May 14, 2003): 1. Available at http://chronicle.com.daily/22003/05/200305140n.htm, accessed June 22, 2003.

CAAP (Collegiate Assessment of Academic Proficiency). Iowa City, Iowa: ACT. Available at http://www.act.org/aap/, accessed March 2, 2004.

California State Polytechnic University, Pomona. "General Program Assessment Home Page." Pomona: California State Polytechnic University, n.d. Available at http://www.csupomona.edu/~academic/programs/assessment/body.htm, accessed August 15, 2003.

———. "Program Assessment: Assessment Tools." Pomona: California State Polytechnic University, n.d. Available at http://www.csupomona.edu/~

academic/programs/assessment/tools_assess.htm, accessed August 15, 2003.

California State University, Monterey Bay. "Academic Information." Seaside: California State University, Monterey Bay, n.d. Available at http:// csumb.edu/academic/colleges/index.html, accessed September 30, 2003.

———. "Academic Program Descriptions: Collaborative Health and Human Services (CHHS)." Seaside: California State University, Monterey Bay, n.d. Available at http://csumb.edu/academic/descriptions/chhs.html, accessed September 30, 2003.

———. "CSUMB Learning Goals." Seaside: California State University, Monterey Bay, n.d. Available at http://csumb.edu/info/academics/goals.html, accessed September 30, 2003.

———. "General Education / University Learning Requirements." Seaside: California State University, Monterey Bay, n.d. Available at http://csumb. edu/info/academics/freshman.html, accessed September 30, 2003.

———. "Technology/Information." Seaside: California State University, Monterey Bay, n.d. Available at http://csumb.edu/academic/ulr/ulr/ technology.html, accessed September 30, 2003.

———. "University Learning Requirements." Seaside: California State University, Monterey Bay, n.d. Available at http://csumb.edu/academic/ulr/, accessed September 30, 2003.

Clayton, Mark. "Backlash Brews over Rising Cost of College." *The Christian Science Monitor* (June 17, 2003). Available at http://www.csmonitor. com/2003/0617/p15s01-lehl.html, accessed June 18, 2003.

College Student Experiences Questionnaire Research Program. Home page. Bloomington: Indiana University, 2003. Available at http://www. indiana.edu/~cseq/, accessed March 2, 2004.

Community College Survey of Student Engagement. Austin: University of Texas, 2003. Available at http://www.ccsse.org/, accessed March 2, 2004.

Conestoga College. Documents—Strategic Plan: "Trends in International Education." Kitchener, Ont.: Conestoga College, n.d. Available at http:// www.conestogac.on.ca/jsp/edocuments/stplan/trends.internationaled trends.jsp, accessed August 15, 2003.

Connecticut College. "E-portfolio Collaboration Project." New London: Connecticut College, n.d. Available at http://www.conncoll.edu/admissions/ admitted.eportdemo/, accessed August 15, 2003.

Cornell University. Office of Distributed Learning. Home Page. Ithaca, N.Y.: Cornell University, n.d. Available at http://www.library.cornell.edu/dl/ aboutus.htm, accessed October 16, 2003.

The Critical Thinking Assessment Project. Chico: California State University, Chico, Department of Philosophy, n.d. Available at http://www. csuchico.edu/phil/ct/ct_assess.htm, accessed March 2, 2004.

The Critical Thinking Consortium. Home page. Dillon Beach, Calif.: Foundation for Critical Thinking. Available at http://www.criticalthinking.org/, accessed March 2, 2004.

Davis & Elkins College. "Assessment at David & Elkins College." Elkins, W.V.: Davis & Elkins College, n.d. Available at http://www.davisandelkins.edu/academics/assessment.htm, accessed March 2, 2004.

Enerson, Diane M., Kathryn M. Plank, and R. Neill Johnson. "An Introduction to Classroom Assessment Techniques." University Park: Pennsylvania State University, Center for Excellence in Learning & Teaching, n.d. Available at http://www.psu.edu/celt/CATs.html, accessed August 15, 2003.

European Network for Quality Assurance in Higher Education. [Home page]. Helsinki, Finland: European Network for Quality Assurance in Higher Education. Available at http://www.enqa.net/index.lasso, accessed March 2, 2004.

Frye, Richard. *Assessment, Accountability, and Student Learning Outcomes*. Bellingham: Western Washington University, n.d. Available at http://www.ac.wwu.edu/~dialogue/issue2.html, accessed August 15, 2003.

George Mason University. "Assessment Plans: Listed by College/Department/Program." Fairfax, Va.: George Mason University, n.d. Available at http://assessment.gmu.edu/programgoals/index.cfm, accessed September 4, 2003.

Government of Ontario. Ministry of Education. Ministry of Training, Colleges and Universities. "Information on Program Outcomes." Ottawa, Ontario: Ministry of Education, 2003. Available at http://www.edu.gov.on.ca.eng/general/postsec/ps_overview.html, accessed August 15, 2003.

Harcourt Assessment. "Watson-Glasier Critical Thinking Appraisal." San Antonio, Tex.: Harcourt Assessment, 2004. Available at http://marketplace.psychcorp.com/PsychCorp.com/Cultures/en-US/dotCom/Assessment+Center/SubPages/Watson-Glaser+Critical+Thinking+Appraisal+(WGCTA)+Forms+A+and+B.htm, accessed March 2, 2004.

Hoey, J. Joseph. "Effectively Sharing Knowledge in Cyberspace: A Comparative Analysis of Faculty Experiences, Student Attitudes and Student Outcomes in Web-Based Courses within the Research University Setting." Paper presented at the Conference of the Consortium for Assessment and Planning Support, Monroe, Louisiana, April 1999. Available at http://courses.ncsu.edu/info/f97_assessment.html, accessed March 2, 2004.

Institute of Museum and Library Services. "Frequently Asked OBE [Outcome-Based Evaluation] Questions." Washington, D.C.: Institute of Museum and Library Services, n.d. Available at http://www.imls.gov/grants/current/crnt_outcomes.htm, accessed March 2, 2004.

iWebfolio. Pittsburgh, Penn.: Nuventive, n.d. Available at http://www.nuventive.com/html/products.htm, accessed March 2, 2004.

James Madison University. "Institution-Specific Measures." Harrisonburg, Va.: James Madison University, n.d. Available at http://roie.schev.edu/four_year/JMU/body.asp?&i=1, accessed September 4, 2003.

———. "Mission Statement." Harrisonburg, Va.: James Madison University, n.d. Available at http://roie.schev.edu/four_year/JMU/body.asp?&m=1, accessed September 4, 2003.

King's College. "The Comprehensive Assessment Program." Wilkes-Barre, Pa.: King's College, n.d. Available at http://www.kings.edu/assessment/index.htm, accessed September 4, 2003.

———. "CORE Curriculum." Wilkes-Barre, Pa.: King's College, n.d. Available at http://www.kings.edu/academics/core.html, accessed September 4, 2003.

Kumar, Anita. "A College FCAT? The Debate Begins." *St. Petersburg Times* (May 1, 2003). Available at http://pqasb.pqarchiver.com/sptimes/access/331459891.html?FMT=FT&FMTS=FT&desc=A+college+FCAT%3f+The+debate+begin, accessed August 12, 2003.

———. "College FCAT? Failure Could Hurt Alma Mater." *St. Petersburg Times* (May 1, 2003). Available at http://www.sptimes.com/2003/05/01/State/College_FCATY_Failure_.shtml, accessed August 15, 2003.

———. "An FCAT for College Juniors?" *St. Petersburg Times* (July 24, 2003). Available at http://pqasb.pqarchiver.com/sptimes/access/374842351.html?FMT=FT&FMTS=FT&desc=An+FCAT+for+college+juniors?, accessed August 12, 2003.

LibQUAL+. Washington, D.C.: Association of Research Libraries, 2003. Available at http://www.libqual.org/index.cfm, accessed September 21, 2003.

López, Cecilia L. "Assessment of Student Learning." *Liberal Education* 84 (Summer 1998): 36–44. Available at EBSCOhost, Academic Search Premier database, accessed June 6, 2003.

Maki, Peggy. "Moving from Paperwork to Pedagogy." *AAHE Bulletin* (May 2002). Available at http://aahebulletin.com/public/archive/paperwork.asp?, accessed June 8, 2003.

———. "Using Multiple Assessment Methods to Explore Student Learning and Development Inside and Outside of the Classroom." *NetResults* [National Association of Student Affairs Professionals] (January 15, 2002): 3. Available at http://www.naspa.org/netresults/article.cfm?ID=558&category=assessment%20/%20Research, accessed November 10, 2003.

MFAT (Major Field Assessment Test). Rolla: University of Missouri, n.d. Available at http://web.umr.edu/~assess/instrumt/mfat.html, accessed March 2, 2004.

Middle States Commission on Higher Education. *Characteristics of Excellence in Higher Education: Eligibility Requirements and Standards for Accreditation.* Philadelphia: Middle States Commission on Higher Education, 2002. Available at http://www.msache.org/pubs.html, accessed August 15, 2003.

Minneapolis Community and Technical College. "Academic Programs." Minneapolis, Minn.: Minneapolis Community and Technical College, n.d. Available at http://www.minneapolis.edu/academicAffairs/index.cfm, accessed September 4, 2003.

———. "Information Literacy Assessment Material." Minneapolis, Minn.: Minneapolis Community and Technical College, n.d. Available at http://www.minneapolis.edu/library/courses/infs1000/assessment/assessment. htm, accessed September 4, 2003.

———. "Information Literacy Tutorial." Minneapolis, Minn.: Minneapolis Community and Technical College, n.d. Available at http://www.minneapolis.edu/library/tutorials/infolit/index.html, accessed September 4, 2003.

———. "Information Studies." Minneapolis, Minn.: Minneapolis Community and Technical College, n.d. Available at http://www.minneapolis.edu/library/courses/infostudies.htm, accessed September 4, 2003.

———. "MCTC Strategic Plan: 1999–2004." Minneapolis, Minn.: Minneapolis Community and Technical College, n.d. Available at http://www.minneapolis.edu/portfolio/planning/strategicPlan.htm, accessed September 4, 2003.

———. "Syllabus: Information Literacy & Research Skills." Minneapolis, Minn.: Minneapolis Community and Technical College, n.d. Available at http://www.minneapolis.edu/library/courses/infs1000/acrobat/Syllabi/Syllabus.pdf, accessed September 4, 2003.

———. "Tutorial: Introduction & Use Guides." Minneapolis, Minn.: Minneapolis Community and Technical College, n.d. Available at http://www.minneapolis.edu/library/tutorials/infolit/tablesversion/home.htm, accessed September 4, 2003.

National Center for Public Policy and Higher Education. *Measuring Up 2000: The State-by-State Report Card for Higher Education*. Washington, D.C.: National Center for Public Policy and Higher Education. Available at http://www.highereducation.org/commentary, accessed October 22, 2003.

National Survey of Student Engagement. Bloomington: Indiana University, n.d. Available at http://www.indiana.edu/~nsse/, accessed March 2, 2004.

North Carolina State University, College of Engineering, prepared by Michael Carter. "Annotated Template for Program Outcomes." Raleigh: North Carolina State University, 2000. Available at http://www.engr.ncsu.edu/abet/criterion-3/template-3.html, accessed August 15, 2003.

North Carolina State University, Division of Undergraduate Affairs. *Assessment for the Division of Undergraduate Affairs*. Raleigh: North Carolina State University, Division of Undergraduate Affairs, 2001. Available at http://www.ncsu.edu/undergrad_affairs/assessment/assess.htm, accessed October 11, 2003.

Pausch, L., and Mary P. Popp. "Assessment of Information Literacy Lessons from the Higher Education Assessment Movement." Chicago: American Library Association, Association of College and Research Libraries, 1997. Available at http://www.ala.org/Content/ContentGroups/ACRL1/Nashville_1997_Papers/Pausch_and_Popp.htm, accessed September 28, 2003.

Pennsylvania State University, "Visual Image User Study." University Park: Pennsylvania State University, n.d. Available at http://www.libraries.psu.edu/vius/, accessed October 16, 2003.

Quality Assurance Agency for Higher Education. "About QAA." Gloucester, Scotland: Quality Assurance Agency for Higher Education, n.d. Available at http://www.qaa.ac.uk/aboutqaa/aboutQAA.htm, accessed August 15, 2003.

Quality Assurance Agency for Higher Education and Peter Williams. "Higher Quality 11." Gloucester, Scotland: Quality Assurance Agency for Higher Education, n.d. Available at http://www.qaa.ac.uk/public/hq/hq11_contents.htm, accessed August 15, 2003.

Roanoke College. "Institutional Effectiveness and Assessment for Academic Majors and Programs at Roanoke College: The Essential Components of Institutional Effectiveness in Academic Departments." Salem, Va.: Roanoke College, n.d. Available at http://www.roanoke.edu/inst-res/assessment/AcadMan.htm, accessed September 4, 2003.

———. "Institutional Effectiveness Program." Salem, Va.: Roanoke College, n.d. Available at http://www.roanoke.edu/inst-res/assessment/, accessed September 4, 2003.

Rodrigues, Raymond. "Want Campus Buy-in for Your Assessment Efforts?" *AAHEBulletin.com* (September 2002). Available at http://aahebulletin.com/member/articles/2002–10-feature02_pf.asp?, accessed June 8, 2003.

Rudd, Peggy D. "Documenting the Difference: Demonstrating the Value of Libraries through Outcome Measurement," in *Perspectives on Outcome Based Evaluation for Libraries and Museums*, 17–24. Washington, D.C.: Institute of Museum and Library Services, 1999. Available at http://www.imls.gov/pubs/pdf/pubobe.pdf, accessed August 15, 2003.

Seiden, Peggy, Kris Szmborski, and Barbara Norelli. "Undergraduate Students in the Digital Library: Information Seeking Behavior in a Heterogeneous Environment." Chicago: Association of College and Research Libraries, 1997. Available at http://www.ala.org/Content/ContentGroups/ACRL1/Nashville_1997_Papers/Seiden_Szmborski_and_Norelli.htm, accessed September 28, 2003.

Sheppard, Beverly. "Outcome Based Evaluation." Washington, D.C.: Institute of Museum and Library Services. Available at http://www.imls.gov/grants/current/crnt_obe.htm, accessed June 22, 2003.

Sinclair Community College. "Assessment of Student Learning." Dayton, Ohio: Sinclair Community College, n.d. Available at http://www.sinclair.edu/about/assessment/outcomes/index.cfm, accessed August 15, 2003.

————. "Guiding Principles." Dayton, Ohio: Sinclair Community College, n.d. Available at http://www.sinclair.edu/about/assessment/reports/index.cfm, accessed August 15, 2003.

————. "Institutional Effectiveness (The Learning Organization)." Dayton, Ohio: Sinclair Community College, n.d. Available at http://www.sinclair.edu/about/assessment/reports/index.cfm, accessed August 15, 2003.

————. "Program Outcomes Reports." Dayton, Ohio: Sinclair Community College, n.d. Available at http://www.sinclair.edu/about/assessment/outcomes/index.cfm, accessed August 15, 2003.

The State Council of Higher Education for Virginia. "Purpose of the Reports of Institutional Effectiveness." Richmond: The State Council of Higher Education for Virginia, n.d. Available at http://roie.schev.edu/, accessed September 4, 2003.

Teaching Quality Enhancement Committee. "Learning and Teaching." London: Higher Education Funding Council for England, 2003. Available at http://www.hefce.ac.uk/Learning/, accessed August 15, 2003.

TracDat. Pittsburgh, Penn.: Nuventive, n.d. Available at http://www.nuventive.com/html/products.htm, accessed March 2, 2004; and http://www.sct.com/Education/Products/Connected_Learning/TracDat.html, accessed March 2, 2004.

Truman University. "Assessment: Component of the Program." Kirksville, Mo.: Truman University, n.d. Available at http://assessment.truman.edu/comp-as.stm, accessed August 15, 2003.

University of Washington. "Student Learning Outcomes: A Faculty Resource on Development and Assessment." Seattle: University of Washington, n.d. Available at http://depts.washington.edu/grading/slo/SLO-Home.htm, accessed September 4, 2003.

University of Washington, Accountability Board. "Student Learning Outcomes: A Faculty Resource on Development and Assessment." Seattle: University of Washington University, n.d. Available at http://depts.washington.edu/grading/slo/SLO-Home.htm, accessed September 4, 2003.

————. "Student Learning Outcomes: Assessing SLOs." Seattle: University of Washington, n.d. Available at http://depts.washington.edu/grading/slo/SLO-Assess.htm, accessed September 4, 2003.

————. "Student Learning Outcomes: The Process of Designing Departmental Outcomes." Seattle: University of Washington, n.d. Available at http://depts.washington.edu/grading/slo/SLO-Issues.htm, accessed September 4, 2003.

University of Washington, Office of Educational Assessment. "Student Writing and Quantitative Skills." Seattle: University of Washington, 1998. Available at http://www.washington.edu/oea/rptsqsr.htm, accessed August 15, 2003.

University of Wisconsin–Madison, Office of the Provost. "Outcomes Assessment: Using Assessment for Academic Program Improvement." Madison: University of Wisconsin–Madison, Office of the Provost, April 2000. Available at http://www.wisc.edu/provost.assess/manual/manual2.html, accessed May 13, 2003. Similar material is now available in section IV.A, *Assessment Manual*, http://www.provost.wisc.edu/assessment/manual/, accessed November 2, 2003.

University of Wisconsin–Whitewater. "The Six Priorities of the Strategic Plan." Whitewater: University of Wisconsin, n.d. Available at http://www.uww.edu/Admin/strplan/prior.htm, accessed September 4, 2003.

———. "Strategic Plan: Priority 1." Whitewater: University of Wisconsin, n.d. Available at http://www.uww.edu/Admin/strplan/prior1.htm, accessed September 4, 2003.

———. "Strategic Planning Assumptions." Whitewater: University of Wisconsin, n.d. Available at http://www.uww.edu/Admin/strplan/assump.htm, accessed September 4, 2003.

———. "Undergraduate Catalog, 2002–2004: Mission Statement." Whitewater: University of Wisconsin, 2002. Available at http://www.uww.edu/Catalog/02–04/Intro/4mission.html, accessed September 4, 2003.

———. "UW-Whitewater Vision Statement." Whitewater: University of Wisconsin, n.d. Available at http://www.uww.edu/Admin/strplan/vision.htm, accessed September 4, 2003.

Vassar College. *Media Cloisters*. Poughkeepsie, N.Y.: Vassar College, n.d. Available at http://mediacloisters.vassar.edu/flash/, accessed October 16, 2003.

Virginia Tech University, Office of Academic Assessment. "Assessment." Blacksburg: Virginia Polytechnic Institute and State University, n.d. Available at http://aappc.aap.vt.edu/, accessed August 15, 2003.

Other Sources

American Association of University Professors. *Policy Documents and Reports*. Washington, D.C.: American Association of University Professors, 1990.

Bresciani, Dean L. *Explaining Administrative Costs: A Case Study*. Ph.d. diss. Tucson: University of Arizona, 1996 (UMI Dissertation Services, 9713408).

Bresciani, Marilee J. *Expert Driven Assessment: Making It Meaningful to Decisionmakers*, ECAR Research Bulletin 21. Boulder, Colo.: Educause, 2003.

Conley, David T. *Understanding University Success: A Report from Standards for Success, a Project of the Association of American Universities and the Pew Charitable Trusts.* Eugene: Center for Educational Policy Research, University of Oregon, 2003.

Council of Regional Accrediting Commissioners. *Regional Accreditation and Student Learning: Principles of Good Practice.* Washington, D.C.: Council of Regional Accrediting Commissioners, May 2003.

Edgerton, R. *Education White Paper.* Philadelphia: Pew Charitable Trusts, 1997.

Ewell, Peter T. "Outcomes, Assessment, Institutional Effectiveness, and Accreditation: A Conceptual Exploration," in *Accreditation, Assessment, and Institutional Effectiveness: Resource Papers for the COPA Task Force on Institutional Effectiveness,* 1–17. Washington, D.C.: Council on Postsecondary Accreditation 1992 (ERIC, ED 343513).

Hogan, Thomas P. "Methods for Outcomes Assessment Related to Institutional Accreditation," in *Accreditation, Assessment, and Institutional Effectiveness: Resource Papers for the COPA Task Force on Institutional Effectiveness,* 37–55. Washington, D.C.: Council on Postsecondary Accreditation, 1992 (ERIC, ED 343513).

North Central Association of Colleges and Schools. *A Collection of Papers on Self-Study and Institutional Improvement.* Chicago: North Central Association of Colleges and Schools, 1996, 1999.

———. *Assessment Workbook.* Chicago: North Central Association of Colleges and Schools, 1991.

Packwood, Gene. "Issues in Assessing Institutional Effectiveness," in *Assessing Institutional Effectiveness in Community Colleges,* edited by Don Doucette and Billie Hughes, 45–51. Laguna Hills, Calif.: League for Innovation in the Community College, 1990 (ERIC, ED 324072).

South Carolina Higher Education Assessment Network. *Recommendations for Defining and Assessing Institutional Effectiveness.* Charleston: South Carolina Higher Education Assessment Network, 1994 (ERIC, ED 393384).

Wolff, Ralph A., and Olita D. Harris, "Using Assessment to Develop a Culture of Evidence," in *Changing College Classrooms: New Teaching and Learning Strategies for an Increasingly Complex World,* edited by D. F. Halpern, 271–288. San Francisco: Jossey-Bass, 1994 (ERIC, ED 368307).

Unpublished Sources

Bresciani, Marilee J. Raleigh: North Carolina State University, Division of Undergraduate Affairs, 2001. Available at http://www.ncsu.edu/undergrad_affairs/, accessed October 15, 2003.

————. "The Assessment of Assessment," submitted for publication to *Assessment Update*, 2002.

————. "Creating a Universitywide Assessment Plan," submitted for publication to *Assessment Update* (2002).

Bresciani, Marilee J., and Keri Bowman. "Assessing the Impact of Our Assessment Process," paper presented at North Carolina State University Assessment Symposium, Raleigh, 2003.

Centre for the Enhancement of Learning and Teaching, Educational and Staff Development Section. "The 'Aims and Learning Outcomes' Approach." Aberdeen, Scotland: The Robert Gordon University, n.d. Available at http://www2.rgu.ac.uk/subj/eds/pgcert/specifying/speci3.htm, accessed August 15, 2003.

Chesebro, J., K. Snider, and A. Venerable. *Measuring Learning Community Effectiveness: Conceptions, an Instrument, and Results.* Paper presented at the Conference of the Consortium for Assessment and Planning Support, Monroe, Louisiana, April 1999.

López, Cecilia L. *Assessment of Student Learning: An Update.* Paper presented at the Working Conference of the Association of American Colleges and Universities, Tampa, Florida, February 1999.

————. *Assessment of Student Learning: A Progress Report.* Paper presented at 103rd Annual Meeting of the North Central Association, Commission on Institutions of Higher Education, Chicago, 1998.

————. *Opportunities for Improvement: Advice from Consultant-Evaluators on Programs to Assess Student Learning.* Chicago: North Central Association of Colleges and Schools, Commission on Institutions of Higher Education, 1997.

Maki, Peggy, and Marilee J. Bresciani. "Integrating Student Outcomes Assessment into a University Culture." Presentation at the American Association of Higher Education Faculty Forum on Roles and Rewards Conference, Phoenix, Arizona, January 2002.

McGregor, Felicity. "Benchmarking with the Best," in *Library Measures to Fill the Void: Assessing the Outcomes*, Fifth Northumbria International Conference on Performance Measurement in Libraries and Information Service. Durham, UK: University of Durham, 2003.

Oehler, D., and D. Sergel. *Performance-Based Assessment of General Education in Missouri: Common Outcomes across Institutions.* Paper presented at the Conference of the Consortium for Assessment and Planning Support, Monroe, Louisiana, April 1999.

Index

About the Editors and Contributors

JAMES ANDERSON (janderson@tamu.edu) assumed the position of vice president and associate provost for Institutional Assessment and Diversity at Texas A & M University (College Station, Texas 77843) on November 19, 2003. He is also a tenured professor in the Department of Psychology. From 1992 to 2003, he served as the vice provost for undergraduate affairs at North Carolina State University. Dr. Anderson has also served on the psychology faculty at Indiana University of Pennsylvania and Xavier University of New Orleans, Louisiana. At Xavier he also served as the department chair. He obtained a B.A. degree from Villanova University and a Ph.D. in psychology from Cornell University. He currently serves on the Board of Trustees at Villanova University. His research and publications focus on three areas: (1) the development of student learning styles across gender, race, culture, and class, and how varied styles respond to different modes of instruction; (2) the formal assessment of student learning in the college classroom; and (3) the examination of how diversity impacts student learning, retention, and overall institutional effectiveness.

RONALD L. BAKER (rbaker@nwccu.org) is the deputy executive director of the Northwest Commission on Colleges and Universities (8060 165th Avenue NE, Suite 100, Redmond, Washington 98052), the higher education regional accrediting agency for the seven-state region comprising Alaska, Idaho, Montana, Nevada, Oregon, Utah, and Washington. Prior to joining the commission, he was the chief academic officer at a new community college where he directed the development of its outcomes-based curriculum. His experience in higher education includes service as the director of distance education for the Oregon community colleges, full-time faculty responsibilities, and a variety of educational administrative positions.

His research interests include institutional values and mission development, alignment of practices to support institutional mission, and identification and assessment of learning outcomes. He holds a B.A. in mathematics from Washington State University, an M.S. in mathematics from New Mexico State University, an M.S. in computer education from Eastern Washington University, and an Ed.D. in community college leadership from Oregon State University.

SANDRA BLOOMBERG (sbloomberg@njcu.edu) has been dean of the College of Professional Studies, New Jersey City University (2039 Kennedy Blvd., Jersey City, New Jersey 07305), since 1998. She has served in the capacity of faculty member, chairperson, and associate dean at several colleges in the Northeast. Since 1982, she has focused her efforts on issues related to student and program assessment. As early as 1983, she worked with colleagues to identify cross-curricular competencies that were then systematically integrated into core courses of a major urban-based, health-care management, baccalaureate degree program. Her work at New Jersey City University has largely focused on encouraging an environment in which student learning is at the center of the teaching-learning process; where evidence is consistently used to inform teaching, learning, and programmatic change; and where faculty and students view each other as collaborators in learning.

ELIZABETH W. CARTER (cartere@citadel.edu) is associate professor and head of reference and instruction at Daniel Library, The Citadel (Charleston, South Carolina 29409). She received a master of librarianship from Emory University in Atlanta, Georgia. Her main areas of interest and research are the study of teaching and learning and assessment of the instruction process. She is the author of a number of published papers and conference presentations on these issues, and is active in the Citadel's Communication Across the Curriculum and Citadel Academy for the Scholarship of Teaching, Learning, and Evaluation. She is active in state and national library associations, holding a variety of section, committee, and executive board positions in the South Carolina Library Association, most recently serving as president, and as chapter liaison to the Association of College and Research Libraries.

ROBERT E. DUGAN (rdugan@suffolk.edu) is the director of the Mildred F. Sawyer Library at Suffolk University (8 Ashburton Place, Boston, Massachusetts 02108). During a thirty-year career in librarianship, he has been a reference librarian, director of public libraries, head of statewide library development, a state librarian, an associate university librarian, and college library director. He has coauthored six books and more than fifty articles on topics such as information policy, technology, outcomes assessment, and library management and operations.

PETER HERNON (peter.hernon@simmons.edu) is a professor at Simmons College Graduate School of Library and Information Science (300 The Fenway, Boston, Massachusetts 02115), where he teaches courses on government information policy and resources, evaluation of library services, research methods, and academic librarianship. He received his Ph.D. from Indiana University in 1978 and has taught at Simmons College, the University of Arizona, and Victoria University of Wellington (New Zealand). He is coeditor of *Library & Information Science Research* and past editor *of Government Information Quarterly* and *The Journal of Academic Librarianship*. He is the author of nearly 200 articles and forty books, including the coauthored *U.S. Government on the Web* (3rd ed., 2003) and *United States Government Information* (2002), a textbook on government information policy.

CECILIA L. LÓPEZ (clopez2@ccc.edu) is the vice president for academic and student affairs at Harold Washington College (30 E. Lake St., Chicago, Illinois 60601), one of the City Colleges of Chicago. For twelve years (February 1991 to February 2003), she was the associate director of the Higher Learning Commission of the North Central Association of Colleges and Schools (NCA). Dr. López received her B.A. and M.A. degrees in English from Florida State University, with the generous assistance of the Southern Scholarship and Research Foundation and the National Hispanic Scholarship Fund. She earned her Ph.D. in Instructional Design and Learning from Arizona State University.

Dr. López has taught at Chabot College, Florida A & M University, and Arizona State University, West Campus. She serves on the Board of Trustees of the Association of American Colleges and Universities (AACU) and the Executive Committee of the Council for the National Postsecondary Education Cooperative (NPEC). She is a member of the National Advisory Board for the NSSE/AAHE project on promoting student success through using student engagement data, the Advisory Board for the Academic of Excellence in Institutional Assessment at

North Carolina State University, and the National Advisory Board for the Policy Center on the First Year of College. Dr. López served for ten years as a reviewer for *Educational Technology, Research and Development (ETR&D)* and now serves as a consulting editor for the *Assessment Update: Progress, Trends, and Practices in Higher Education*. On March 2000, the Hispanic Caucus of the American Association for Higher Education (AAHE) selected her as the first female to receive the Alfredo G. de los Santos Jr. Award for Distinguished Leadership in Higher Education.

Her research on issues affecting higher education, particularly issues relating to assessment of student learning and general education, has been published in articles appearing in *Liberal Education* (Summer 1998 and Summer 1999) and the *Journal of Academic Librarianship* (November 2002), and in the numerous papers she has presented at international, national, regional, and statewide conferences on assessment of student learning.

PEGGY L. MAKI (PeggyMaki@aol.com), Ph.D., is an educational consultant (35 Atlantic Road, Gloucester, Massachusetts 01930). Previously she was a senior scholar with Assessing for Learning, American Association for Higher Education (AAHE). Her articles on assessing student learning have appeared in *AAHE's Bulletin, Change, The Journal of Academic Librarianship, Assessment Update, NetResults*, and AAHE's Inquiry and Action series. Over the last several years, she has conducted more than 200 workshops on assessment nationally and internationally. Before joining AAHE, she served as associate director of the Commission on Institutions of Higher Education, New England Association of Schools and Colleges; vice president, academic dean, dean of faculty, and professor of English, Bradford College, Massachusetts; and chair of English, theater arts, and communication, associate professor of English, and dean of continuing education, Arcadia University, Pennsylvania. She is a recipient of a Lindback Award for Distinguished Teaching. Her book, *Assessing for Learning: Building a Sustainable Institutional Commitment*, was published in spring 2004.

MELAINE MCDONALD (mmcdonald@njcu.edu) is assistant dean (acting) of the College of Professional Studies (New Jersey City University, 2039 Kennedy Boulevard, Jersey City, New Jersey 07305) and a doctoral student in the Higher Education Administration program at Seton Hall University. Her work and research interests at New Jersey

City University have focused on faculty development, student and program assessment, and leadership styles.

DANUTA A. NITECKI (danuta.nitecki@yale.edu) has been associate university librarian at Yale University Library (P.O. Box 208240, New Haven, Connecticut 06520–8240) since 1996. She has held administrative and public service positions at three other academic research libraries since 1972. Her Ph.D. dissertation (University of Maryland, 1995) about evaluating library service quality received two national awards. Dr. Nitecki also holds master of science degrees in library and information science (Drexel University, 1972) and communications (University of Tennessee, 1976). Active in professional associations and services, she has had more than fifty articles and compilations published, and she has made presentations to regional, national, and international groups.

WILLIAM RANDO (william.rando@yale.edu) is founding director of the McDougal Graduate Teaching Center and dean's advisor on teaching and learning at Yale University Graduate School of Arts and Sciences (Yale University Graduate School, P.O. Box 208236, New Haven, Connecticut 06520). He has been working and writing in the field of faculty development since 1985. His Ph.D. dissertation (Northwestern University, 1992) addressed the formation of implicit theories of teaching and learning among new college teachers. In his previous positions, he has actively engaged collaboration between the teaching center and the library, and in 1996, he codeveloped the Information Literacy Initiative, a library-based faculty development program at the Florida International University. In 1992, Dr. Rando coauthored "Learning from Students," and he has written numerous articles on teaching, learning, and assessment.

OSWALD M. T. RATTERAY (oratteray@msache.org) has been the assistant director for constituent services and special programs, Middle States Commission on Higher Education (3624 Market St., Philadelphia, Pennsylvania 19104) since 1994. He has joint responsibility for the commission's incoming information, collecting and analyzing the data that colleges and universities are required to submit annually as well as occasional surveys on such special topics as the self-study process, peer review, information literacy, and outcomes assessment. He also is responsible for coordinating the commission's outgoing information in the form of training workshops, annual conferences, conferences on special topics, print publications, and World Wide Web publications. A graduate of Howard University, he worked as a wordsmith in Washington, D.C., for twenty-seven years, specializing for much of that time in corporate management and summarizing information. He also served on the task force, sponsored by the Association of College and Research Libraries, to *Develop Information Literacy Standards for Higher Education* (2000).